Stravinsky on Stage

Frontispiece:
Portrait of Igor Stravinsky, 1961,
by Théodore Strawinsky.
Photo: Raymond Asseo.

Stravinsky on Stage

ALEXANDER SCHOUVALOFF
VICTOR BOROVSKY

STAINER & BELL: LONDON

ISBN 0 85249 604 4

Typeset by Pierson LeVesley Ltd

Printed in Great Britain
by Sackville Press Billericay Ltd

Designed and produced
by Editorial and Production Services Ltd

Contents

In memoriam

Igor Fedorovitch Stravinsky

Oranienbaum, St Petersburg,
17 June 1882 –
6 April 1971

Acknowledgements

The preparation of this book has been a collaboration between the two authors but each of them has also worked independently. We would both like to express our foremost thanks to Monsieur Théodore Strawinsky for the frontispiece and for his picture, as a child of twelve, of the first night of *Histoire du Soldat*. Without the generous agreement of Eric Walter White, who allowed us to use his numbering of Stravinsky's compositions, the book would have been a mass of confusions. We are also most grateful to Robert Craft who kindly helped with a number of problems and, in particular, the vexing one of the titles of Stravinsky's works.

My grateful thanks are to Martin Cooper, John Roberts and Judith Baum, who helped me in so many different ways with my essay.

Victor Borovsky

Without being able to undertake a world cruise lasting many months, if not years, I have often had to rely on the help of others for the compilation of the statistics in this book. My particular thanks to Sarah C.Woodcock, who put up with my changes of mind and late requests for pictures with angelic patience and who, when we discovered that the original designs for *Jeu de Cartes* no longer exist, found a colour photograph of the first production; and to Pip Dyer who, with his extraordinary eye and memory, found and identified many photographs. My thanks also to Madame André Barsacq for vital illustrations of *Perséphone*; to Claire de Robilant who gave me so much information about South America; to Anne Vivarelli who defied the notorious Italian postal service by getting me a crucial book; to Asya Chorley who so promptly found some important but elusive pictures; to Harold Rosenthal who not only allowed me to delve through his collection of pictures but also let me see the proofs of his new edition of *Annals of the Opera*; to Monsieur Boris Kochno for confirming certain facts and dispelling certain doubts; to Heinrich Huesmann for such efficient replies about Germany; to David Hockney for his generosity in letting me reproduce photographs of his models for *The Nightingale*; to Robert L.Parkinson of the Circus World Museum who troubled to send me an essential document; to Antony Hippisley-Coxe whose unrivalled knowledge of the circus finally put me on the right track; to Richard Buckle who many times paved my way and resolved many questions; to Tony Palmer who made it possible for the backcloth of *The Firebird* to be hung in a large enough space for it to be photographed; to Nikita Lobanov Rostovsky for his many helpful suggestions; to Wendy Fisher who faultlessly typed the manuscript and constantly gave invaluable advice and meticulous help in spite of having been driven temporarily back to smoking; and to Lord and Lady Oxford whose generous hospitality allowed me to be such a bad guest that I could finish the book.

And to Daria, my wife, who suffered more than anyone but always remained a calm and indispensable support. At least the sun was usually shining in the early mornings.

Alexander Schouvaloff

Our thanks also to many others, unidentified, who were pestered by telephone calls and telegrams asking for irritating facts, and always supplied the answer. Nor would it have been possible without the encouragement and enthusiasm of Dr Allen Percival of Stainer and Bell; John Maddison our designer and Daphne Terry our editor; and Graham Brandon, who painstakingly and with great sensitivity took many of the photographs.

Introduction

Now, a hundred years after his birth and ten years after his death, there is probably a performance of one of Stravinsky's works taking place somewhere in the world every night of the year.

It was not always like this. Although Stravinsky became internationally famous overnight with his first work *The Firebird* when it was performed in 1910, and although he consolidated that early success with *Petrushka* in 1912 and *Le Sacre du Printemps* in 1913, it was some time before companies other than Diaghilev's Ballets Russes began to attempt these works. Later works, which were also first produced by Diaghilev, were more theatrically experimental and therefore not only more difficult to stage but, at first, not so popular because they were also difficult to fit into a programme in a large theatre.

Because of their instant success the early productions of Stravinsky's works for the stage seemed to seal the way in which they should be performed. Both Fokine's choreography for the first two ballets and Benois' designs for *Petrushka* and Gontcharova's for *The Firebird* (1926) were somehow felt to be the only way of doing these ballets. And it was George Balanchine's choreography which set the seal for Stravinsky's later works. Only relatively recently have new choreographers and new designers tried to think of new ways of staging Stravinsky's work. It takes time in the theatre to forget the impact of the first production of new work. But if the text of a play, or, in Stravinsky's case, the score, can stand up to revival then in order to go on living and meaning something to contemporary audiences new ways of interpretation have to be found. Paradoxically some of the staging of Stravinsky's works suffered from those early impacts, because it is only fairly recently that a new generation of people working in the theatre has discovered the marvel of Stravinsky's music for new interpretations.

Stravinsky wrote twenty works specifically for performance. Choreographers and dancers have used many of his other compositions for their ballets. Many, many books and articles have been written about Stravinsky and about his music. He was a huge figure in the history of 20th century theatrical art and his works have always attracted the greatest contemporary artists and interpreters. The first productions of his works from 1910-1957 provide prodigious evidence for the development of art and taste in the theatre through that time.

The illustrations in this book show that development. They have been chosen wherever possible to illustrate both the first productions and some of the subsequent ones. The majority of the illustrations are taken from the collections of the Theatre Museum, Victoria and Albert Museum.

The introductory essay describes particularly the Russian influences on Stravinsky and his new art, and the development of his own ideas about theatre. The second part of the book gives details of the first performances of each work followed by those of other important performances and productions. *Danses Concertantes* has been included in this part because, although it was not specifically composed for the theatre, it is a suite of dances and was quickly staged by Balanchine. In each case, the title used is either the one which is known to have been preferred by Stravinsky himself or the one used by Robert Craft in his book *Stravinsky in Pictures and Documents*. Each composition is also identified by an EWW number. Eric Walter White has most generously agreed to allow the numbering which he gives in his comprehensive book *Stravinsky – The Composer and his Works* (2nd edn) to be used here. Wherever possible the details about the productions and performances have been gleaned from programmes in the archives of the Theatre Museum. Where it has not been possible to consult the original programme it has been thought preferable to include such details as have been discovered, however sparse, than to ignore the event altogether.

Finally, the section at the end of the book lists productions of works on stage which were not originally composed for the theatre. It cannot be an exhaustive catalogue because, apart from anything else, new works are being produced all the time.

The statistics in this book bear out what Clive Barnes has said: that every other 'Tom, Dick or Heinrich, particularly Heinrich', is doing Stravinsky. Some of it is good, some of it is not so good, but what is true is that Stravinsky's music continues to inspire others and will always do so.

Alexander Schouvaloff
Mells, 19 July 1981

PART 1
by Victor Borovsky

Stravinsky's Theatre

Igor Stravinsky on 24 June 1962 at the Staatsoper, Hamburg during the celebrations for his 80th birthday. *Photo: F.Peyer*

I love whatever I am doing at a given moment and
with each new work I feel that at last I have found
the way and have begun to compose.

Igor Fedorovich Stravinsky

Stravinsky is one of the most brilliant figures of the century. An extraordinary individualist, transforming 'influences' into original and very personal creations, he resembles no other composer. To measure the extent of his own effect on others is no easy task; already more than one generation of composers and creative artists working in the theatre has experienced the powerful influence of his art. Much has been written about Stravinsky's musical influence, but less attention has been paid to his influence on the theatre as such, to those theatrical innovations that were prompted by his work.

Without becoming trapped in a new dogma of his own devising, Stravinsky established one fashion after another, each championed by a devoted following. Yet he himself continued to progress unswervingly, faithful, as Herbert Read reminds us in *Stravinsky and the Dance* (New York, 1962), to 'the principle of speculative volition'. Nearly every one of his chief works, surprising and unexpected in character with their new revelations in style and imagery, provoked immediate arguments in which devotees of 'yesterday's' Stravinsky often attacked the composer. Yet the incomprehension of today soon became the universal fashion of tomorrow – while the originator of that fashion was already moving on to new frontiers and discoveries.

Many who acclaimed *Petrushka* were perplexed by *Le Sacre du Printemps*. Even Diaghilev, Stravinsky's friend and collaborator of long standing, was bewildered by the traditionalism of *Le Baiser de la Fée*. Later, at a time when the old opera, with its emphasis on the conventions of concert arias and ensembles, appeared to have become obsolete and merely an object of derision, Stravinsky resuscitated the genre in a pure and uncompromising form with the dazzling stylisation of *The Rake's Progress*. Stravinsky may in fact be compared to an actor of genius, able to transform himself completely into any character and impossible to type-cast.

Nothing superfluous is to be found in Stravinsky's works for the stage; each is a fully disciplined production, with no room for improvisation. Nonetheless, those engaged on a Stravinsky production are presented with generous possibilities of discovering new forms and means of expression. Stravinsky assumed complete responsibility for the musical text: there was no question of adapting or changing anything. That time-honoured tradition of the theatre, 'working with the author', was unheard of during the production of a new Stravinsky work, although conductor, choirmaster, choreographer, instrumentalist, singer and dancer had every opportunity to display their skill.

Paradoxically, many of Stravinsky's works not intended for the stage have since been used in creative exploration within the theatre. Concert works attracted, and continue to attract, the attention of choreographers. This interest was first aroused in the early years of the century by Isadora Duncan and, independently of her, by the choreographers Alexander Gorsky and Michel Fokine. According to the commemorative book *Stravinsky and the Dance* published to mark Stravinsky's 80th birthday, in 1962 more than forty of his works, in addition to his fourteen ballets, had by then been choreographed. Twenty years have passed since then and that number has increased. Such figures persuasively testify to the enormous significance of Stravinsky's music for the ballet of the 20th century. The reasons for this will be considered later. An impressive number of works for the concert hall, varying in both form and content, are mentioned in the final part of this book. Stravinsky's many links with 20th century theatre do not require proof, although the fate of his ballets was not always as happy as might have been expected. Why this should have been so is difficult to say: neither the public's conservatism nor the producers' lack of invention seems to offer an adequate explanation. The fact remains that Stravinsky's music was sometimes received with more enthusiasm in the concert hall than in the theatre.

Unfortunately, Stravinsky never had at his disposal a theatre company in which a stable tradition of interpreting his ballets and operas could gradually have taken shape. Apart from links with Serge Diaghilev and the Ballets Russes, and later his co-operation with George Balanchine, no ties exist between Stravinsky's music and any particular company; both premières and subsequent productions of his works were scattered among different theatres around the world.

Stravinsky nevertheless continued all his life not only to write for the theatre but also to keep up his search for diverse stage forms. Thus, in the course of 55 years, he composed 20 works for the stage, and the challenges of theatrical problems occupied him for much of his life, although the degree of his interest naturally fluctuated. From an early age he found himself in contact with literary and artistic circles. As the son of an outstanding singer at the Maryinsky Theatre in St Petersburg he met many of his father's colleagues. Stasov, Mussorgsky, Dostoevsky and Rimsky-Korsakov had been among the visitors to the family home, and from his earliest years Stravinsky had absorbed the spirit of the theatre, its atmosphere of constant change. As a young man he moved in the highest circles of St Petersburg's artistic intelligentsia, took part in 'Evenings of Contemporary Music' and later came into close contact with the members of the artistic group *Mir Iskusstva* (The World of Art) and through them, with the man who was to play a decisive role in the development and establishing of his career as a composer: Serge Pavlovich Diaghilev.

It was Diaghilev who revealed Stravinsky's genius to the world. He linked the young composer's first efforts in the theatre to his own refined taste and imagination, and he assisted at the birth of *The Firebird, Petrushka* and *Le Sacre*

Igor Stravinsky in 1914 at Leysin (Canton de Vaud), Switzerland. It was here that he composed the final scenes of *The Nightingale.*   *Theatre Museum, V & A.*

du Printemps. Perhaps it is best to quote Stravinsky's own words from *Chronicle of my Life*: 'The quality of his intelligence and mentality also attracted me. He had a wonderful flair, a marvellous faculty for seizing at a glance the novelty and freshness of an idea, surrendering himself to it without pausing to reason it out.' During twenty years of intense activity Diaghilev introduced Western Europe to Russian art.

Diaghilev's interests, like those of the other members of *Mir Iskusstva* (who included at various times Alexander Benois, Leon Bakst, Alexander Golovine, Mikhail Vrubel and Nicolai Roerich), were not limited solely to pictorial art. The group's goal was the affirmation of 'culture in the artistic sense, and artistic synthesis as the highest aim of culture'. This idea found its fullest expression in the realms of music theatre, especially, in its early days, in the work of S.I. Mamontov's private opera company in Moscow. From the very beginning the *Mir Iskusstva* artists were not satisfied with the role of designer of a production; they understood their task in a much broader sense and saw themselves as the practical creators of a production. The underlying, unifying theme of a production was often implicit in their scenery, and it is no longer disputed that such painters became the true directors of a production.

Several times in his memoirs Fedor Chaliapin emphasised the great influence of theatre designers on his development as a performer. He was certainly not the only person to be so influenced; the effects of these painters' work were felt in all quarters of the theatrical world. This new conception of the designer's role had been called into existence by the needs of the times. On the threshold of the 20th century artists were revealing a new outlook on the natural values of the world. They reflected in their works the joy in new discovery of old treasures: light, air, colour. In those uncertain times all Russians involved in the arts were striving to foresee the fate of Russia, hardly an easy task when a kind of indecipherable puzzle hovered constantly before their eyes. This produced a propitious situation for the arts and it became possible for artists to liberate themselves from the restrictions of conventional realism. Images conveying a multiplicity of meanings inevitably sprang out of this forced rejection of every-day life. Diaghilev's associates, in spite of differences of personality and serious disagreements of opinion, were united by a dominant interest in visual effects, in local colour; and this interest manifested itself in work of widely differing character: in the cold misty tones depicting aristocratic St Petersburg, in the formal lines of Versailles with its pavilions, summerhouses and parks, in the brilliant hues of Russian popular prints.

The sphere of profound experiences and reflections produced by man's conflict with reality and the psychological labyrinth of the human soul, held little attraction for the *Mir Iskusstva* group. In this sense the cultural traditions of 19th century Russian were alien to them. No form of art should, in their view, ever in any way reproduce reality. Art was concerned with the independent search for the meaning of beauty and artistic imagination. Valery Bryusov, poet and theorist of the new art, loved to cite Franz Grillparzer's elegant aphorism: 'Art is related to reality as wine is to grapes.' In the theatre of which these innovators dreamed, stage action would poetically transform reality and concentrate attention on the significant, essential moments of life. Such a theatre

16

would withdraw from life and condense reality, intensifying or enhancing events, often imparting another dimension to them. The creative artist would perceive and distil the essence hidden beneath that everyday surface. Such a conception of the theatre placed great emphasis on the free will of the creator.

Stravinsky was deeply impressed by these views, although at this time, of course, he had not yet contemplated a radical reform of music theatre. He felt first a desire to renew the genre, without any clear understanding of how to go about it. It was not, therefore, a matter of chance that the innovation of his first works for the stage – *The Firebird*, *Petruskha* and later *Le Sacre du Printemps* – was evident more in the music than in the stage treatment. No definitive answers to concrete questions about stage practice were contained in the broad theatrical programme envisaged at the beginning of the century. The answers were provided by various people in the theatre; the one who should be mentioned first and foremost is Vsevolod Meyerhold.

It may be supposed that in those years Stravinsky was well acquainted with Meyerhold's published pronouncements on stage practice. Even a superficial glance reveals the common ground in the art of Stravinsky and that of Meyerhold. Among the many similarities are the vital role played by the grotesque, the interest in the traditional Italian Commedia dell'Arte, the play-acting and the use of different masks hiding the actors' faces, the subordination of the actors to the complicated counterpoint of the music's rhythm and plasticity.

The nature of Stravinsky's art can be considered in a broader context. The inherent theatricality of his thought inclined him from the very beginning towards stylised theatre, not towards the 'psychological concreteness' of art as a whole and the theatre in particular. Obviously it is very difficult to draw a dividing line between the two: in the real world the two approaches often overlap and interact. Strictly speaking, neither stylised theatre nor the naturalistic theatre of 'direct, live experience' exists at all. Stylisation is an innate feature of the theatre, and the most determined efforts to make a production life-like come up against the stylisation of the box-stage, the stylised temporary erection of the non-existent fourth wall. The difference between stylised and naturalistic theatre consists simply in the manner of realising the action and characters on stage.

In the years when Stravinsky was beginning to compose, part of the Russian theatre, opposed to life-like illusion on the stage, was trying a carnival type of performance with stylised, decorative designs, with interludes interrupting the action, and asides to the audience. This is yet another similarity between Stravinsky's music and the theatre's experiments in the early years of the century – the special festival spirit, the theatricality, what might more precisely be termed the principle of play-acting which stands out as a specific feature of Stravinsky's art. The real main reason for the theatre's existence was, in his opinion, play-acting. In every production based on this premise an unspoken agreement exists between performers and spectators about the rules of the game, but the constant factor is the dominant role of unrestricted play-acting and theatricality, the atmosphere of carnival.

It was in 1909 that Diaghilev first became acquainted with the young Stravinsky's works at St Petersburg concerts. By this time the 'Russian Seasons' organised by Diaghilev in Paris had aroused considerable interest. In 1906 Diaghilev had arranged an exhibition of Russian painting, followed in 1907 by concerts of Russian symphonic music, and in 1908 by productions of Russian opera. Many Russians from all branches of the arts were gripped by Diaghilev's ideas and eagerly came forward to participate in his projects. This desire to show Europe as much of Russian art as possible led to the idea of forming a Russian ballet company.

There were serious obstacles in the way of such an enterprise. In organising operatic productions and symphonic concerts Diaghilev was able to draw on the works of Mussorgsky, Borodin and Rimsky-Korsakov, whereas ballet on Russian themes had to be composed specially. Very few ballets with Russian motifs had been preserved in the repertoire of the Imperial Ballet, and even such works as had been retained were old-fashioned and had been composed by foreigners (for example, *The Little Hump-backed Horse* by Pugni and St Léon in 1864, and *The Goldfish* by Minkus and St Léon in 1866). At the beginning of the 20th century these ballets looked naive and dated.

Michel Fokine was invited to be the ballet-master of Diaghilev's new venture. Although his work as a choreographer had only just begun, Fokine had already shown himself to be an innovator. Developing the best traditions of the Russian ballet, his work marked the beginning of a new epoch in the theatre. Fokine rejected the idea of classical dance being the universal and only means of realising a ballet production, and he employed different, expressive forms according to the theme of each ballet. For him the expressiveness of dancing was directly linked to its concrete meaning and in this sense he condemned the classical dancing of the old ballets as a meaningless pattern of lines in a moving drawing. 'Ballet must be drama, only plastic drama,' he observed in his *Memoirs of a Ballet-master*.

In historical perspective Fokine's reform can be seen to have provided the means by which the art of the ballet moved into a new era. Theatrical history contains a remarkable number of instances of the appearance of different talents suited to the needs of the times, and even of the union of these talents in creative associations. Sometimes fate does not permit artists to meet, but all great achievements have their appointed time. Thus, to select at random a few examples from Russian art, the underrated operas of Mussorgsky and Rimsky-Korsakov found their true expression in Mamontov's Private Opera Company in Moscow, where the real splendour of these composers' music was revealed in the picturesque designs by Korovin, Vrubel and Serov and in the stage performances of Zabella-Vrubel, Tsvetkova, Sekar-Rozhansky and, above all, of Chaliapin. Almost at the same time a new theatre company under the direction of Stanislavsky and Nemirovich-Danchenko made its appearance in Moscow; here, after a resounding failure on the Imperial stage in St Petersburg, Chekhov's *The Seagull* was successfully staged, and over the next few years the foundations of Chekhovian theatre were established. A new style of performing was developed, a new type of actor was born – the actor of the Moscow Art Theatre. So too occurred the inevitable meeting of those who were to direct Russian music theatre onto a new course: Diaghilev, Stravinsky, Fokine, Benois, Golovine and later, in the 1920s, Balanchine, to name a few of those involved. Once

18

again the creative co-operation that sprang up was not a matter of chance. The times brought various, often dissimilar, creative personalities together.

The 1909 summer season in Paris consisted of both ballet and operatic productions, including the third act of Borodin's *Prince Igor* in which Chaliapin appeared and for which Fokine choreographed the Polovtsian Dances. A suggestion was made to present a ballet on a Russian folk theme and this was how the idea of *The Firebird* was born. Who actually made this suggestion? Benois, in his *Reminiscences of the Russian Ballet*, says that *The Firebird* was composed jointly, from a combination of various fairy-tales.

'The fundamental elements of the subject were inspired by the young poet Potiomkin. The working out of these elements was undertaken by a sort of committee in which Cherepnin, Fokine, the painters Steletzky, Golovine and I took part. Our excellent writer Remizov, who was not only a great eccentric, but also a great lover of all things Russian, was carried away with our idea. During the two meetings I had with him, his whole attitude seemed to give life to our joint work.

'But, alas, the path leading to the fulfilment of our enterprise was a difficult one and most of those who had taken part in the "committee" gradually fell away. Among them was Cherepnin . . .' Once Cherepnin lost interest the score was commissioned from Lyadov. He accepted the commission but time passed and nothing was heard of the music. At last Diaghilev proposed to give the scenario to Stravinsky, whose music had made an enormous impression on him. 'Diaghilev and I,' recalled Fokine, 'were thrilled with this music, for it contained the element we wanted for *The Firebird*. The music was on fire, burning brightly and sending off sparks.'

In the meantime it became clear that too much time had elapsed for *The Firebird* to be staged during the 1909 summer season. But news of the ballet had already reached the press. The ever resourceful Diaghilev therefore included in the programme the pas-de-deux of the Bluebird and the Enchanted Princess from Tchaikovsky's *Sleeping Beauty*, dressed the dancers in gold costumes, and called the number – *The Firebird*. The position of the new ballet was further complicated because at that time Stravinsky was fully engaged on a completely different task: he was writing an opera based on the lyrical fairy-tale by Hans Christian Andersen about a Chinese emperor and two nightingales. When Stravinsky received Diaghilev's proposal, he had already completed sketches of the opera and had written the first act. Now Diaghilev's bursting, indomitable energy and unique ability to attract people to his schemes were revealed in full measure. He persuaded Stravinsky to put *The Nightingale* (as the opera was called) to one side and take up *The Firebird*.

Stravinsky and Fokine would sit together for hours at a time, discussing the music and evolving the complicated interaction of the music and its plastic expression. Fokine described their method of working in his memoirs: 'Stravinsky visited me with his first sketches and basic ideas, he played them for me, I demonstrated the scenes to him. At my request he broke up his folk themes into short phrases corresponding to the separate moments of a scene, separate gestures and poses.

I remember how he brought me a beautiful Russian melody for the entrance

Igor Stravinsky with Serge Diaghilev at the Alfonso XIII Hotel, Seville, in 1921.

of the Tzarevich Ivan. I suggested not presenting the complete melody all at once, but just hinting at it, by means of separate notes, at the moments when Ivan appears at the wall, when he observes the wonders of the enchanted garden, and when he leaps over the wall.

Stravinsky played, and I interpreted the role of the Tzarevich, the piano substituting for the wall. I climbed over it, jumped down from it, and crawled, horror-struck, looking around – my own room. Stravinsky, watching, accompanied me with patches of the Tzarevich melodies, playing mysterious tremolos as background to depict the garden of the sinister Immortal, Kashchei.'

By 1910 the score of *The Firebird* was ready. The première took place that same year at the Opera House in Paris and was a sensation. The papers wrote that the ballet was a miracle of entrancing balance in every detail. Later, when years had gone by and Stravinsky looked back on the past, he wrote that the choreography for *The Firebird* always seemed to him too 'complicated and overburdened with plastic detail'. Moreover, he came to the conclusion that 'the dances were somewhat limp'. What was the production really like? After all, there is no doubt that *The Firebird* of Stravinsky, Fokine and the designer, Golovine was the beginning of a new epoch in the history of the ballet, and has proved an evergreen masterpiece. A well-known contemporary writer on ballet, Vera Krasovskaya, (author of a four-volume history of the Russian ballet) gives a convincing answer to this question: 'In the 1930s, when Stravinsky wrote *Chronicle of My Life*, his meeting with Balanchine, the choreographer who was reviving the art of Marius Petipa according to 20th century symphonic principles,

20

had already taken place and he categorically stated that "the evolution of the classical dance and its problems now seem more real to me, and touch me more closely than the distant aesthetics of Fokine".' It was this that caused him to write of the 'limpness' of the dances.

Krasovskaya goes on to say: 'Fokine believed in drama where the action developed logically. He introduced mime in which the precise, economic, poetic gesture, the pose, the free and natural movement of the whole body united with the stylistic conception dictated by the music and the artist's designs for a production. He selected and combined the colours characterising each role. The logic of the actions and the acuteness of the plastic characteristics of Fokine's ballet then became law for choreographers who acknowledged the dramatisation of action as the sine qua non of dance productions.'

Between them the production of *The Firebird* and Stravinsky's music constituted an entirely new treatment of the Russian theme in ballet; Diaghilev's quest was crowned with great success. The distant fairy-tale past of Russia was presented before the audience in living and highly coloured symbols. Recalling the production which, except for Bakst's costumes for the Firebird and the Tzarevna, was designed by Golovine, Fokine wrote: 'The garden was like a Persian carpet interwoven with fantastic vegetation, and the architecture of the castle was unbelievably sinister-looking. All the scenery was in dark tones, with the golden apples shining eerily.'

The choreographic images flowed organically out of the musical images, a feat not easily achieved. For the aesthetics of ballet in this period Stravinsky's music was full of unexpected and unusual peculiarities: the irregularity and capricious mutability of rhythms and themes, the sudden changes of accent, the number of episodes/scenes which had to be organised into a unified whole. But it was precisely these not entirely 'convenient' features that set in motion the regeneration of modern choreography. It was necessary to reinterpret the old methods, to reconsider previous conceptions of the interdependence of music and dance that had now proved unserviceable.

According to Stravinsky's way of thinking, a special contrapuntal correspondence between the music and the choreography must be achieved. It was necessary not to 'count the beats' to the accompaniment of the music, but to recast the musical form in a plastic rendering that would express the complicated interweaving of the accents of music and dance. In such choreography musical and dance rhythms and beats rarely coincide, and did so only as a carefully planned device deliberately introduced into the choreographic design. In other words, the ballet was discovering the 'principle of the director' whereby, as in the straight theatre, everything is subordinated as far as possible to the logic of a single idea permeating all that is seen and heard on stage.

The use of new means of expression presented the ballet with new potential for the revelation of character. At the première the part of the Firebird was danced by one of Russia's greatest ballerinas – Tamara Karsavina. And although Stravinsky would initially have preferred Anna Pavlova, he confessed years later: 'Though circumstances had decided otherwise than I had planned, I had no cause for complaint, since Karsavina's rendering of the bird's part was perfect, and that beautiful and gracious artist had a brilliant success in it.' The magnificence of the powerful enchantress was combined with a touching timidity when she found herself a prisoner of Prince Ivan (danced by Fokine himself), while the airy lightness and brilliance of her dancing created the impression of a bird's flight.

The Firebird's success and the French public's interest in Russian art spurred on the directors of the 'Russian Seasons' to further efforts in this direction. A year later, on 13 June 1911, the première of Stravinsky and Fokine's second ballet, *Petrushka*, took place at the Théâtre du Châtelet. This ballet became a kind of symbol of the 'Russian Seasons', establishing a new standard for its creators' artistic achievements. For Stravinsky, Fokine and Benois *Petrushka* marked the turning point in their respective careers. It was Stravinsky's first step along the road of long and splendid activity in the vanguard of contemporary music.

'Even at the end of the 1920s,' wrote Boris Asafiev, 'the score of *Petrushka* was utterly different from that of *The Firebird*, but even more pellucid and stunning. With *Petrushka* Stravinsky finally became his own master; with *Petrushka* the entire generation of contemporary musicians yielded first place to him. Everyone who did not want to be a "living corpse" understood then that a great event was taking place, that Russian music had achieved something really new and unprecedented. In *The Firebird* everything was directed towards inventiveness, here it was towards expressiveness. It was as if Russian intonations had been turned into living musical speech.' Of course there were 'living corpses', as Francis Routh pointed out in his book *Stravinsky* (London, 1975): 'The audiences who applauded (*The Firebird*) were not at all anxious, subsequently, to follow its creator into fresh, more original, uncharted territories.'

Petrushka is a hero of Russian folk fantasy. For generations he has been brought to life in various ways, from performances by live actors to portrayals by handmade wooden puppets. At the beginning of the 20th century there was a new wave of interest in Petrushka among Russian artists. Cunning, quick-witted, able to extricate himself from scrape after scrape, Petrushka underwent a transformation at the turn of the century from a merry and amusing clown to an unhappy and tragic figure. Now the fool's cap and mask hid the clown's true feelings, as he tried to protect his individuality from the vulgarity and coarseness of life; under his multi-coloured costume he unexpectedly revealed a bitterly lonely and easily wounded soul. The harlequinade, summoned from the past by painters, actors, composers and writers, came into direct contact with modernity and was endowed with a new meaning. In an atmosphere of anxiety, by a wavering and uncertain light, and in a sombre but luxurious setting, brief scenes passed one after the other. Their insubstantial content made few demands on the audience but behind the amusing trivialities lay a symbolic meaning. Rough street theatre acquired a bitter and bloody tint. Everything was at once ridiculous but significant, stupid but profound. The enjoyment of the moment, the fleeting instant of play gave place to desperate terror in the face of Fate's arbitrary disposal of events. The bold challenge beneath the clowning, the despair without hope of victory, the fight to the death with reality – became the principal theme of Stravinsky's new ballet.

It is interesting to read Stravinsky's own account of the time when he was

22

composing *Petrushka*: 'Before tackling *Le Sacre du Printemps*, which would be a long and difficult task, I wanted to refresh myself by composing an orchestral piece in which the piano would play the most important part – a sort of *Konzertstück*. In composing the music, I had in my mind a distinct picture of a puppet, suddenly endowed with life, exasperating the patience of the orchestra with diabolical cascades of *arpeggi*. The orchestra in turn retaliates with menacing trumpet blasts. The outcome is a terrific noise which reaches its climax and ends in the sorrowful and querulous collapse of the poor puppet. Having finished this bizarre piece, I struggled for hours, while walking beside Lake Geneva, to find a title which would express in a word the character of my music and consequently the personality of this creature. One day I leapt for joy. I had indeed found my title – *Petrushka*, the immortal and unhappy hero of every fair in every country.'

Stravinsky probably worked on none of his other compositions with such enthusiasm; he literally felt his hero to be a living person with whom he was well acquainted. In a letter to his mother of 9 November 1910, he wrote: 'My Petrushka reveals more and more unsympathetic traits in his character every day, but what delights me is that he is absolutely devoid of hypocrisy.' After Stravinsky had shown the sketches of the music to Diaghilev, who went into raptures over them, someone had to be found to create the scenario of the future ballet. It is impossible not to be surprised again and again by Diaghilev's unique ability to find the very person for the task in hand. He turned to Alexandre Benois, although they had fallen out. But Diaghilev's instinct did not fail him. Benois replied with an immediate and unconditional acceptance of the offer.

For him, as for Stravinsky, the work on *Petrushka* was linked with precious childhood memories: wandering about the Champ de Mars in St Petersburg during the holidays and watching the lively shows of the annual Shrovetide Fair. In his memoirs Benois wrote: 'My delight in Stravinsky was so great that out of reverence I was prepared to efface myself utterly before the undoubted genius of his music – all the more so because the initiative in everything was wholly his. I only helped to create concrete stage forms. I was responsible almost entirely for the creation of the ballet, the characters and their personalities, the opening and development of the action, the majority of various details . . .' Later in his memoirs we read: 'As regards the personality of Petrushka himself, I immediately felt a kind of "obligation for old time's sake" to immortalise him on the modern stage. But I was even more attracted by the idea of depicting Shrovetide on stage – the dearly loved fair booths, the great joy of my childhood that had been my father's joy too.'

This interest contains both a personal aim and an artistic purpose. Although Benois does not link his enthusiasm with circumstances at the time of *Petrushka*'s composition, the enormous influence of the harlequin theme on Russian art, mentioned above, cannot be dismissed. The ideal image of the actor in the new theatre could be found in the puppet who could express feelings and ideas that had a far more general application than those of a live actor. The poet Andrei Bely even had the idea of opening a special theatre for puppets, whose characteristic means of expression seemed to him particularly alluring: puppets easily convey the grotesque, the lonely and anguished inability to come to terms with

The Royal Ballet production of *Petrushka*, 1957, with the Benois scenery and costumes, and dancers Margot Fonteyn, Alexander Grant, Peter Clegg and Frederick Ashton.   *Photo: Houston Rogers. Theatre Museum, V & A.*

the surrounding world, the insignificance and essential farcicality of human life.

The scenes of the future ballet, its images and plot soon took shape in Benois' mind. On his return to St Petersburg later in 1910 Diaghilev had a look at the outlined scenario. It told of Petrushka's hopeless love for a ballerina and his death at the hands of his rival, the Moor. The action unfolded by turn in the Shrovetide Fair and in the Showman's fairground theatre. In December Stravinsky arrived in St Petersburg; he showed Benois those parts of the music he had already completed and discussed the details of the libretto with him. Thus, although the scenario and music were composed at the same time, the work on each was carried out independently. Fokine, the ballet's choreographer, came into even less contact with Stravinsky and Benois at this time; he started rehearsing when the libretto had been finished and work on the music was nearing completion. Naturally some changes had to be made during the drafting

24

of the final version, but it is clear that the linking up of the co-authors' independent work resulted in an intensification of what they had composed. Thus, to take one example, Benois described his vision of the ballet's finale, the scene of the murder, in one of his first letters to Stravinsky in 1910; although the ballet does not after all end in this way (Benois suggested the murder of the Moor by Petrushka, in accordance with the traditions of puppet pantomime), the atmosphere of the projected scene seems to be describing the music – whereas Benois had in fact not yet seen the music.

It is interesting to note both the intentional effect of the puppets' transformation that Benois had already devised and the characteristics of the music of the final dance. 'The fight takes place in a blue-grey, almost lilac twilight. The murder must be presented 'au sérieux', and this entire scene must be performed with a slight but genuine sadness (in the music). Commotion, hubbub. People look for a doctor, the policeman bursts in, forces aside the group surrounding the victim. Petrushka has locked himself in his little booth and refuses to appear when summoned. The ballerina is in the other booth. Suddenly the Showman appears, bends over the victim and . . .lifts up the puppet Moor whose cardboard nose he pulls off with a smile, then goes to Petrushka's booth, unlocks it with his key and pulls out a puppet, the stupid, idiotic puppet Petrushka. The same takes place with the ballerina . . . Here general relief and immeasurable joy: carousels, fairground rides, entertainments . . .a torchlight bacchanalia begins . . .a general wild, devilish dance goes on . . .a counterpoint of twenty themes (at the very least) – jingling, little bells and perhaps even an accordion as an orchestral instrument.' (*I.F. Stravinsky, Articles and Source Material*, Moscow, 1973, page 158.)

Stravinsky insisted on changing the finale so that Petrushka fell at the hands of his happy rival, the Moor, yet Benois' work was in perfect harmony with Stravinsky's basic ideas. Stravinsky had no quarrel, for instance, with the way in which Benois added depth to Petrushka's image through his subjection to the magic of the Showman who, in Benois' scenario, was the prime cause of all Petrushka's troubles: he 'dared to give his toy a heart and soul'. In the music, in Benois' decor and in Fokine's choreography the sense of tragedy extended far beyond the limits of an intimate puppet play. Events established the appropriate scale, emphasising the idea of human solitude, incomprehension and impotence. Thus, starting with a sentimental desire to recreate tenderly remembered scenes from childhood, the authors of *Petrushka* went on to tell of man's tormented fate when he is forced to spend his life obeying laws which are abhorrent to his true self and which force him to compromise with his conscience. In this way the unending conflict both with oneself and with the surrounding world is born. Vaslav Nijinsky's brilliant interpretation of the character of the human puppet harmonised perfectly with the creation of Stravinsky, Benois and Fokine; in fact, Nijinsky could rightly be called the fourth co-author of the ballet. Stravinsky hailed him as the greatest performer of the role of Petrushka. Fokine echoed Stravinsky's praise: 'I never again beheld such a Petrushka. No one else could so catch the innermost meaning of a gesture.'

Petrushka has a special place in the ballet's heritage. Much has been written about this brilliant ballet, by the English writer Joan Lawson for example. In her

History of the Ballet and its Makers (London, 1964), she devotes many pages to *Petrushka* and shows how Fokine was the first to succeed completely in conveying unspoken feelings through dance movements alone. There is one particular aspect that deserves attention. Although Stravinsky believed *Petrushka* to be Fokine's finest work, he was nonetheless dissatisfied with the direction of the crowd on stage. 'It was a pity that the movements of the crowd had been neglected,' he wrote. 'I mean that they were left to the arbitrary improvisation of the performers instead of being choreographically regulated in accordance with the clearly defined exigencies of the music.'

Stravinsky described the character of the crowd in various way. After the lively, merry, festive hubbub of the strolling crowd comes the image of a dull, indifferent herd whose members are linked to each other only by a common desire for amusement. Everyone concentrates on himself and his narrow personal interests. Stravinsky came to the conclusion that such a crowd, stupid and cruel and indifferent to the fate of others, was one of the basic reasons for Petrushka's downfall. In the choreography for the crowd Fokine painstakingly worked out a dramatic picture, like that of a painting, suggesting to the performers bright individual characteristics. This method of staging crowd scenes entered both opera and ballet from the Moscow Art Theatre. In their first productions the crowd was perceived as an association of concrete individuals. Crowd scenes were interpreted as the overall effect of separate figures, in which each performer had to find the 'kernel' of his own character, his own external characteristics and experience, the line of conduct peculiar to him. This was a daring but dangerous course. At that time Stanislavsky's method of directing was often accused of concentrating the spectators' attention on individuals in separate episodes not connected with the general course of events, and of thereby distracting attention from the essential action at a given moment.

This approach, which Fokine chose to adopt in *Petrushka*, did not prove unsatisfactory simply because it clashed with Stravinsky's active dislike of improvisation and his oft-repeated dictum that a strict and clear form, rule and order must constantly prevail over the haphazard and arbitrary. The real problem with Fokine's approach was that the principle on which it was based was only marginally suitable for music theatre. Here the single characteristic of music seems to level individuality, forcing all the performers to react in one way to a given event. In *Petrushka* Stravinsky gave the crowd just such a single characteristic. As time passed the evolution of the director's approach in music theatre (at first on the operatic stage) led to the application of another method more in keeping with Stravinsky's own views: the unity of the crowd, enveloped by common concerns and desires, was now emphasised. Under these conditions the dividing lines between members of the crowd were not obliterated, but each person was subordinated to the underlying idea at the basis of the action.

If *Petrushka* marks one of the high points of Stravinsky's creativity, containing many features in its store of dramatic, figurative and stylistic methods that were developed in his subsequent works, *Le Sacre du Printemps* became in its turn a revelation in the history of twentieth century music and theatre. As he explains in his memoirs, the idea for this ballet had come to Stravinsky much earlier when he was 'finishing the last pages of *The Firebird* in St Petersburg. I

26

Nicolai Roerich's costume design for one of the maidens in *Le Sacre du Printemps*, Part I.   *Bakhrushin Museum, Moscow.*

had a fleeting vision which came to me as a complete surprise, my mind at the moment being full of other things. I saw in imagination a solemn pagan rite: sage elders, seated in a circle, watched a young girl dance herself to death. They were sacrificing her to propitiate the god of spring. Such was the theme of *Le Sacre du Printemps*. I must confess that this vision made a deep impression on me, and I at once described it to my friend, Nicolai Roerich, he being a painter who had specialised in pagan subjects. He welcomed my inspiration with enthusiasm, and became my collaborator in this creation. In Paris I told Diaghilev about it, and he was at once carried away by the idea, though the realisation was delayed by the subsequent events.' (We already know that one of the 'subsequent events' that delayed *Le Sacre du Printemps* was the composition of *Petrushka*.)

Jean Cocteau's caricature of Stravinsky playing *Le Sacre du Printemps*.
© SPADEM. *Theatre Museum, V & A.*

Stravinsky's new work was set in the landscape of primitive pagan Russia. There are no 'individuals': almost nothing distinguishes the inhabitants of the world from the world of nature with its mysterious vital energy. Nicolai Roerich, who designed the ballet, said in an interview in the summer of 1910: 'The new ballet will present a series of scenes of a sacred night among the ancient Slavs. The action begins on a summer night and ends before sunrise, as the first rays of light are revealed. Strictly speaking the choreographic aspect consists of ritual

28

dances. This will be the first attempt to reproduce the distant past without a defined dramatic subject.'

The score of *Le Sacre du Printemps*, whose première caused a famous scandal, proved to be a work which the world could not ultimately dismiss. In Stravinsky's own creativity and in the theatre's search for new directions in the twentieth century this work became a beacon illuminating many subsequent years. As he expressed it in one of his letters, Stravinsky himself was conscious of the ballet's novelty 'as if twenty, and not merely two, years had passed since the composition of *The Firebird*.' A work was offered for theatrical interpretation in which the customary emphasis was displaced. This ballet concentrated neither on subjective experiences, nor on personal, psychologically directed relations to events. Instead it focused attention on the essence of that which is enduring and deeply rooted in the human consciousness, transmitted from generation to generation for thousands of years. Stravinsky's concern was now, as it would often be in the future, with the revelation of the suprapersonal, filtered by centuries but eternally present in the human mind.

The astonishing novelty of Stravinsky's musical language demanded a new theatrical approach. In *Le Sacre du Printemps*, to quote Asafiev again, 'the heart of the matter is movement, incessant swelling up, branching out, expanding or contracting of the material. It is as if the material breathes, first full of air and expanding, then reduced to one or two lines.' 'The whole thing must be presented in dancing form – without mime,' insisted Stravinsky time and time again. But how was this to be achieved? The choreography had to reject the concrete meaning of the ballet's thirteen episodes and find a form of action expressive of the music. In addition the repudiation of individual thought and feeling, the freedom from the constraint of a plot, the whole movement of musical ideas inclined the theatre towards the creation of symphonic ballet. Thus the classical ballet gained a new lease of life, though in another form. The classical tradition was already developing on a new basis, and with it Stravinsky's theatre moved towards a new unity with the new choreographers.

Fokine's method of choreography, which emphasised the concrete meaning of events, was not suitable for *Le Sacre du Printemps*, and Diaghilev asked Nijinsky to stage the ballet. Stravinsky claims in his memoirs that he was not satisfied with the ballet. Several times he returns to a discussion of Nijinsky, always stressing his admiration for Nijinsky as a dancer but at the same time denying him any ability as a choreographer; in fact, Stravinsky writes that he had his doubts about Nijinsky in the latter capacity from the very beginning and that he told Diaghilev so repeatedly during rehearsals. Diaghilev, however, 'persisted in pushing Nijinsky along that path... (Nijinsky) appeared to be quite unconscious both of his inadequacy and of the fact that he had been given a role which, to put it plainly, he was incapable of filling in so serious an undertaking as the Russian Ballet'.

Was this really the case? For an answer to this vexed question we must again turn to Professor Krasovskaya. In the chapter devoted to *Le Sacre du Printemps* she cites several comments made by Stravinsky in 1913, the year of the première. From these, and indeed from many other of his comments, as well as from the testimony of contemporaries, it is clear that time altered Stravinsky's views. Several hours before the beginning of the première Stravinsky said: 'I am happy that in Nijinsky I have found the ideal collaborator.' Three weeks after the première with its accompanying scandal and stormy passions, he once again summed up his views: 'Nijinsky's choreography is incomparable. With a very few exceptions, everything was as I wished. We must wait a long time for the public to become used to our idiom. I *believe* in what we did and this gives me the strength for further work.'

It is clear, not just from the juxtaposition of Stravinsky's contradictory comments, that the production choreographed by Nijinsky was a great artistic achievement in the art of ballet. Later years in the ballet's development revealed that this powerful production set ballet on a new course, with a sudden mighty lurch. The innovations made by Nijinsky were viewed by his contemporaries as a sick insult. 'But in the history of world choreography,' writes Krasovskaya, 'his creative ideas proved to be a fresh graft on to the trunk of theatrical dance and stimulated the growth of new branches: what Nijinsky revealed was granted the same right of citizenship as the music of *Le Sacre du Printemps* and may be detected in the works of various choreographers throughout the world, who often have no inkling of their predecessor's discoveries.'

The same could hardly be said of George Balanchine. As Bernard Taper remarks in his biography of Balanchine (New York & London, 1974,) 'Almost single-handed, Balanchine has kept the classic tradition of ballet alive in our epoch . . .(at the same time) he has boldly explored realms of movement not seen before in ballet.' It was from Stravinsky's music that Balanchine made one of his most important discoveries; 'gestures have certain family relations which, as groups, impose their own laws.' The clarity of the score for *Apollo* brought home to him that he must not mix various styles of movement; instead he must select the only possible style for the music. This realisation has influenced all Balanchine's subsequent work. But it was not until 1927 that Balanchine worked with Stravinsky on *Apollo*. Their creative collaboration had not yet begun in 1913 when Nijinsky choreographed *Le Sacre du Printemps* and the scandal erupted on the ballet's first night. In the intervening years Stravinsky had written many other works.

In 1913 he completed his lyrical operatic fairy-tale, *The Nightingale*, which he had abandoned several years previously in favour of *The Firebird*. The opera was first performed by Diaghilev's troupe in Paris in the following year, and a little later the symphonic suite, *The Song of the Nightingale*, made its appearance. The production was designed by Benois and the opera was in Stravinsky's words, 'performed incomparably'. According to Stravinsky it was not his own idea to return to his first work for the stage, but the suggestion of the Svobodny Teatr (Free Theatre), which had only just been established in Moscow. For a time Stravinsky hesitated. His musical idiom had changed significantly during the four years that had elapsed. He was afraid that the music of the scenes still waiting to be composed would be too noticeably different from the music of the prologue. He then realised that 'the forest, with its nightingale, the pure soul of the child who falls in love with its song . . . All this gentle poetry of Hans Andersen's could not be expressed in the same way as the baroque luxury of the Chinese Court, with its bizarre etiquette, its palace fêtes, its thousands of little bells and lanterns, and the grotesque humming of the mechanical Japanese nightingale . . .in short, all this exotic fantasy obviously demanded a different musical idiom.'

In its turn the 'different musical idiom' acted as a creative stimulus and inspired the masters of the stage to set out once again in search of new means of theatrical expression. The original artistic ideas concealed in Stravinsky's scores helped the formation of new theatrical forms and expanded the vocabulary of the stage. The theatrical innovators found in Stravinsky's music opportunities for the clearer definition of these new forms.

Obviously Stravinsky's stage practice and its artistic results were not solely Stravinsky's creation, he united in himself a number of ideas that were in the air, brought out and expressed important fundamental artistic tendencies of the period, apprehended and expressed in different ways. But throughout this search the essential idea of theatrical stylisation stands out, as does Stravinsky's indefatigable search for new possibilities in the complex, contradictory but indissoluble union of music and theatre. Thus, for example, the idea of the separation of performing roles was employed during the production of *The Nightingale* by Diaghilev's troupe in Paris. This method was first tried out in the production of Rimsky-Korsakov's *The Golden Cockerel* in the spring of 1914. Choreographed by Fokine and designed by Gontcharova, this production treated the composer's last work as an opera-ballet. The singers sat on the stage, holding their scores, while dancers and mimes conveyed the action of the drama. In his memoirs Benois gives a description of the rapture with which this production was received. Despite a certain violence done to Rimsky-Korsakov's opera, the experiment had great significance for many of Stravinsky's subsequent works, and considerably influenced the music theatre of the 20th century.

As already mentioned, a similar principle was used as the basis of the Paris production of *The Nightingale* (directed by Alexandre Benois and Alexandre Sanine, choreographed by Romanov and designed by Benois). Four years later, on 30 May 1918, Vsevolod Meyerhold presented *The Nightingale* on the stage of the Maryinsky Theatre in St Petersburg. According to the production's designer, Golovine, Stravinsky himself chose Meyerhold. This choice was not haphazard. As a director of both straight and music theatre during this period, Meyerhold had expressed views that approached the solution of similar problems of theatrical form; Stravinsky's musical innovations intrinsically suited Meyerhold's transformations on the operatic stage.

Meyerhold's production of *The Nightingale* was also based on the separation of the musical and stage elements; this approach again strongly emphasised the principle of stylisation. Konstantin Ruznitsky, author of a definitive work on Meyerhold (*Meyerhold the Director*, Moscow, 1969), writes: 'In front of each performer stood a music-stand bearing his music. As they moved from place to place, the characters carried their music-stands with them, placed them where necessary; beginning their solos at a signal from the conductor, they looked at their music while singing, and, having finished their parts, sat (or stood) with vacant expressions on their faces.' Here Meyerhold declared open war on the dramatisation of opera, on the attempt to introduce into operatic art the verisimilitude of a dramatic performance. Opera was regarded as musical action in costume. In accordance with this aim, Meyerhold placed on the right and left of the proscenium stationary choral groups and severely restricted the main characters' movement about the stage. The soloists and chorus were condemned to immobility but at the same time silent actors vividly mimed the action.

The principles tested in Paris and fully developed under Meyerhold were not, as it seemed at the time, simply a fashionable experiment. To Stravinsky these principles meant a great deal. In this instance the practice of the theatre anticipated the musical form of many of his future works, a form that was developed in its fullest extent in the opera-oratorio *Oedipus Rex*, where the 'performers' had to create the impression of living statues, as Stravinsky put it. Even before Meyerhold's production of *The Nightingale* Stravinsky had written *Renard*, in which the principle of separating the functions of the singers and actors was openly displayed and defined by the composer himself. In essence this work is a pantomime performed by ballet dancers and acrobats to the accompaniment of a vocal quartet and instrumental ensemble. In *Renard* Stravinsky employed the device of sub-dividing the image, of consciously not synchronising the concrete stage character of the hero with the words pronounced by him. The characters' words are given to singers or even to an entire chorus placed in the orchestra.

In *Pulcinella* the singers, who were also placed in the orchestra, were given texts taken from various operas and cantatas that were quite unconnected with the action of the ballet on stage. This contrast was matched by the contrast of modern and traditional in Stravinsky's reinterpretation of 18th century music. In an article in the April 1981 issue of *Dance Magazine* Marilyn Meeker shows how this treatment of the music influenced the décor and choreography of the ballet. Picasso was able to make experiments in stage design, contrasting the muted colours of his cubist sets with the bright colours of the traditional costumes, and lighting the stage for the first time completely from above; Massine similarly introduced contrasting methods into his choreography, combining comic gesture and popular dance styles with the techniques of classical ballet.

A narrator appears in *Histoire du Soldat*, and most episodes are performed on stage in the form of a musical pantomime. The characters are depicted by various artistic methods: whereas the Devil both acts and dances, the Princess only dances and the Soldier only mimes, although in a later version the Soldier and the Devil are given words to say. In *Les Noces*, begun before *Renard* in 1914, as later in *Perséphone* and at the end of his life in *The Flood*, Stravinsky in various ways constantly exposes facets of the theatrical cornerstone of stylisation and play-acting. Sometimes the singers sit together with the orchestra while the stage is given over to mimes, sometimes total immobility is juxtaposed with living action – or it may happen that all these features are incorporated in a single work. In *Les Noces* the performers, the chorus, the dancers, four pianos and the percussion instruments are all on stage where they can be seen by the audience.

Hand in hand with the stylistic approach went another specific feature of Stravinsky's works – the grotesque. Already making an appearance in his first work (in the third scene of *Petrushka*), the grotesque in Stravinsky's music passed through various stages of development but was always used as one of the techniques of the stylistic method. This interest in satirical, grotesque devices was stimulated by the possibilities they offered. Viewed from an unusual angle different manifestations of life and human character were made to reveal many-sided, paradoxical combinations. This in turn gave full scope to the element of play-acting itself, to the contrasting and confronting of opposing ideas and images. Such an approach is common in the literature and art of the 20th century, and it was natural to Stravinsky's sharp, ironic mind. To be convinced of this one has only to open his dialogues with Robert Craft at any page, or to look through his correspondence or his numerous interviews. His penetrating power of observation, his sharp, subtle pronouncements, his amazing sense of humour, his profound culture, the stunning originality and depth of his ideas – all command attention. In exactly the same way one is gripped by the many nuances in the rich individual character of Stravinsky's theatrical works.

'But the manner of their presentation,' writes Mikhail Druskin in his work on Stravinsky (Leningrad, 1979), 'is usually the same: the dominant free element of play-acting and theatricality. Stravinsky affirms the festival spirit in its true, direct sense. He loves to open a work with an introductory fanfare, as in *Agon*, or with a marching entrance like the parade around the ring which is common to the circus, the hippodrome and the bullring. Thus, *Renard* opens with a march to whose music the actors make their entrance (they exit to the sound of the same march); and in *Histoire du Soldat* the performance opens with a march, as do *Danses Concertantes* and each of the three scenes of *Jeu de Cartes*.' In such frankly emphasised theatricality, moments of play-acting are highlighted. They are present in the apotheoses (dithyrambs) which conclude *Apollo*, in *Le Baiser de la Fée*, in the *Duo Concertante* for violin and piano, in *Scènes de Ballet* and in *Orpheus*. Of course the diversity of stage forms in Stravinsky's theatre has not yet been exhausted. The majority of his works cannot be pigeon-holed in the traditional framework of opera or ballet, but it is precisely these works that have exerted the greatest influence on theatre practice in the 20th century.

Stravinsky's works did not by any means always break with tradition and bring about radical change in the theatre. Sometimes it was his love of tradition which actually inspired him. For example, the ballet *Pulcinella* was 'a first return to the past, the first of similar infatuations of mine', as Stravinsky recalled. These journeys into the past were above all connected with a special feeling of affection for earlier times. It might be affection for some particular artistic event, or some personal reminiscence which he especially valued. At times the present and past are united in a fantasy: the idea that it is possible to 'fuse specifically Russian elements with the spiritual richness of the West'.

The opera-buffa *Mavra* is dedicated to Pushkin, Glinka and Tchaikovsky, but the influence of Western artistic ideas of the time is indisputable. Stravinsky reinterpreted Pushkin's charming, lyrical and slightly mournful poem 'The Little House at Kolomna'. The opera is based on the use of the grotesque in the development of a situation. The librettist Boris Kochno had the difficult task of adding a new text to Pushkin's verses. This he managed to do skilfully and with great delicacy and tact. The characters of the opera are to a certain extent a continuation of the Russian vaudeville tradition. They are conventional figures

A scene from the production of *The Rake's Progress* at the Staatsoper, Hamburg, 1967, with Edith Lang as Mother Goose, Tom Krause as Nick Shadow and Loren Driscoll as Tom Rakewell.   *Photo: F.Peyer.*

rather than specific images or personalities. Anyone acquainted with Russian music will have no difficulty in finding echoes of the operas of Dargomijsky, Tchaikovsky and Rimsky-Korsakov in *Mavra*, and the tunes of old popular songs. The material, which is easily recognisable, is distorted in a grotesque fashion, and thus creates an original effect. *Mavra* has been imitated many times and by many people – for example by Shostakovich in his first opera, *The Nose*.

Stravinsky's longest opera, *The Rake's Progress*, which was created under the influence of Hogarth's paintings, is also based on the idea of a grotesque spectacle, a game. The scenes follow thick and fast one after the other. As in *Mavra*, the past is viewed through the filter of the grotesque. The plot, which is typical of the classical period, is tinged with the author's ironical attitude. The choice of form allowed Stravinsky to make use of the logic and methods of opera composition of the 17th and 18th centuries. The work abounds with brilliance and energy.

It is not easy, in fact it seems almost impossible, to specify the precise limits of Stravinsky's influence on contemporary theatre. When one is dealing with such a many-sided creative personality, any definition must be tentative. Stravinsky's genius incorporated features drawn from a wide range of artistic systems. Yet this amazing ability to blend such distinctive elements, to combine the cultural achievements of the past harmoniously with the most modern way of expressing

34

ideas about life, cannot obscure Stravinsky's individuality: he can be recognised behind all styles and masks.

Stravinsky's long life contained a number of crucial personal and professional changes, and it is interesting that in times of crisis his most important works were often linked with the theatre. Changes in his musical poetics and style are linked likewise with changes in his views on the theatre, although his own logic can be detected throughout; the stormy dynamics of his art have an inner consistency. Stravinsky was a man of the theatre and he effected many changes in the theatre. Combining a diversity of forms and means of expression, Stravinsky sought in his theatrical works to comprehend the realm of broad philosophical and poetic speculation. Addressing themselves to both the hearts and minds of the spectators, his theatrical works force people to re-examine and reassimilate their familiar, accustomed world. This constant challenge to human consciousness has proved a continuing stimulus to artistic creation and to the quest for fresh ideas.

It is impossible to speak of Stravinsky and of the theatre he created in the past tense. The contemporary theatrical repertoire remains heavily indebted to him and perpetually returns to replenish its forces from his inexhaustible treasury of ideas, feelings, thoughts and images, embodying the joys and sorrows of 20th century life.

Igor Stravinsky on 24 June
1962 at the Staatsoper,
Hamburg during the
celebrations for his 80th
birthday.   *Photo: F.Peyer*

PART 2
by Alexander Schouvaloff

Works composed for performance

Productions from other compositions

Marc Chagall: Squared-up drawing for the front cloth.   © *SPADEM*.

The Firebird

Russian fairy story in two scenes
adapted by Michel Fokine
45 minutes (EWW 16)

Alexander Golovine designed the scenery and all the costumes for the first production except for the Firebird herself and the Beautiful Tzarevna. These costumes were designed by Leon Bakst.

According to Boris Kochno, the other known costume designs by Bakst for *The Firebird* were done later, when he tried unsuccessfully to persuade Diaghilev to revive the production. But they were never used because when Diaghilev finally did revive the production in 1926 in London the scenery and costumes were designed by Natalia Gontcharova. The production was then also used by the Ballets Russes all over the world. New designs by Gontcharova, based on the old, were also used by the Royal Ballet for their production, which is still in the repertoire. At first it was expected that Anna Pavlova would dance the leading role but her place was eventually taken by Tamara Karsavina.

The first performance, choreographed by Michel Fokine, made Stravinsky into an instant international success. Much later Stravinsky was to say that he did not really like Fokine's choreography, but much preferred Balanchine's in 1949, made to the Concert Suite version of the score of 1945 with designs by Chagall. These had first been used by Adolf Bolm in 1945 for his production with Alicia Markova as the Firebird, although he did not see them until very late, and apparently hated them.

In a programme note for the performance by the Ballet du XXe siècle at the Théàtre royal de la Monnaie, Brussels, on 15 March 1973, with Ivan Marko (Firebird) and Niklas Ek (Phoenix), Maurice Béjart commented: '... Let us ...try to free ourselves from the emotion that runs through the succession of "numbers" in the score as it has been arranged, by rediscovering the two striking elements which caused such a stir at its first performance:
– Stravinsky the Russian musician,
– Stravinsky the revolutionary musician.
The dance, then, is to give abstract expression to these two elements which are present throughout the music . . .
– the Firebird is the phoenix that is reborn out of these ashes,
– the poet, like the revolutionary, is a bird born out of fire.'

First Performance 25 June 1910

Theatre:	Théâtre national de l'Opéra, Paris
Company:	Les Ballets Russes de Serge Diaghilev
Conductor:	Gabriel Pierné
Choreographer:	Michel Fokine
Scenery:	Alexander Golovine
Costumes:	Alexander Golovine & Leon Bakst (the Firebird and the Beautiful Tzarevna)
Principal Dancers:	Tamara Karsavina (the Firebird)
	Vera Fokina (the Beautiful Tzarevna)
	Michel Fokine (Ivan Tzarevitch)
	Alexei Bulgakov (Kashchei)

Synopsis

Ivan Tzarevitch strays into Kashchei's garden at night and sees the Firebird, enticed there by a tree with golden apples. He catches the bird. She begs him to let her go, but he only releases her after she gives him a magic feather. He then meets thirteen beautiful princesses who are captive under the magic spell of Kashchei, and falls in love with one of them. At dawn they have to go back to the palace. Ivan breaks open the gates to follow them but is taken prisoner by Kashchei's monster guards. He remembers the feather. He waves it three times. The Firebird appears and makes Kashchei and his monsters dance until they fall exhausted. The Firebird then shows Ivan Tzarevitch the egg which contains the life and death of Kashchei. Ivan Tzarevitch breaks the egg on the ground. Kashchei dies, and the princesses are freed. The two lovers are reunited and celebrate their betrothal.

Leon Bakst's costume design for Tamara Karsavina for the first performance.
© *Sotheby Parke Bernet.*

41

Tamara Karsavina as the Firebird.
Photo: Bert. Theatre Museum, V & A.

The extravagant detail of Bakst's design, particularly of the head-dress, had to be simplified, for obvious practical reasons.

Sketch of Tamara Karsavina made during the performance. Valentine Gross, a young artist living in Paris, was dazzled by the arrival of the Russian Ballet in the West, and spent nearly all her evenings in the theatre making sketches in the dark. Her quick, sure lines capture the thrill of the performance better than any photograph. Tamara Karsavina herself thought that this one gave the most accurate impression of her dancing. *Theatre Museum, V & A, Valentine Gross Archive.*

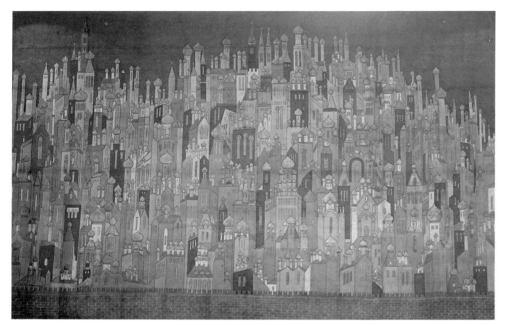

Natalia Gontcharova's
backcloth for the final scene
made for the revival of 1926.
This was among the major
acquisitions made for the
Theatre Museum by Richard
Buckle at one of the famous
auctions of scenery and
costumes of the Ballet Russe
held by Sothebys in the '60s.
Theatre Museum, V & A.

The final scene as presented by
Colonel de Basil's Ballet Russe
with Tamara Grigorievna as the
Tzarevna and Boris Kniaseff as
Ivan Tzarevitch. *The Firebird*
was one of the most regularly
performed ballets in the
repertoire. After Diaghilev's
death in 1929, Colonel de Basil
continued the company.
Theatre Museum, V & A.

Opposite: Margot Fonteyn as the Firebird and Michael Somes as Ivan Tzarevitch in the Royal Ballet production of 1954. Action photography at its most telling: Houston Rogers, standing in the wings of the Royal Opera House, Covent Garden, freezes the action, but the Firebird is hovering.
Photo: Houston Rogers. Theatre Museum, V & A.

Maria Tallchief as the Firebird and Francisco Moncion as Ivan Tzarevitch in the New York City Ballet production, 1949.
Photo: George Platt Lynes. Theatre Museum, V & A.

Other Major Productions

1921 Petrograd, Maryinsky

Conductor: Emil Cooper
Choreographer: Fedor Lopukhov
Scenery & Costumes: Alexander Golovine
Principal Dancers: Elena Lukom (Firebird), Boris
Shavroff (Tzarevitch)

25 November 1926 London, Lyceum

Choreographer: Michel Fokine
Scenery & Costumes: Natalia Gontcharova
Principal Dancers: Lydia Lopokhova (Firebird), Lubov
Tchernicheva (Tzarevna), Serge Lifar (Tzarevitch),
Georges Balanchin* (Kashchei)
Revival by les Ballets Russes de Serge Diaghilev.

* At this date he had not yet 'anglicised' his name to
George Balanchine.

16 December 1927 Berlin, Deutsche Oper

Choreographer: Lizzie Maudrik
Scenery & Costumes: Alexandre Benois

1927 Stockholm, Royal Opera

Choreographer: Lisa Steier
Scenery & Costumes: Isaac Grunewald

3 December 1928 Copenhagen, Det Kongelige Teater

Choreographer: Kaj Smith
Scenery: Ove Christian Pederson
Costumes: Axel Brunn

1929 Düsseldorf, Opernhaus

Choreographer: Ruth Loeser
Scenery & Costumes: Hellmut Jurgens

1929 Königsberg, Opernhaus

Choreographer: Marion Hermann

1931 Buenos Aires, Teatro Colon

Conductor: Ernest Ansermet
Choreographer: Michel Fokine
Scenery & Costumes: Ivan Bilibine
Principal Dancers: Olga Spessiva*, Maria Ruanova,
Dora Del Grande, Keith Lester
* Or Spesivtseva

1933 Zurich, Stadttheater

Choreographer: Helmut Zehnpfennig
Scenery & Costumes: Roman Clemens

1937 Karlsruhe

Choreographer: Valeria Kratina
Scenery & Costumes: Zircher

1940 Zurich, Stadttheater

Choreographer: Hans Macke
Scenery & Costumes: Roman Clemens

1940 Los Angeles, Hollywood Bowl

Choreographer: Adolf Bolm
Scenery & Costumes: Nicolas Remizov

2 February 1941 Milan, La Scala

Conductor: Nino Sanzogno
Choreographer: Nives Poli after Michel Fokine
Scenery: Nicola Benois
Principal Dancers: Nives Poli (Firebird), Ermanno
Savaré (Kaschchei), Marcel Fenchel (Tzarevitch), Nadia
Colombo (Tzarevna)

December 1944 Lima, Teatro Municipal

Company: Original Ballet Russe
Conductor: Eugene Fuerst
Choreographer: Michel Fokine
Scenery & Costumes: Natalia Gontcharova

24 October 1945 New York, Metropolitan Opera House

Company: Ballet Theatre
Choreographer: Adolf Bolm
Scenery & Costumes: Marc Chagall
Principal Dancers: Alicia Markova, Anton Dolin, John
Taras, Diana Adams

28 August 1947 London, Royal Opera House

Conductor: Richard Beck
Choreographer: Michel Fokine
Scenery & Costumes: Natalia Gontcharova
Principal Dancers: Olga Morosova (Firebird), Helene
Komarova (Tzarevna), Roman Jasinsky (Tzarevitch),
Vladimir Dokoudovsky

1947 Munich, Staatsoper

Choreographer: Marcel Luipart
Scenery & Costumes: Janni Loghi

27 November 1949 New York, City Center

Company: New York City Ballet
Choreographer: George Balanchine
Scenery & Costumes: Marc Chagall (sets from 1945
production)
Lighting: Jean Rosenthal
Principal Dancers: Maria Tallchief (Firebird), Francisco
Moncion (Tzarevitch)

To the music of the Third Concert Suite (1945)

31 December 1949 Milan, La Scala

Conductor: Issay Dobrowen
Choreographer: Margherita Wallmann
Scenery & Costumes: Alberto Savinio
Principal Dancers: Yvette Chauviré (Firebird), Olga
Amati (Tzarevna), Ermanno Savaré (Kashchei),
Wladimir Skouratoff (Tzarevitch)

1950 Riga, Latvian Opera and Ballet Theatre

Company: Riga Opera Ballet
Choreographer: Alexandra Fedorova-Fokin
Scenery & Costumes: Ludolfs Liberts

1953 Tokyo

Company: Komaki Ballet Company
Choreographer: Masahide Komaki after Michel Fokine
Scenery: Kotaro Maki
Costumes: Masakazu Yoshimura
Principal Dancers: Nora Kaye (Firebird), Antony Tudor
(Tzarevitch)

7 April 1954 Paris, Théâtre national de l'Opéra

Company: Paris Opera Ballet
Choreographer: Serge Lifar
Scenery & Costumes: Georges Wakhevitch
Principal Dancers: Nina Vyroubova (Firebird), Youly
Algaroff (Tzarevitch), Christiane Vaussard (Tzarevna),
Serge Lifar (Kashchei)

23 August 1954 Edinburgh, Empire Theatre

Company: The Royal Ballet
Choreographers: Original reconstructed by Serge
Grigoriev, Lubov Tchernicheva and Tamara Karsavina
Scenery & Costumes: Natalia Gontcharova
Principal Dancers: Margot Fonteyn (Firebird), Michael
Somes (Tzarevitch), Svetlana Beriosova (Tzarevna),
Frederick Ashton (Kashchei)

26 March 1962 Leningrad, Maly Theatre

Company: Maly Theatre Opera Ballet Company
Choreographer: Konstantin Boyarski
Scenery: S. Solomko
Costumes: Tatiana Bruni
Principal Dancers: Ludmilla Safronova (Firebird), Adol
Khamzin (Tzarevitch), Natalya Yananis (Tzarevna),
N. Filippovski (Kashchei)

17 November 1962 Munich, Bayerische Staatsoper

Company: Bavarian State Opera Ballet
Choreographer: Heinz Rosen
Scenery: Rudolph Heinrich
Costumes: Charlotte Fleming

4 March 1964 Berlin, Deutsche Oper

Choreographer: John Cranko
Scenery & Costumes: Jürgen Rose

20 May 1964 Stuttgart, Württemburgische Staatstheater

Company: Stuttgart Ballet
Choreographer: John Cranko
Scenery & Costumes: Jürgen Rose

1 June 1966 Budapest, State Opera House

Conductor: Péter Tóth
Choreographer: Michel Fokine
Scenery: Zoltán Fülöp
Costumes: Tivadar Mark
Principal Dancers: Zsuzsa Kun, Ferenc Haras, Jacqueline Menyháir

1 November 1967 New York, Broadway Theatre

Company: Harkness Ballet
Choreographer: Brian Macdonald
Scenery & Costumes: Rouben Ter-Arutunian
Principal Dancers: Jeanett Vobdersaar alternating with Manola Asensio

19 March 1970 Frankfurt, Opernhaus

Company: Frankfurt Opera Ballet
Choreographer: John Neumeier
Scenery & Costumes: Dorothee Zippel
Principal Dancers: Heidrun Schwarz, Beatrice Cordua, Riccardo Duse, André Doutreval

A new version in a science fiction setting. Kashchei is a robot; the Tzarevitch a space explorer, called just A Young Man.

28 May 1970 New York, NY State Theatre

Company: New York City Ballet
Choreographers: George Balanchine & Jerome Robbins
Scenery & Costumes: Marc Chagall: scenery executed by Volodia Odinokov, costumes by Barbara Karinska

31 October 1970 Paris, Palais des Sports

Company: Paris Opera Ballet
Choreographer: Maurice Béjart
Costumes: Joëlle Roustan & Roger Bernard
Lighting: Christian Boeckx
Principal Dancer: Paolo Bortoluzzi

To the music of the *Third Concert Suite* (1945). Maurice Béjart's version of the ballet was subsequently performed at the Cirque Royal, Brussels (17 November 1970), the Théâtre national de l'Opéra, Paris (12 April 1973), Teatro dell'Opera, Rome (23 October 1973), Grand Theatre, Geneva (10 January 1974), La Scala, Milan (23 February 1974), Teatro Verde, Venice (19 June 1975), The London Coliseum (18 April 1977)

10 November 1972 Stockholm, Royal Opera House

Company: Royal Swedish Ballet
Choreographer: Eske Holm
Scenery & Costumes: Josef Svoboda

23 February 1974 Milan, La Scala

Conductor: Pier Luigi Urbini
Choreographer: Maurice Béjart
Scenery & Costumes: Roger Bernard & Joëlle Roustan
Principal Dancers: Jorge Donn, Gildo Cassani, Mara Cavangnini, Antonio di Giovanni, Rosalie Kovacs, Tiziano Mietto

10 March 1974 Würzburg, Städtisches Theater

Choreographer: Klaus Meyer

5 May 1974 Zurich, Opernhaus

Choreographer: Geoffrey Cauley
Scenery: Kaspar Wolfensberger
Principal Dancers: Helena Villarvoya (Firebird), Roberto Dimitrievitch (Tzarevitch), Angelica Bornhausen (Tzarevna), Eve Trachsel (Kashchei)

28 March 1975 New York, Vandam Theatre

Company: Les Ballets Trocadéro de Monte Carlo
Choreographer: Marian Hovosko
Scenery: Richard Strahan & Joseph De Angelis
Costumes: Anthony Bassae

1975 Leningrad, Kirov Theatre

Company: Kirov Ballet Company
Choreographer: Boris Eifman

2 March 1976 Mulhouse, Théâtre Municipal

Company: Ballet du Rhin
Conductor: Paul Capolongo
Choreographer: Peter Van Dijk
Scenery & Costumes: Walter Gondolf

21 February 1977 Los Angeles, Dorothy Chandler Pavilion

Company: American Ballet Theatre
Choreographer: Christopher Newton after Michel Fokine
Scenery & Costumes: after designs by Natalia Gontcharova
Principal Dancers: Natalia Makarova (Firebird), Clark Tippet (Tzarevitch), Marcos Paredes (Kashchei), Marie Johansson (Tzarevna)

28 April 1977 Mannheim, Nationaltheater

Choreographer: Lothar Höfgen
Scenery: Wolf Wanninger
Costumes: Winnie Schneider
Principal Dancers: Christine Treisch (Firebird),
Christine Pelz (Tzarevna), Vaclav Slovenak
(Tzarevitch), Hans Wrona (Kashchei)

14 January 1979 Karlsruhe, Badisches Staatstheater

Company: Ballett des Badisches Staatstheaters
Choreographer: Germinal Casado
Scenery & Costumes: Günther Weidinger
Principal Dancers: Marina Michalopoulou (Firebird),
Peter Vondruska (Tzarevitch), Melinda Lewis
(Tzarevna), Igor Iwanoff (Kashchei)

Frederick Ashton as
Kashchei, 1954.
Photo: Houston Rogers.
Theatre Museum, V & A.

Petrushka

Burlesque ballet in four scenes
by Igor Stravinsky and Alexandre Benois
43 minutes (EWW 18)

The original choreographer, Michel Fokine, and the original designer, Alexandre Benois, provided the definitive staging of Stravinsky's second ballet for more than 60 years. The part of Petrushka, created and made legendary by Nijinsky, has also enticed every star dancer since 1911 into trying to imitate him. The drawing by Valentine Gross of Nijinsky was done after seeing his performance in Paris; the photograph by Houston Rogers of Nureyev taken many years later almost uncannily seems to be a mirror image of that drawing.

Benois designed many productions of the ballet and many others were based on his designs. He also drew many versions of the original costume design for Petrushka and, because Nijinsky had made the part so famous, he used to inscribe them 'Petrushka Nijinsky, 1911'. This makes them often impossible to date accurately. The original 'original' design, however, is in Russia.

Maurice Béjart finally broke the spell of tradition with his production in 1977. He is the great reinterpreter of Stravinsky for the second half of the 20th century, creating his own traditions which he began with his first work for the Ballet du XXe siècle, *Le Sacre du Printemps*, in 1959 and continued with *The Firebird* in 1970.

Opposite: Rudolf Nureyev as Petrushka at the Royal Opera House, Covent Garden, 1963. *Photo: Houston Rogers. Theatre Museum, V & A.*

Drawing of Vaslav Nijinsky as Petrushka, made by Valentine Gross after seeing his performance in Paris. *Theatre Museum, V & A, Valentine Gross Archive.*

First Performance 13 June 1911

Theatre:	Théâtre du Châtelet, Paris
Company:	Les Ballets Russes de Serge Diaghilev
Conductor:	Pierre Monteux
Choreographer:	Michel Fokine
Scenery & Costumes:	Alexandre Benois
Principal Dancers:	Tamara Karsavina (the Ballerina)
	Vaslav Nijinsky (Petrushka)
	Alexandre Orlov (the Moor)
	Enrico Cecchetti (the Showman)

Synopsis

Scene I: Admiralty Square, St Petersburg. The Shrovetide Fair in 1830. A crowd is enjoying the fair. A drumroll heralds the appearance of the Showman from behind a curtained booth. The curtains open to reveal three puppets: a Moor, a Ballerina and Petrushka. At a command from the Showman, the puppets dance. The Moor and Petrushka are in love with the Ballerina. She prefers the Moor. Petrushka, jealous, attacks the Moor. The Showman ends the performance. The puppets collapse motionless.

Scene II: Petrushka's room. Petrushka is kicked into the room by the Showman. He tries in vain to escape. The Ballerina appears. Petrushka expresses his love awkwardly. The Ballerina does not respond, and leaves him alone and in despair.

Scene III: The Moor's room. The Moor, alone, is content to play with a coconut. The Ballerina enters and dances to excite him. He embraces her. Petrushka enters and threatens the Moor. He chases Petrushka away.

Scene IV: Admiralty Square (the same as Scene I, but later). The crowd is still dancing. Suddenly Petrushka rushes out of his booth, chased by the Moor brandishing a scimitar. The Moor stabs and kills Petrushka. A policeman arrives, but the Showman picks up the body and to everyone's relief shows that Petrushka was only a puppet. The Showman is left alone, holding the puppet. As he goes back towards the booth the ghost of Petrushka appears above it, and threatens the Showman and everyone else for refusing to believe that he is not just a puppet.

Alexandre Benois' preliminary drawings showing the first scene and the Showman. *Theatre Museum, V & A.*

Alexandre Benois' design for the Moor's room.
Photo: © Sotheby Parke Bernet, New York.

The Moor's Room in the first production, 1911, with Tamara Karsavina, Alexander Orlov and Vaslav Nijinsky.
Photo: Bert. Theatre Museum, V & A, Valentine Gross Archive.

The actual set, compared with the design, shows that although Benois changed the detail of the scenery he kept the original shape and 'feel'.

Tamara Karsavina as the Ballerina, from *Comœdia Illustré.*
Theatre Museum, V & A.

Alexandre Benois: costume design for the Ballerina. The drawing is certainly an early one because it is so like the photograph of the original costume. Later, with Baronova and Fonteyn, the details have changed (see pages 24, 57). *Theatre Museum, V & A, Arts Council of Great Britain Collection.*

Alexandre Benois: costume design for Petrushka. This is one of the versions of the design which Benois made after the ballet had become so famous with Nijinsky in the title part. *Theatre Museum, V & A, Arts Council of Great Britain Collection.*

Ewald Dülberg's design for Scene 1, Krolloper, Berlin production, 1928. The
Krolloper was an important and influential experimental company directed by
Otto Klemperer. The artistic policy was to perform new or modern works and,
although the experiment lasted only four years, the company produced a number
of Stravinsky's works. The evening when *Petrushka* was performed also included
a production of *Mavra*. Dülberg's design was the first to give a new interpretation
to the setting. The scenario requires the booths but there is nothing particularly
Russian about the atmosphere. The letters on the banners only approximate to
cyrillic characters and have no meaning as words.

56

Col. de Basil's Ballets Russes production with Yurek Shabelevsky as Petrushka, Irina Baronova as the Ballerina and David Lichine as the Moor, c 1935.
Photo: Gordon Anthony. Theatre Museum, V & A, London Archives of the Dance.

Scene from the production by the Ballet du XXe siècle. Without discarding tradition but upsetting traditionalists Maurice Béjart has given new interpretations of Stravinsky's major works to a new generation of spectators. His choreography is a rediscovery of 'classic' Stravinsky – shocking some, inspiring many. As Béjart remarked in a programme note; 'Petrushka, the Ballerina, and the Moor are the Eternal Triangle of universal comedy, just as Pierrot, Columbine and Harlequin are of Commedia dell'Arte and the Husband, the Wife and the Lover are of bourgeois drama.'

VASSILIEV

BEJART

STRAVINSKY

PETROUCHKA

"THE GREATEST DANCER IN THIS GENERATION"

No DANCER on the stage to-day, it is said, does such remarkable character dancing as Warslav Nijinsky, here shown in the fascinating little doll play, "Petrouchka." His artistic skill, combined with humor and magnetic personality, amounts to positive genius.

Maurice Béjart and Vladimir Vassiliev rehearsing for the Ballet du XXe siècle production. From an advertising leaflet of the Théâtre royal de la Monnaie, Brussels. *Theatre Museum, V & A.*

Vaslav Nijinsky as Petrushka, from a contemporary magazine. *Theatre Museum, V & A.*

58

Other Major Productions

4 February 1913 London, Royal Opera House

Company: Les Ballets Russes de Serge Diaghilev
Conductor: Pierre Monteux
Choreographer: Michel Fokine
Scenery & Costumes: Alexandre Benois
Principal Dancers: Tamara Karsavina (Ballerina),
Vaslav Nijinsky (Petrushka), Kotchetovsky (Moor),
Enrico Cecchetti (Showman)

24 January 1916 New York, Century Theatre

Company: Les Ballets Russes de Serge Diaghilev
Choreographer: Michel Fokine
Scenery & Costumes: Alexandre Benois
Principal Dancers: Leonide Massine, Lydia Lopokhova,
Adolf Bolm

6 February 1919 New York, Metropolitan Opera House

Conductor: Pierre Monteux
Choreographer: Adolf Bolm after Fokine
Scenery & Costumes: John Wenger
Principal Dancers: Rosina Galli (Ballerina), Adolf Bolm
(Petrushka), Guiseppe Bonfiglio (Moor), Ottakar Bartik
(Showman)

Revived 13 March 1925 with the same principals but
with scenery and costumes by Serge Soudeikine and
conducted by Tullio Serafin.

3 May 1919 London, Alhambra

Company: Les Ballets Russes de Serge Diaghilev
Choreographer: Michel Fokine
Scenery & Costumes: Alexandre Benois
Principal Dancers: Lydia Lopokhova (Ballerina),
Leonide Massine (Petrushka), Nicolas Zverev (Moor),
Enrico Cecchetti (Showman)

20 November 1920 Petrograd, Marinsky

Company: Kirov Ballet
Conductor: Emil Cooper
Choreographer: Leonid Leontiev
Scenery & Costumes: Alexandre Benois
Principal Dancers: Leonid Leontiev (Petrushka), Elena
Lukom (Ballerina), Vassili Vainonen (Moor)

14 October 1925 Copenhagen, Det Kongelige Teater

Company: Royal Danish Ballet
Choreographer: Michel Fokine
Scenery & Costumes: Alexandre Benois

1925 Buenos Aires, Teatro Colon

Choreographer: Adolf Bolm
Scenery & Costumes: Rodolfo Franco
Principal Dancers: Adolf Bolm, Ruth Page

9 May 1926 Milan, La Scala

Conductor: Igor Stravinsky
Choreographer: Boris Romanov
Scenery & Costumes: Alexandre Benois
Principal Dancers: Vincenzo Celli (Moor), Cia Fornaroli
(Ballerina), Obouchoff (Petrushka), Egidio Rossi
(Showman)

1926 Hanover, Städtische Bühnen

Company: Hanover Opera Ballet
Choreographer: Yvonne Georgi
Scenery & Costumes: Georg Kirsta

1926 Budapest, State Opera House
Choreographer: Ede Brad

20 March 1927 Milan, La Scala

Conductor: Antonino Votto
Choreographer: Giovanni Pratesi
Scenery & Costumes: Alexandre Benois
Principal Dancers: Cia Fornaroli (Ballerina), Mascagno (Moor), Vincenzo Celli (Petrushka), Enrico Cecchetti (Showman)

25 February 1928 Berlin, Krolloper

Conductor: Otto Klemperer
Choreographer: Max Terpis
Scenery & Costumes: Ewald Dülberg
Principal Dancers: Edith Moser, Rudolf Kölling, Walter Junk

1928 Karlsruhe, Badisches Staatstheater

Choreographer: Furstenau

1930 Paris, Théâtre des Champs-Elysées

Company: Opéra Russe à Paris
Choreographer: Bronislava Nijinska
Scenery & Costumes: Orest Allegri, after Alexandre Benois

1930 Essen, Staatsoper

Choreographer: Kurt Jooss
Scenery & Costumes: Hein Heckroth

17 June 1931 London, Lyceum

Company: Opéra Russe à Paris
Conductor: Eugene Goossens
Choreographer: Leon Woizikowsky, after Fokine
Scenery & Costumes: after Alexandre Benois
Principal Dancers: Vera Nemtchinova (Ballerina), Leon Woizikowsky (Petrushka), Algeranoff (Moor), Moyseenko (Showman)

1931/32 New York, Intimate Theatre Studio

Company: Dance Center, New York
Choreographer: Senia Gluck-Sandor

16 June 1932 Berlin, Deutsche Oper

Choreographer: Lizzie Maudrik
Scenery & Costumes: Wilhelm Reinking

1932 Stockholm, Royal Opera

Choreographer: Julian Algo
Scenery & Costumes: John Jon-And

1933 Riga, Latvian Opera and Ballet Theatre

Company: Riga Opera Ballet
Choreographer: Anatole Wiltzak

1933 Budapest, State Opera House

Choreographer: Aurel Milloss
Scenery & Costumes: Gustav Oláh

1933 Brescia, Teatro Grande

Choreographer: Bronislava Nijinska

1933 Rome, Teatro Reale

Choreographer: Paul Petrov
Scenery & Costumes: Alexandre Benois

10 January 1934 New York, St James Theatre

Company: Ballet Russe de Monte Carlo
Choreographer: Michel Fokine
Scenery & Costumes: Alexandre Benois

10 September 1935 London, Coliseum

Company: Ballets de Leon Woizikowsky
Choreographer: Leon Woizikowsky, after Fokine
Scenery & Costumes: after Alexandre Benois: scenery executed by Orest Allegri, costumes by Barbara Karinska
Principal Dancers: Nina Tarakanova (Ballerina), Leon Woizikowsky (Petrushka), André Eglevsky (Moor), Sapiro (Showman)

1936 Buenos Aires, Teatro Colon

Conductor: Igor Stravinsky
Choreographer: Bronislava Nijinska
Scenery & Costumes: after Alexandre Benois
Principal Dancers: Maria Ruanova, Leticia de la Vega, Dora Del Grande, Michel Borovsky

15 May 1936 London, Alhambra

Company: Ballets de Monte Carlo
Choreographer: Michel Fokine
Scenery & Costumes: Alexandre Benois
Principal Dancers: Vera Nemtchinova (Ballerina), Anatole Wiltzak (Petrushka), André Eglevsky (Moor), Nicolas Zverev (Showman)

29 October 1937 Copenhagen, Det Kongelige Teater

Company: Royal Danish Ballet
Choreographer: Michel Fokine, staged by Harald Lander
Scenery & Costumes: Alexandre Benois

1937 Stuttgart, Staatstheater

Choreographer: Lina Gerzer

1939 Zurich, Stadttheater

Choreographer: Hans Macke
Scenery & Costumes: Roman Clemens & Jürg Stockar

21 November 1940 New York, 51st Street Theater

Company: Original Ballet Russe
Choreographer: Michel Fokine
Scenery & Costumes: Alexandre Benois

27 August 1942 Mexico City, Palacio de Bellas Artes

Company: Ballet Theatre of New York
Choreographer: Michel Fokine
Scenery & Costumes: Alexandre Benois
Principal Dancers: Irina Baronova (Ballerina), Yura Lazovsky (Petrushka), David Nillo (Moor), Simon Semenoff (Showman).

This production was performed in New York for the first time on 8 October 1942 at the Metropolitan Opera House, with the same principals except Richard Reed (Showman). It was first staged in London at the Royal Opera House, Covent Garden on 11 July 1946, with principal dancers Lucia Chase (Ballerina), Michael Kidd (Petrushka), André Eglevsky (Moor), Stanley Herbert (Showman).

1942 Rome, Teatro Reale

Choreographer: Aurel Milloss
Scenery & Costumes: Nicola Benois

1943 Zurich, Stadttheater

Choreographer: Hans Macke
Scenery & Costumes: Théodore Strawinsky

1943 Stockholm

Choreographer: George Gué
Scenery & Costumes: Lars Runsten

21 November 1946 Frankfurt, Opernhaus

Conductor: Werner Bitter
Choreographer: Dominik Hartmann

1946 Berlin, Staatsoper

Choreographer: Tatiana Gsovski
Scenery & Costumes: Willi Schmidt

22 February 1947 Milan, La Scala

Conductor: Tullio Serafin
Choreographer: Aurel Milloss
Scenery & Costumes: Alexandre Benois
Principal Dancers: Wanda Milly Clerici (Ballerina), Ugo Dell'Ara (Moor), Aurel Milloss (Petrushka), Ermanno Savaré (Showman)

1947 Vienna, Staatsoper

Choreographer: Erika Hanka
Scenery & Costumes: Robert Kautsky

7 April 1948 Paris, Théâtre national de l'Opéra

Company: Paris Opera Ballet
Choreographers: Serge Lifar & Nicholas Zverev, after Fokine
Scenery: Maurice Moulène, after Alexandre Benois
Costumes: H. and M. Mathieu, after Alexandre Benois

19 January 1949 Budapest, State Opera House

Conductor: András Kórodi
Choreographer: Ernö Vashegyi
Scenery: Gustav Oláh & Zoltán Fülöp
Costumes: Tivadar Mark
Principal Dancers: Istvan Rab, Vera Pasztor, Ernö Vashegyi

June 1949 Lima, Teatro Municipal

Company: Ballet Alicia Alonso
Conductor: Seymour Finkelstein
Choreographer: Michel Fokine
Scenery: Márquez
Costumes: Andrés

1949 Buenos Aires, Teatro Colon

Choreographer: Aurel Milloss

28 October 1950 London, Stoll

Company: Festival Ballet
Conductor: H. Foster Clark
Choreographer: Nicolas Beriosoff after Fokine
Scenery & Costumes: Alexandre Benois
Principal Dancers: Natalie Krassovska (Ballerina), Anton Dolin (Petrushka), Anthony Burke (Moor)
Production revived, Royal Festival Hall, London, July 1955.

1950 Melbourne

Company: Borovansky Australian Ballet
Choreographer: Edouard Borovansky, after Fokine
Scenery & Costumes: William Constable

September 1952 Santiago, Chile, Teatro Municipal

Company: Ballet Nacional Chileno
Conductor: Victor Tevah
Choreographer: Ernest Uthoff
Scenery & Costumes: Hedy Krasa
Principal Dancers: Virginia Roncal/Malucha Solario
(Ballerina), Octavio Cintolesi/Joachim Frowin (Moor),
Willi Maurer/Heinz Poll (Petrushka), Jean Cebron
(Showman)

31 December 1952 Milan, La Scala

Conductor: Nino Sanzogno
Choreographer: Aurel Milloss
Scenery & Costumes: Alexandre Benois
Principal Dancers: Ugo Dell'Ara (Petrushka), Violetta
Elvin (Ballerina), Giulio Perugini (Moor), Giuseppe
Pessina (Showman)

Performed again 7 March 1954 with the same principals
except Gilda Majocchi (Ballerina).

2 December 1955 Copenhagen, Det Kongelige Teater

Company: Royal Danish Ballet
Choreographer: Michel Fokine, staged by Niels Bjørn
Larsen
Scenery & Costumes: Alexandre Benois

18 April 1953 Frankfurt, Opernhaus

Conductor: Bruno Vondenhoff
Choreographer: Herbert Freund
Scenery & Costumes: Josef Fenneker

1956 Catania, Teatro Bellini

Choreographer: Ganca Bartolemei, after Fokine
Scenery & Costumes: after Alexandre Benois

19 January 1957 Düsseldorf, Deutsche Oper am Rhein

Choreographer: Otto Krüger
Scenery & Costumes: Dominik Hartmann

26 March 1957 London, Royal Opera House

Company: The Royal Ballet
Conductor: Sir Malcolm Sargent
Choreographer: Michel Fokine, produced by Serge
Grigoriev & Lubov Tchernicheva
Scenery & Costumes: Alexandre Benois
Principal Dancers: Margot Fonteyn (Ballerina),
Alexander Grant (Petrushka), Peter Clegg (Moor),
Frederick Ashton (Showman)

17 March 1958 Vienna, Staatsoper

Choreographer: Leonide Massine, after Fokine
Scenery & Costumes: Alexandre Benois

6 June 1958 Milan, La Scala

Conductor: Luciano Rosada
Choreographer: Serge Grigoriev & Lubov
Tchernicheva, after Fokine
Scenery & Costumes: Alexandre Benois
Principal Dancers: Fiorella Cova (Ballerina), Giulio
Perugini (Moor), Mario Pistoni (Petrushka), Giuseppe
Pessina (Showman)

12 May 1961 Leningrad, Maly Theatre

Company: Maly Theatre Opera Ballet Company
Conductor: Sergei Prokhorov
Choreographer: Konstantin Boyarski after Fokine
Scenery & Costumes: V.Kuper & E.Leshchinsky, after
Alexandre Benois
Principal Dancers: Elbrus Gioev (Petrushka), Maria
Mazun (Ballerina), A.Miretsky (Moor)

30 January 1964 Bonn, Bonn Opera

Company: Bonn Opera Ballet
Choreographer: Giuseppe Urbani

1 June 1966 Budapest, State Opera House

Conductor: Gyula Borbely
Choreographer: Michel Fokine
Scenery: Gabor Forray
Costumes: Gizella Szeitz
Principal Dancers: Levente Sipeki, Gabriella Lakatos,
Laszlo Peter

26 May 1968 Copenhagen, Det Kongelige Teater

Company: Royal Danish Ballet
Choreographer: Michel Fokine, staged by Niels Bjørn
Larsen & Kirsten Ralov
Scenery & Costumes: Henrik Bloch, after Alexandre
Benois

12 March 1970 New York, City Center

Company: City Center Joffrey Ballet
Choreographer: Yura Lazovsky, after Fokine
Scenery: John Burbridge, after Alexandre Benois
Costumes: Jane Greenwood, after Alexandre Benois
Principal Dancers: Edward Verso (Petrushka), Christian Holder (Moor), Erika Goodman (Ballerina), Yura Lazovsky (Showman)

Leonide Massine was originally credited with the choreography, but withdrew his name.

19 June 1970 New York, NY State Theatre

Company: American Ballet Theatre
Choreographer: Dimitri Romanoff & Yura Lazovsky, after Fokine
Scenery & Costumes: Oliver Smith, after Alexandre Benois
Principal Dancers: Eleanor D'Antuno (Ballerina), Ted Kivitt (Petrushka), Bruce Marks (Moor), Dennis Nahat (Showman)

1 December 1971 Berlin, Deutsche Oper

Choreographer: John Taras
Scenery & Costumes: Georges Wakhevitch

1971 Florence, Teatro Comunale

Choreographer: Aurel Milloss
Scenery & Costumes: Sylvano Bussotti

10 December 1971 Milan, La Scala

Conductor: Bruno Maderna
Choreographer: Aurel Milloss
Scenery & Costumes: Alexandre Benois
Principal Dancers: Liliana Cosi (Ballerina), Mario Pistoni (Petrushka), Bruno Telloli (Moor), Walter Venditti (Showman)

1972 Paris, Théâtre national de l'Opéra

Choreographer: Nicolas Beriosoff

7 April 1972 Pittsburgh, Heinz Hall

Company: Pittsburgh Ballet Theatre
Choreographer: Vitale Fokine
Scenery: William Black
Costumes: Budd Hill

18 March 1973 Warsaw, Teater Wielki

Choreographer: Leon Woizikowsky
Scenery & Costumes: Andrej Majewski

16 May 1973 Bordeaux, Grand Théâtre

Company: Compagnie de Ballet du Grand Théâtre
Conductor: Yvon Leenart
Choreographer: Wladimir Skouratoff, after Fokine
Scenery & Costumes: L.Nifontoff after Benois
Principal Dancers: Yvette Chauviré (Ballerina), Patrice Bart (Petrushka), Wladimir Skouratoff (Moor)

29 September 1973 Oslo, Norske Opera

Conductor: Per Åke Anderson
Choreographer: Poul Gnatt, after Fokine
Scenery & Costumes: Alistair Powel
Principal Dancers: Ellen Kjellberg (Ballerina), Rudolf Nureyev (Petrushka), Antony Geeves (Moor), Poul Gnatt (Showman)

1973 Toulouse, Théâtre du Capitole

Company: Toulouse Théâtre du Capitole Ballet
Choreographer: Serge Golovine
Scenery & Costumes: after Alexandre Benois

Revived at the Théâtre national de l'Opéra, Paris in 1976 with Serge Golovine (Petrushka) and Serge Peretti (Showman).

1973/74 Teheran, Roudaki Hall

Company: Iranian National Ballet Company
Choreographer: Tilde Urseanu
Scenery: Theo Lau
Costumes: Homa Partovi

September 1974 Basle, Stadttheater

Choreographer: Heinz Spoerli
Scenery & Costumes: Herbet Leupin

3 November 1975 Cork, Opera House

Company: Cork Ballet
Conductor: Aloys Fleischmann
Choreographer: Geoffrey Davidson, after Fokine
Scenery: Patrick Murray, after Alexandre Benois
Costumes: Maeva Coakley, after Alexandre Benois
Lighting: Raymond Casey
Principal Dancers: Lavinia Anderson (Ballerina), Domy Reiter-Soffer (Petrushka), Shaun Higgins (Moor), Michael Glendinning (Showman)

14 May 1976 Schwetzingen Festival

Company: Hamburg Staatsoper Ballet
Choreographer: John Neumeier

As 'Petruskha-Variationen', from *Trois mouvements de Petrouchka* for piano.

15 November 1977 Brussels, Forest-National

Company: Ballet du XXe siècle
Choreographer: Maurice Béjart
Scenery & Costumes: Joëlle Roustan & Roger Bernard
Lighting: Allan Burrett
Masks: Werner Strub
Principal Dancers: Vladimir Vassiliev (Petrushka), Rita Poelvoorde, Bertrand Pie (the Friends)

14 May 1981 Florence, Teatro Comunale

Conductor: Bruno Bartoletti
Choreographer: Nicholas Beriosoff
Scenery & Costumes: Alexandre Benois
Principal Dancers: Rudolf Nureyev (Petrushka), Marga Nativo (Ballerina), Francesco Bruno (Moor)

Programme of the first performance in Paris, 13 June 1911.

Grande Saison de Paris. — Direction : G. ASTRUC & Cie

Les Ballets Russes

organisés par M. Serge de Diaghilew

DIRECTEUR CHORÉGRAPHIQUE
M. Michel Fokine

DIRECTEUR ARTISTIQUE
M. Alexandre Benois

PROGRAMME DE LA SOIRÉE

PÉTROUCHKA

Scènes burlesques en quatre tableaux de MM. IGOR STRAVINSKI et ALEXANDRE BENOIS

Musique de M. IGOR STRAVINSKI
Scènes et Danses composées et réglées par M. FOKINE. Maître de Ballet
des Théâtres Impériaux de Saint-Pétersbourg.
Décors et Costumes dessinés par M. ALEXANDRE BENOIS
Décors exécutés par M. ANISFELD
Costumes exécutés par MM. CAFFI et VOROBIEV

La Ballerine. ... ... Mme TAMAR KARSAVINA
Pétrouchka. ... ... MM. NIJINSKI
Le Maure... ... ... ORLOV
Le vieux Charlatan. ... ... CECCHETI

Les nourrices : Mmes BARANOVITCH I, BARANOVITCH II, A. VASSILIEVA, M. VASSILIEVA, GASHEVSKA, TCHERYCHEVA, LASTCHILINA, SAZONOVA, BIBER.
Les cochers : MM. LASTCHILINE, SEMENOV, PETROV, V. ROMANOV, ORLIK.
Les palefreniers : MM. ROSAÏ, A. MOLOTSOV.
Le marchand fêtard : M. KOUSSOV.
Les tziganes sans foi ni loi : Mmes SCHOLLAR, REISEN.
Les danseuses de rue : Mmes NIJINSKA, VASSILIEVSKA.
Premier joueur d'orgue : M. SERGHEIEV.
Second joueur d'orgue : M. KOBELEV.
Le compère de la foire : M. B. ROMANOV.
Le montreur de vues d'optique : M. OGNEV.
Masques et travestis : Mmes LARIONOVA, KANDINA. — MM. LEONTIEV, KREMNIEV, OULANOV, S. MOLOTSOV, DMITRIEV, GOUDNINE, KOTCHETOVSKY, MASSLOV, GUERASSIMOV, CHRISTAPSON, LAROSOV.

Marchands, marchandes, officiers, soldats, seigneurs, dames, enfants, bonnes, cosaques, agents de la police, un montreur d'ours, etc.

Le Sacre du Printemps

(The Rite of Spring)
Tableau of pagan Russia in two acts
by Igor Stravinsky and Nicolas Roerich
35 minutes (EWW 21)

The first night was a riot. It has become the stuff of myth. The reality is impossible to capture because all those who wrote about it at the time joined the mythological bandwagon. It is not even clear how many performances there were – some say six, others say seven. But it was a fact, it did happen. Valentine Gross was in the audience on that first night: 'I thought there was something wonderful about the titanic struggle which must have been going on in order to keep these inaudible musicians and these deafened dancers together, in obedience to the laws of their invisible choreographer.' That choreographer was Nijinsky, and what was happening on stage as well as what was coming out of the pit must indeed have been revolutionary, and shocking. Valentine Gross with her pencil and pastel drawings describes those first performances better than any words. Seven years later, one of the 'women', Maningsova, had become Sokolova and danced 'the Chosen Virgin' in Massine's restaging of the ballet. She must have remembered something, but, comparing the few photographs that exist of both productions, the frenzied, pagan fire of the first was somewhat dampened by the time of the second.

Nicolai Roerich designed the first production but his drawings bear little relation to the actual costumes. Many works by him called *Sacre du Printemps* are not really costume or scene designs but paintings based on the costumes which were finally made for the first production and also used in the 1920 revival.

Maurice Béjart in 1959 started another revolution. Marie Rambert, as Ramberg, one of the Maidens in the first production, later founded her own company, Ballet Rambert, which produced the ballet in 1980.

There were 6 performances in 1913, on 29 May, 4 June and 6 June in Paris and on 11, 14 and 23 July in London. It was announced for 18 July, but was not performed. The programme was changed that evening to *Petrushka*, *Scheherazade*, *le Spectre de la Rose* and *Prince Igor-Polovtsian Dances*.

First Performance 29 May 1913

Theatre:	Théâtre des Champs-Elysées, Paris
Company:	Les Ballets Russes de Serge Diaghilev
Conductor:	Pierre Monteux
Choreographer:	Vaslav Nijinsky
Scenery & Costumes:	Nicolai Roerich
Principal Dancers:	Maria Piltz (the Chosen Virgin)
	Konstantin Woronzow (the Sage)

Synopsis

Part I: The Adoration of the Earth. Ritual dances celebrating the return of Spring.

Part II: The Sacrifice. The victim is chosen and is sacrificed.

The following was the synopsis provided for the first performances in London:

This, the third and most recent of M. Stravinsky's ballets has for theme the ritual of primeval mysticism and, for setting, the Muscovy of dimmest antiquity. Its two scenes evoke the worship of Iarillo, God of Light, on the return of spring, with ceremonies that include the sacrifice of a young girl – who represents the mother of the future's unborn springs – and divers rites symbolising and exalting the benignant earth's fertility, the majesty of the great forces of nature, and the mystery of everlasting stars.

It is a luminous spring evening in the first scene, and an aged woman of the tribe is instructing the young men in the season's appropriate incantations. Soon the young girls come up from the river side, and there are dances and symbolic games. Part of the rite is a simulated abduction. Now approaches a procession of elders of the tribe escorting the most venerable, the high priest of the cult, who pronounces solemn blessing on the earth's unfailing fruitfulness and seeks omens in the enigmatic calm of nature's face. In the second scene, that of the sacrifice, the maiden-victim is chosen by hazard in the mazes of a dance of the young girls. In a dance of heroic nature the rest of the girls then do her honour, and there are pious ceremonies by the elders in evocation of the spirit of their ancestors and in preparation for the mystic marriage. The bride meanwhile has lain rigid in a kind of trance. On a sudden she stirs and begins a dance of religious exaltation. The exaltation turns to frenzy, the frenzy fades to exhaustion, and the girl expires – the sacrifice accomplished.

Opposite: Pastel drawings by Valentine Gross of the first and second parts, made after seeing the performances in Paris. These (and two others) are the only accurate impressions of those first performances, and retain a spontaneity which her 'finished' pastels of some other ballets lack.
Theatre Museum, V & A, Valentine Gross Archive.

Nicolai Roerich's designs for one of the
youths in Part I and one of the maidens
in Part II.
Bakhrushin Museum, Moscow.

Opposite: The costumes worn by Maria
Piltz and Konstantin Woronzow in the
first production, as they were seen in the
exhibition *Spotlight* at the Victoria and
Albert Museum, London, 1981. The
decorative patterns, simplified from the
original designs, are all painted on the
cloth. Roerich subsequently painted
scenes of *Le Sacre du Printemps* which
have figures wearing costumes very like
those used in the first production; but
they are wrongly called 'designs'.
Theatre Museum, V & A.

Three Productions:

Postcard of the 1948 production at the Teatro alla Scala, Milan. This was a re-creation by Massine and Roerich of the first revival by Diaghilev in 1920. *Theatre Museum, V & A, London Archives of the Dance.*

Ballet du XXe siècle at the London Coliseum, 1980. This production was first produced by Maurice Béjart in 1959. He said in a programme note: 'Let this ballet, stripped of all pictorial artifice, be a hymn to that union of Man and Woman at their innermost being, union of heaven and earth, dance of life or death, timeless as the spring.'

Ballet Rambert production, 1981, with Yair Vardi as the Sage and Sally Owen as the Chosen One. *Photo: Peter O'Rourke ARPS.*

Monica Mason as the Chosen Maiden, the Royal Ballet, 1962.
Photo: Houston Rogers. Theatre Museum, V & A.

Other Major Productions

11 July 1913 London, Drury Lane

Company: Les Ballets Russes de Serge Diaghilev
Conductor: Pierre Monteux
Choreographer: Vaslav Nijinsky
Scenery & Costumes: Nicolai Roerich
Principal Dancers: Konstantin Woronzow (Sage), Maria
Piltz (Chosen Virgin)

15 December 1920 Paris, Théâtre des Champs-Elysées

Conductor: Ernest Ansermet
Choreographer: Leonide Massine
Scenery & Costumes: Nicolai Roerich
Principal Dancer: Lydia Sokolova (Chosen Virgin)
Revival by les Ballets Russes de Serge Diaghilev.

27 June 1921 London, Princes

Company: Les Ballets Russes de Serge Diaghilev
Conductor: Ernest Ansermet
Choreographer: Leonide Massine
Scenery & Costumes: Nicolai Roerich
Principal Dancer: Lydia Sokolova (Chosen Virgin)

11 April 1930 Philadelphia, Academy of Music

Company: League of Composers
Choreographer: Leonide Massine, with Martha Graham
Scenery & Costumes: Nicolai Roerich (new)
Principal Dancer: Martha Graham (Chosen Virgin)

1932 Buenos Aires, Teatro Colon

Conductor: Juan José Castro
Choreographer: Boris Romanov
Scenery & Costumes: Wladimir Acosta
Principal Dancers: Dora Del Grande, Boris Romanov

5 August 1937 Los Angeles, Hollywood Bowl

Company: Dance Theatre (Lester Horton)
Choreographer: Lester Horton
Costumes: William Bowne

27 March 1941 Rome, Teatro Reale dell'Opera

Conductor: Tullio Serafin
Choreographer: Aurel Milloss
Scenery & Costumes: Nicola Benois
Principal Dancer: Attilia Radice

24 April 1948 Milan, La Scala

Conductor: Nino Sanzogno
Choreographer: Leonide Massine
Scenery & Costumes: Nicolai Roerich
Principal Dancers: Luciana Novaro (Chosen Virgin),
Ermanno Savaré (Sage)

1949 Munich, Prinzregententheater

Choreographer: Rudolf Kölling
Scenery & Costumes: Willy Hempel
Principal Dancer: Irina Kladivova (Chosen Virgin)

30 April 1956 Stockholm, Royal Opera

Company: Swedish Royal Ballet
Choreographer: Leonide Massine

24 September 1957 Berlin, Deutsche Oper

Company: Städtische Oper Ballet
Choreographer: Mary Wigman
Scenery & Costumes: Wilhelm Reinking

7 December 1959 Brussels, Théâtre royal de la Monnaie

Conductor: André Vandernoot
Choreographer: Maurice Béjart
Scenery & Costumes: Pierre Caille
Principal Dancers: Tania Bari, Germinal Casado

18 April 1960 London, Sadler's Wells

Company: The Ballet of the TRM, Brussels; The Western Theatre Ballet; The Ballet Theatre of Maurice Béjart
Conductor: André Vandernoot
Choreographer: Maurice Béjart
Scenery & Costumes: Pierre Caille
Principal Dancers: Tania Bari (Chosen Virgin), Germinal Casado (Chosen Man)

Performed at the Théâtre des Nations, Paris, on 11 May 1960 with Sadler's Wells Opera production of *Oedipus Rex*.

3 May 1962 London, Royal Opera House

Company: The Royal Ballet
Conductor: Colin Davis
Choreographer: Kenneth MacMillan
Scenery & Costumes: Sidney Nolan
Principal Dancer: Monica Mason (Chosen Virgin)

31 March 1963 Budapest, State Opera House

Conductor: András Kórdi
Choreographer: Imre Eck
Scenery: Zoltán Fülöp
Costumes: Twadar Kórodi
Principal Dancer: Zsuzsa Kun (Chosen Virgin)

24 May 1964 Santiago, Chile, Teatro Municipal

Company: Ballet Nacional Chileno
Choreographer: Patricio Bunster
Scenery & Costumes: Julio Escamez
Lighting: Victor Segura

Produced with the title *Uka-Ara*.

23 April 1965 Paris, Théâtre national de l'Opéra

Company: Ballet de l'Opéra de Paris
Conductor: Pierre Boulez
Choreographer: Maurice Béjart
Scenery & Costumes: Pierre Caille
Principal Dancers: Jacqueline Rayet, Cyril Atanassof

28 June 1965 Moscow, Bolshoi

Conductor: Gennadi Rozhdestvensky
Choreographers: Natalia Kasatkina and Vladimir Vassiliev
Scenery & Costumes: A.D. Goncharov
Principal Dancers: Yuri Vladimirov, Nina Sorokina, Natalia Kasatkina

19 April 1970 Düsseldorf, Deutsche Oper am Rhein

Choreographer: Erich Walter
Scenery; Heinrich Wendel

7 April 1972 Pittsburg, Heinz Hall

Company: Pittsburg Ballet Theatre
Choreographer: Nicholas Petrov

25 November 1972 Frankfurt, Städtische Bühnen

Choreographer: John Neumeier

9 December 1972 Milan, La Scala

Conductor: Bruno Maderna
Choreographer: John Taras
Scenery & Costumes: Marino Marini
Principal Dancer: Natalia Makarova (Chosen Virgin)

17 April 1974 Munich, Bayerische Staatsoper

Company: Bavarian State Opera
Conductor: Hans Zender
Choreographer: Glen Tetley
Scenery & Costumes: Nadine Baylis
Principal Dancers: Ferenc Barbay (Chosen Man), Konstanza Vernon, Frederic Werner

16 May 1974 Amsterdam, Stadsschouwburg

Company: Het Nationale Ballet
Choreographer: Hans van Manen
Scenery & Costumes: Jean-Paul Vroom
Lighting: Howard Eldridge
Principal Dancers: Hans Ebbelaar, David Loring, Sandor Némethy, Alexandra Radius, Monique Sand, Francis Sinceretti, Anja Licher

10 May 1975 Lyon, Opéra

Choreographer: Vittorio Biagi
Scenery & Costumes: Roger Bernard

1 October 1975 Buenos Aires, Teatro San Martin

Choreographer: Oscar Araiz

26 October 1975 Hamburg, Staatsoper

Conductor: Klauspeter Seibel
Choreographer: John Neumeier
Principal Dancer: Beatrice Cordua

3 December 1975 Wuppertal, Opernhaus

Choreographer: Pina Bausch

21 June 1976 New York, Metropolitan Opera House

Company: American Ballet Theatre
Choreographer: Glen Tetley
Scenery & Costumes: Nadine Baylis
Lighting: John B. Read
Principal Dancers: Mikhail Baryshnikov, Martine van Hamel, Clark Tippet, Nanette Glushak, Rebecca Wright, Frank Smith, Charles Ward

5 November 1977 Berlin, Deutsche Oper

Choreographer: Valery Panov
Scenery: David Sharir
Costumes: Valery Panov

7 April 1978 Oakland, California, Paramount Theatre

Company: Oakland Ballet Company
Choreographer: John Pasqualetti

February 1979 Toronto

Company: National Ballet of Canada
Choreographer: Constantin Patsalas

6 March 1981 London, Sadler's Wells

Company: Ballet Rambert
Choreographer: Richard Alston
Scenery & Lighting: Peter Mumford
Costumes: Anne Guyon
Principal Dancers: Yair Vardi (Sage), Sally Owen (Chosen Virgin)

To an arrangement for two pianos.

3 December 1981 New York, Metropolitan Opera House

Company: Metropolitan Opera Ballet
Conductor: James Levine
Choreographer: Jean-Pierre Bonnefous
Scenery & Costumes: David Hockney

Drawings by Valentine Gross made in the theatre during the first performance in Paris.
Theatre Museum, V & A. Valentine Gross Archive.

The Nightingale

(Le Rossignol)
A musical fairy story
by Igor Stravinsky and Stepan Mitusov
after the story by Hans Andersen

45 minutes (EWW 24)

Stravinsky had had the idea for this, his first opera, before composing *The Firebird*, and had written the first act. The last two acts were not written until after *Le Sacre du Printemps*, which explains a certain unevenness in the score.

Although the designs by Alexandre Benois were perfect in their way the opera was not a resounding success. Perhaps audiences had by now become over-expectant whenever a new work by Stravinsky was announced. It is also a difficult work to fit into a ballet company's programme.

For many years it was performed very infrequently, but in the 1960s it began to be more popular. In the revivals by the Ballet Théâtre Contemporain in 1972 and the Metropolitan Opera Company in 1981 when it was the central work in an all Stravinsky programme it was given its proper place. When David Hockney, after the success of his *Parade*, was asked to design three other works for the Metropolitan the idea was to do two works by Stravinsky – *Le Sacre du Printemps* and *Oedipus Rex* and one by Schönberg – *Erwartung*. But clearly this was unfortunate programme building, and it was David Hockney who suggested *The Nightingale* instead of *Erwartung*. Hockney links the three different works by the same composer by using the visual symbol of the circle.

First Performance 26 May 1914

Theatre:	Théâtre national de l'Opéra, Paris
Company:	Les Ballets Russes de Serge Diaghilev
Conductor:	Pierre Monteux
Choreographer:	Boris Romanov
Scenery & Costumes:	Alexandre Benois
Principal Cast:	Paul Andreev (the Emperor of China)
	Aurelia Dobrovolska (the Nightingale)
	Elisabeth Petrenko (Death)

Synopsis

Act I: A forest by the sea. A fisherman sings in his boat about the beauty of the Nightingale's song. Then the Nightingale herself is heard. But she is interrupted by the arrival of the High Chamberlain, the Cook, the Bonze (High Priest) and other courtiers from the Emperor's palace. They invite the Nightingale to sing at the palace for the Emperor.

Act II: The Palace. The royal procession enters, the Nightingale sings and the Emperor is moved to tears. Three envoys from the Emperor of Japan arrive with a mechanical nightingale. When it begins to sing the real Nightingale flies away. The Emperor of China is so angry that he banishes the real Nightingale from his empire. The fisherman is heard singing of the coming of death.

Act III: The Emperor is ill. He is watched over by Death wearing the Emperor's crown and accompanied by ghosts. The Nightingale returns and sings so beautifully that Death and the ghosts are chased away. When the courtiers arrive they see the Emperor quite well again in all his splendid robes. And the fisherman proclaims that the song of the Nightingale has conquered death.

Alexandre Benois' costume
design for the Emperor and
scene design for the Emperor's
Throne Room for the first
production, 1914.
Ashmolean Museum, Oxford.

The Emperor's Throne Room at the Teatro Comunale, Florence, 1961, with Marcello Cortis as the Emperor and Marga Nativo as the Nightingale.
Photo: Marchiori. Harold Rosenthal Collection.

Ballet Théâtre Contemporain production, 1972, with Michel Llado as the Emperor.
Photo: Daniel Keryzaouën.

David Hockney's models for the first scene by the sea, the forest, and the palace, for the Metropolitan Opera House, New York production, 1981. Hockney has gone back to the original Chinese feeling by using Chinese pottery and the famous willow pattern as his inspiration for the shapes and the colours, but they do not obstruct his own fertile originality as a designer for the theatre.
Photo: Courtesy the artist.

Other Major Productions

18 June 1914 London, Theatre Royal, Drury Lane

Company: Les Ballets Russes de Serge Diaghilev
Directors: Alexandre Benois & Alexandre Sanine
Choreographer: Boris Romanov
Scenery & Costumes: Alexandre Benois
Principal Singers: Paul Andreev (Emperor), Aurelia
Dobrowolska (Nightingale), Elisabeth Petrenko
(Death), Marie Brain (Cook), Alexandre Warfolomeiew
(Fisherman), Nicolas Goulaiew (High Priest), Alexandre
Belianine (High Chamberlain)

30 May 1918 Petrograd, Maryinsky

Director: Vsevolod Meyerhold
Scenery & Costumes: Alexander Golovine

12 November 1919 London, Royal Opera House

Conductor: Eugene Goossens
Principal Singers: Frederic Austin (Emperor), Sylvia
Nelis (Nightingale), Kathleen Moore (Death), Edith
Clegg (Cook), Maurice D'Oisly (Fisherman), Foster
Richardson (High Priest), Arthur Wynn (High
Chamberlain)

6 March 1926 New York, Metropolitan Opera House

Conductor: Tullio Serafin
Director: Samuel Thewman
Scenery & Costumes: Serge Soudeikine
Principal Singers: Marion Talley (Nightingale), Ina
Bourskaya (Cook), Ralph Errole (Fisherman), Adamo
Didur (Emperor), Gustav Schützendorf (Chamberlain),
James Wolfe (Priest)

14 May 1926 Milan, La Scala

Conductor: Igor Stravinsky
Director: Giovacchino Forzano
Scenery: Antonio Rovascalli
Costumes: S.A.Caramba
Principal Singers: Laura Pasini (Nightingale), Cesira
Ferrari (Cook), Nello Palai (Fisherman), Carlo Walter
(Emperor), Eugenio Sdanowski (Chamberlain), Amleto
Galli (High Priest)

1927 Berlin, Staatsoper

Scenery & Costumes: Nicola Benois

27 February 1928 Rome, Teatro dell'Opera

Conductor: Igor Stravinsky
Scenery & Costumes: Urbano
Principal Singers: Laura Pasini (Nightingale), Cesira
Balenti (Cook), Alfredo Tofanetti (Fisherman), Ernesto
Dominici (Emperor), Debora Fambri (Death), Silvio Seri
(Chamberlain), Lorenzo Pasquariello (High Priest)

25 April 1960 London, Sadler's Wells

Company: New Opera Company
Conductor: Brian Priestman
Director & Scenery: Colin Graham
Costumes: Annena Stubbs
Principal Singers: Marion Studholme (Nightingale),
Johanna Peters (Death), Kenneth Bowen (Fisherman),
James Atkins (High Priest), Frederick Westcott (High
Chamberlain), Harold Blackburn (Emperor)

2 May 1960 Cologne, Opernhaus

Conductor: Joseph Rosenstock
Director: Hans Bauer
Choreographer: Marcel Luipart
Scenery & Costumes: Teo Otto
Principal Singer: Erika Köth (Nightingale)

16 December 1961 Florence, Teatro Comunale

Conductor: Vittorio Gui
Director: Michel Crochot
Choreographer: Nives Poli
Scenery & Costumes: Emanuele Luzzati
Principal Singers: Mattiwilda Dobbs (Nightingale), Anna Maria Canali (Cook), Amalia Pini (Death), Giuseppe Baratti (Fisherman), Marcello Cortis (Emperor), Carolo Badioli (High Chamberlain), Alessandro Maddalena (High Priest)
Principal Dancers: Marga Nativo (Nightingale), Delio Cioni (Death), Renato Fiumicelli (Fisherman), Antonietta Davino (Mechanical Nightingale)

10 January 1962 Rome, Teatro dell'Opera

Conductor: Armando La Rosa Parodi
Director: Alessandro Manetti
Scenery & Costumes: Emanuele Luzzati
Principal Singers: Jolanda Meneguzzer (Nightingale), Giuseppe Baratti (Fisherman)
Principal Dancer: Marga Nativo (Nightingale)

1 August 1962 Santa Fe, New Mexico, Santa Fe Opera, Stravinsky Festival

Conductor: Igor Stravinsky
Director: Bliss Hebert
Scenery & Costumes: Henry Heymann
Principal Singers: John McCollum (Fisherman), Jeanette Scovotti (Nightingale), Maria di Gerlando (Cook), Therman Bailey (High Chamberlain), John West (Bonze), Elaine Bonazzi (Death)

3 October 1963 New York, City Center

Company: New York City Opera
Conductor: Walter Susskind
Director: Bliss Hebert
Choreographer: Thomas Andrew
Scenery & Costumes: Gordon Micunis
Principal Singers: Arthur Graham (Fisherman), Patricia Brooks (Nightingale), Elisabeth Carron (Cook), Donald Gramm (Emperor), Rochelle Zide (Mechanical Nightingale), Jean Kraft (Death)

24 April 1964 Brussels, Théâtre royal de la Monnaie

Conductor: André Vandernoot
Director: Jean-Marc Landier
Scenery & Costumes: Raymond Renard
Principal Singers: Claudine Arnaud, Gilberte Danlée, Henri De Jonghe, Maurice de Groot, Jules Bastin, Roger Godfrin, Claud Mansy

1967 Vienna, Volksoper

Conductor: Peter Maag
Principal Singers: Colette Boky, Suzanne Dacksler, Marcel Cordes, Erich Witte

1967 Mexico City, Palacio de Bellas Artes

Principal Singers: Maria Salinas, Jorge Lagunes

14 December 1968 Chicago, Lyric Opera

Choreographer & Director: Luciana Novaro
Scenery & Costumes: Emanuele Luzzati
Principal Dancers: Carla Fracci (Nightingale), Peter van Ginkel (Emperor), Kenneth Johnson
Principal Singers: Christiane Eda-Pierre (Nightingale), Ottavio Garaventa (Fisherman)

1 August 1969 Sante Fe, New Mexico, Santa Fe Opera

Conductor: Robert Baustian
Director: Bliss Hebert
Scenery & Costumes: Willa Kim
Principal Singers: Stuart Burrows (Fisherman), Jeanette Scovotti (Nightingale), Doris Yarick (Cook), Ray Hickman (High Chamberlain), James Morris (Bonze), Jean Kraft (Death)

1969 Amsterdam

Company: Netherlands Opera Foundation
Conductor: Jean Fournet
Director: Jan Bouws
Scenery & Costumes: Nicols Wijnberg
Principal Singer: Eliane Manchet

14 January 1970 Cambridge, Mass., Loeb Dance Centre

Conductor: Günther Schuller
Director: Ian Strasfogel
Scenery & Costumes: Eric Martin
Principal Singers: Alexander Stevenson (Fisherman), Susan Spacagna (Nightingale), Gwendolyn Little (Cook), Terrence Tobias (Chamberlain), Robert Vian (High Priest), Patricia Pease (Death)

17 July 1970 Santa Fe, New Mexico, Santa Fe Opera

Conductor: Robert Baustian
Director: Bliss Hebert
Scenery & Costumes: Willa Kim
Principal Singers: Sidney Johnson (Fisherman), Judith Blegen (Nightingale), Betty Lane (Cook), John White (High Chamberlain), Howard Chadwick (Bonze), Jean Kraft (Death)

April 1972 Venice, La Fenice

Company: Ballet Théâtre Contemporain
Director: Jacques Demy
Choreographer: Françoise Adret
Scenery & Costumes: Pham Ngoe Tuan
Principal Singers: Jean-Pierre Chevalier (Fisherman),
Patricia Dupont/Anne-Marie Rodde (Nightingale),
George Jollis (High Priest), Michel Hubert
(Chamberlain), Danielle Grima (Cook), Michel Llado
(Emperor), Danielle Grima (Death)

First performed 14 June 1972, Théâtre de la Ville, Paris

3 August 1973 Santa Fe, New Mexico, Santa Fe Opera

Conductor: Robert Baustian
Director: Bliss Hebert
Scenery & Costumes: Willa Kim
Principal Singers: Stuart Burrows (Fisherman), Rita
Shane (Nightingale), Barrie Smith (Cook), William
Dansby (High Chamberlain), John Hall (Bonze), Isola
Jones (Death)

3 December 1981 New York, Metropolitan Opera
House

Conductor: James Levine
Director: John Dexter
Scenery & Costumes: David Hockney
Principal Singers: Gwendolyn Bradley, Claudia Catania,
Phillip Creech, Morley Meredith, John Cheek

The production included a *pas de deux* choreographed
by Frederick Ashton and danced by Natalia Makarova
and Anthony Dowell.

Histoire du Soldat

To be read, played and danced in two parts
Libretto by Charles-Ferdinand Ramuz
35 minutes (EWW 41)

War. The echo of misery. Living in Switzerland. Friendship with Ramuz. The idea of a simple touring theatre, like the cart for mystery plays. The Russian popular story about a Soldier and the Devil. Recitation, acting, dancing, music: experimental theatre.

The idea of doing something 'on the cheap' became inevitably more complex and expensive. It is always expensive to do something simple really well. The danger is to destroy the simplicity and therefore the impact of this original and moving story by theatrical over-elaboration. Even though the first performance, so touchingly visualised by the 12-year-old son of the composer, Théodore, took place in a large red theatre, the simple idea must have been perfectly realised.

The Edinburgh Festival production in 1954 was perfect too, because all those who took part were in total sympathy with the work.

Stravinsky and Ramuz succeeded in their intention of creating something popular. It is often performed at Festivals when organisers can get together a good 'team', or by student theatre groups. On several occasions it has been produced by puppet companies.

The trap, as is so often the case in the theatre, is that the work's very simplicity gives the illusion that it is easy to stage. Simple is not the opposite of sophisticated.

First Performance 28 September 1918

Theatre:	Théâtre Municipal, Lausanne
Conductor:	Ernest Ansermet
Directors:	Georges and Ludmilla Pitoëff
Designer:	René Auberjonois
Principal Cast:	Elie Gagnebin (Narrator)
	Gabriel Rosset (the Soldier)
	Jean Villard (the Devil – spoken)
	Georges Pitoëff (the Devil – danced)
	Ludmilla Pitoëff (the Princess)

Synopsis

Joseph, the soldier, is going home on leave. He sits down by a stream and plays his violin. The Devil appears as an old man with a butterfly net. He persuades the soldier to give him the violin in exchange for a magic book and to teach him how to play it. The Devil delays Joseph not for three days but for three years. When Joseph finally returns to his village all his friends and relatives, who had given him up for dead, shun him as if he were a ghost. The Devil reappears disguised as a cattle merchant. As Joseph is about to attack him, the Devil reminds him of the book and how it will make him rich. Joseph becomes rich but remains unhappy. He throws the book away and the Devil reappears again disguised as an old woman. Joseph tries to buy the violin back. The old woman will only sell it if he can play. He tries to play it, but no sound comes out. He flings it away and tears up the book.

Joseph has gone to another country where the king's daughter has an unknown illness. Whoever cures her will marry her. The soldier is tempted to try, then meets the Devil disguised as a virtuoso violinist and plays cards with him. He plays to lose and by losing all his money overcomes the Devil. He recovers his violin and begins to play. His playing cures the Princess. The Devil warns that if Joseph should ever cross the frontier then he will be in his power for ever and the Princess will fall ill again.

The Narrator: 'You must not seek to add to what you have or once had.'
  'You have no right to share what you are with what you were.'
  'No-one can have it all, that is forbidden; you must learn to choose between.'

Joseph thinks he has everything. But the Princess tempts him to take her to visit his mother. Joseph goes ahead to find the frontier, strays over it and is snatched by the Devil.

Théodore Strawinsky's watercolour of the first night at the Théâtre Municipal, Lausanne, made when he was 12 years old. From right to left: the reader's table, the cloth designed by Auberjonois, Georges Pitoëff as the Devil in one of his disguises, Ernest Ansermet the conductor.   *Courtesy the artist.* © *SPADEM.*

The scene on stage at the Edinburgh
Festival, 1954, with the band conducted
by Hans Schmidt-Isserstedt, Robert
Helpmann as the Devil, Terence
Longdon as the Soldier, Moira Shearer
as the Princess and Anthony Nicholls as
the Narrator.
Photo: Paul Shillabeer FRPS.

The Bayerische Staatsoper production
at the Nationaltheater, Munich, 1976.
Photo: Sabine Toepffer.

Because *Histoire du Soldat* is
'experimental' it cannot be put into any
particular category. It is not a play. It is
not a ballet. It is not a recitation. It has
therefore appealed to many different
kinds of companies, including puppet
theatres. But if it is presented 'straight'
then there is always a remarkable
resemblance in the staging of the
different productions. The
experimentation was Stravinsky's
alone.

Marina Sokolova's scene design for the Bolshoi Theatre, Moscow production, 1964. The production was done as a ballet.   *Bakhrushin Museum, Moscow.*

Jean Maillot's scene design for production at the Théâtre de l'Université, Tours, 1975.

Villagers. Figures designed and made by Lyndie Wright for the Little Angel Marionette Theatre production, Queen Elizabeth Hall, London, 1968.
Photo: Courtesy Little Angel Marionette Theatre.

Other Major Productions

18 January 1925 Hamburg, Stadttheater

Conductor: Egon Pollak
Director: Leopold Sachse
Scenery & Costumes: Johannes Schröder
Principals: Leopold Sachse (Narrator), Degler (Soldier), Elschner (Devil), Holz (Princess)

10 July 1927 London, Arts Theatre Club

Conductor: Edward Clark
Scenery & Costumes: Nicolas Galitzine & Vera Soudeikine
Principals: Harcourt Williams (Reader), Ivan Firth (Soldier), Frank Cochrane (Devil), Lydia Lopokhova (Princess)

1927 Münster, Städtische Bühnen

Choreographer: Kurt Jooss
Scenery & Costumes: Hein Heckroth

25 March 1928 New York, Jolson (later Century)

Company: League of Composers
Choreographer: Michio Ito
Scenery & Costumes: Donald Oenslager
Principals: Tom Powers (Narrator), Blake Scott, Lilly Lubel

11 October 1928 Berlin, Krolloper

Conductor: Otto Klemperer
Director: Jacob Geis
Scenery & Costumes: Traugott Müller
Principals: George Schdanow (Soldier), Paul Bildt (Devil), Elisabeth Grube (Princess), Carl Ebert (Reader)

1930 Düsseldorf, Stadttheater

Scenery & Costumes: Hellmut Jurgens

12 April 1931 New York, Guild Theatre

Choreographer: Ruth Page
Scenery & Costumes: Nicolas Remisov

1935 Florence, Sala Bianca

Choreographer: Hermann Scherchen

1940 Rome, Teatro delle Arti

Choreographer: Enrico Fulchingnoni
Scenery & Costumes: Renato Guttuso

1944 Cape Town, Ballet Club

Choreographer: John Cranko
Scenery & Costumes: Hanns Ebenstein

9 March 1946 Copenhagen, Det Kongelige Teater

Director: Torben Anton Svendsen
Choreographer: Borge Ralov
Scenery & Costumes: Richard Mortensen

1 May 1946 Paris, Théâtre des Champs-Elysées

Conductor: Ernest Ansermet
Director: Alfred Roulet
Scenery & Costumes: Gaston Faraval, after Auberjonois
Principals: Elie Gagnebin (Narrator), François Simon (Soldier), Jean Valois (Devil), Alexandra Sava (Princess), Willy Flay (Devil – danced)

Based on original production; first performed in Geneva on 9 February 1945 and in Lausanne on 23 March 1945.

29 June 1946 Mannheim, Nationaltheater

Conductor: Joachim Popelka

11 November 1946 Hamburg, Schauspielhaus

Conductor: Ewald Lindemann
Director: Günther Rennert
Scenery & Costumes: Alfred Mahlau

1946 Munich, Staatsoper

Choreographer: Walter Jokisch
Scenery & Costumes: Dominik Hartmann

1946 New York, ISCM

Choreographer: Elsa Kahl
Scenery & Costumes: Tryggvadottir

30 April 1947 Frankfurt, Opernhaus

Conductor: Werner Bitter
Director: Walter Jokisch
Scenery & Costumes: Dominik Hartmann

1948 Buenos Aires, Teatro Colon

Choreographer: Margherita Wallmann
Scenery & Costumes: Hector Basaldua

1948 New York, ISCM

Choreographer: Elsa Kahl
Scenery & Costumes: Kiesler

1 April 1951 London, Whitehall

Company: Under Thirty Theatre Group
Conductor: Ionel Patin
Choreographer & Director: Bert Stimmel
Scenery & Costumes: Bertram Tyrer
Principals: Kenneth Mackintosh (Narrator), Maurice Kaufmann (Soldier), Gérard Guillaume (Devil), Eleanor Fazan (Princess)

6 September 1954 Edinburgh, King's Theatre

Conductor: Hans Schmidt-Isserstedt
Director: Günther Rennert
Scenery & Costumes: Alfred Mahlau
Principals: Moira Shearer (Princess), Robert Helpmann (Devil), Terence Longdon (Soldier), Anthony Nicholls (Narrator)

18 December 1954 New York, Kaufman Auditorium

Choreographer: Anna Sokolow
Scenery & Costumes: Paul Sherman
Lighting: Doris S. Einstein

1954 Essen, Städtische Bühnen

Conductor: Paul Belker
Director: Hans Hartleb
Scenery & Costumes: Friedholm Strenger

5 February 1955 Hamburg, Staatsoper

Conductor: Leopold Ludwig
Director: Günther Rennert
Scenery & Costumes: Teo Otto

28 March 1955 New York, Phoenix Theatre

Choreographer: Edward Caton
Costumes: Stanley Simmons
Libretto by N. Richard Nash based on original.

11 July 1955 Stratford, Ontario, Festival Concert Hall

Conductor: Paul Sherman
Director: Douglas Campbell
Costumes: Clarence Wilson
Principals: Lilian Jarvis (Princess), Marcel Marceau (Devil), William Needles (Narrator), Douglas Rain (Soldier)

7 August 1955 Munich, Residenz Courtyard

Company: Bayerische Staatsoper
Conductor: Julius Karr-Bertoli
Principal: Gerd Seid (Soldier)

3 November 1956 Gelsenkirchen, Städtische Bühnen, Grillo-Gymnasium

Conductor: Ljubomir Romansky
Director: Jost Dahmen
Scenery & Costumes: Theo Lau
Principals: Ruth Dechant (Princess), Walter Kohls (Soldier), Rolf Niehus (Devil), Rolf Sebastian (Narrator)

1956 Montreal

Company: Les Ballets Chiriaeff
Choreographer: Ludmilla Chiriaeff
Scenery: Alexis Chiriaeff
Costumes: Claudette Picard

89

22 July 1958 London, Sadler's Wells

Company: New Opera Company
Conductor: Keith Darlington
Director: Colin Graham
Choreographer: Elizabeth West
Scenery: Colin Graham
Costumes: Annena Stubbs
Principals: Gordon Jackson (Narrator), Job Stewart (Soldier), Lee Montague (Devil), Hazel Merry (Princess)

18 March 1959 Stockholm, Marionetteatern

Director: Michael Meschke
Scenery & Costumes: Gilbert Regazzoni
Puppet Manipulators: Renata Centenari, Zanza Lidums, Agnetta Ginsburg, Michael Meschke, Ulla Nygren

5 April 1959 New York, Kaufman Auditorium

Company: Joseph Gifford Dance Theater
Conductor & Choreographer: Joseph Gifford
Costumes: Bernice Mendelsohn
Principals: Joseph Gifford (Devil), Douglas Watson (Soldier)

26 June 1961 Cologne, Bühnen der Stadt

Conductor: Miltiades Caridis
Director: Hans Bauer
Scenery & Costumes: Teo Otto
Principals: Carmen Panader, Peter Fricke, Alois Garg, Harald Kreutzberg

The programme also included new productions of *Renard* with choreography by Aurel Milloss and *Mavra* directed by Helmuth Matiasek.

14 July 1964 Moscow, Bolshoi

Conductor: A.Kopilov
Choreographer: E.Suve
Scenery & Costumes: Marina Sokolova

4 September 1967 Edinburgh, Assembly Hall

Company: Scottish Opera
Conductor: Alexander Gibson
Director: Wendy Toye
Scenery & Costumes: Carl Toms
Lighting: Charles Bristow
Principals: Gordon Jackson (Narrator), Nicky Henson (Soldier), Patrick Wymark (Devil), Una Stubbs (Princess)

14 January 1968 New York, Kaufman Auditorium

Company: Bertram Ross and Company
Choreographer, Scenery & Costumes: Bertram Ross
Principal: James Cahill (Narrator)

15 August 1968 London, Queen Elizabeth Hall

Company: Little Angel Puppet Theatre
Conductor: Daniel Barenboim
Scenery & Costumes: Lyndie Wright
Principals: Michael Flanders (Narrator), Little Angel Marionettes

28 September 1970 London, Young Vic

Conductor: Michael Lankester
Director: Wendy Toye
Scenery & Costumes: Carl Toms
Principals: Gordon Jackson (Narrator), Nicky Henson (Soldier), Desmond McNamara (Devil), Una Stubbs (Princess)

28 December 1971 Washington, DC, Kennedy Center

Company: American Ballet Theatre
Conductor: Akira Endo
Choreographer: Eliot Feld
Costumes: Frank Thompson
Lighting: Jennifer Tipton
Principals: Daniel Levans (Soldier), Eliot Feld (Pimp), Sallie Wilson, Paula Tracy (Whores), Buddy Balough, Robert Brassel, Richard Cammack, David Coll, Warren Conover, Rory Foster, Frank Smith, Bojan Spassoff, Luis Vallaneuva (Soldiers)

To music from the Concert Suite version (1920), with a new libretto by Eliot Feld.

1971 Colorado Springs

Director: Herbert Beattie
Principal: Herbert Beattie (Narrator)

1971 Aix en Provence, Cours Mirabeau

Conductor: Diego Masson
Principals: Jean Babilée (Devil), Alain Bory (Soldier)

3 June 1972 The Hague, Het O-Theater

Conductor: Edo de Waart
Director: Erik Vos
Scenery & Costumes: Neils Harmel

21 March 1973 Bologna, Teatro Comunale

Conductor: Marcello Panni
Choreographer: Amadeo Amodio
Director: Carlo Emanuele Crespi
Scenery & Costumes: Giocomo Manzu
Principals: Amadeo Amodio (Soldier), Roberto Pistone (Devil), Luciana Savignano (Princess), Fernando Caiati (Narrator)

14 June 1975 Cardiff, Sherman

Company: Welsh Dance Theatre
Conductor: Boris Brott
Director: Nicholas Ferguson
Choreographer: William Louther
Costumes: Peter Docherty
Lighting: Richard Caswell
Principals: Mikloth Bond (Soldier), Graeme Edler (Devil), Francis Rozelaar Green (Narrator), Alice Stopczynski (Princess)

18 June 1975 Tours, Théâtre de l'Université

Conductor: Jean-Michel Vaccaro
Director: Jean-Pierre Ryngaert
Scenery & Costumes: Jean Maillot, assisted by Philippe Poirier
Principals: Philippe Desboeuf (Narrator), Vincent Ridard (Soldier), Jacques Roehrich (Devil), Isabelle Ball (Princess)

18 October 1976 New York, Shakespeare Festival Public Theatre

Choreographer: Eliot Feld
Costumes: Theoni V.Aldredge
Lighting: Thomas Skelton

Revision of 1971 version by Eliot Feld.

19 December 1976 Munich, Nationaltheater

Company: Bayerische Staatsoper
Conductor: Miltiades Caridis
Director: Hans Korte
Scenery & Costumes: Günther Schneider-Siemssen
Costumes: Silvia Strahammer
Principals: Joachim Bissmeier (Soldier), Jürgen Feindt (Devil)

6 June 1977 Bath, Theatre Royal

Conductor: Mark Elder
Director: David William
Choreographer: Geraldine Stephenson
Scenery & Costumes: Alan Barlow
Principals: Christopher Hancock (Narrator), Kevin Williams (Soldier), Edward Atienza (Devil), Melanie Parr (Princess)

Staged by Nash Ensemble Productions.

12 July 1977 London, Little Angel, Islington

Company: Little Angel Marionette Theatre
Director: John Wright
Scenery & Costumes: Lyndie Wright
Principals: Alan Judd (Narrator), Barrie Smith (Devil), Chris Leith (Soldier)
Puppet Operators: June Bond, Susanne Forster, Nigel Plaskitt, Ronnie le Drew, Chris Leith, Juliet Middleton

1 June 1978 Birmingham, Repertory Theatre

Conductor: Christopher Lyndon Gee
Choreographer & Director: Andy Adamson
Scenery & Costumes: Judith Park
Lighting: Simon Kahn
Principals: Alec Wallis (Devil), Robert Gill (Soldier), Bob Smith (Devil), Susanne Hywel, Karen Bowen (Dancers)

8 July 1980 Oxford, Playhouse

Company: Oxford Music Theatre
Conductor: Henry Ward
Directors & Choreographers: Eleanor Fazan, Terry Gilbert, Gordon McDougall
Scenery & Costumes: Martyn Bainbridge
Lighting: Raymond Cross
Principals: Valentine Dyall (Narrator), Neil McCaul (The Earl of Essex), Sylvester McCoy (The O'Neill), Rosamond Attwood (the O'Neill's daughter/The Red Queen)

6 February 1981 London, Queen Elizabeth Hall

Conductor: David Atherton
Director: Peter Adam
Scenery & Costumes: Peter Adam and Nicholas Ormerod
Principals: Alec McCowen (Narrator), Wayne Sleep (Soldier), Murray Melvin (Devil)

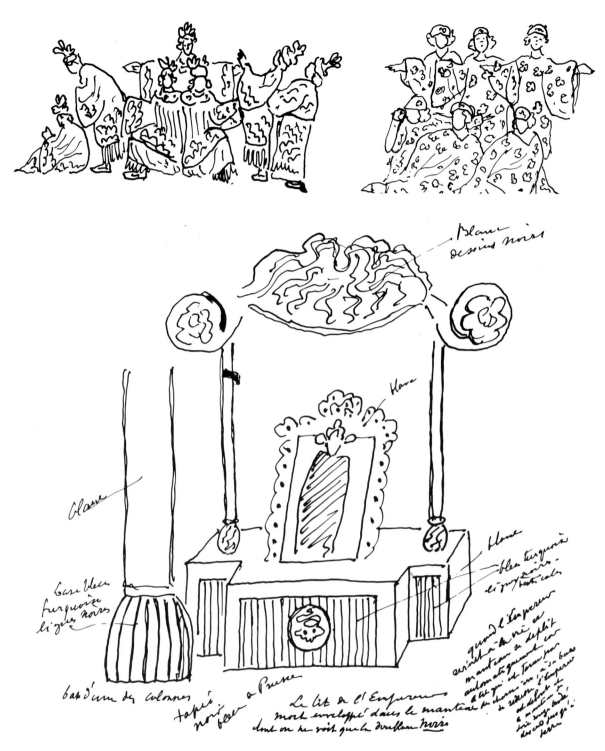

Henri Matisse's design for Dancers of the Emperor (top left), Dancers: Lantern Carriers (top right), and the Emperor's bed. The annotation reads, in translation: 'The bed of the dead Emperor enveloped in the cloak of which we see only the black lining. When the Emperor comes back to life this cloak folds back automatically as the bed, which is hinged at its foot, is gradually up-ended until the Emperor is standing erect and the red silk embroidered cloak hangs to the ground.'

Photo: Bibliothèque Nationale, fonds Kochno.

The Song of the Nightingale

(Le Chant du Rossignol)
Symphonic poem in three parts
20 minutes (EWW 24A)

When Diaghilev asked Stravinsky to make his opera *The Nightingale* into a ballet he also asked Fortunato Depero, the Italian futurist painter, to design it.

It was the time of great theatrical experiment and aesthetic manifestos. The Italians had published two in 1915 defining their futurist theories about theatre and about scene design, and Diaghilev, always the eager experimentalist, himself directed probably the first 'light show' in a set which he commissioned from Giacomo Balla to the music of Stravinsky's *Feu d'Artifice*. Balla's idea was that the stage itself, without actors, even without marionettes, should be the spectacle.

His set was made up of a variety of three-dimensional translucent shapes. In just over four minutes there were 44 lighting cues, lighting the shapes both from in front and from inside as well as casting different shadows onto the cyclorama.

Depero also wanted to reject all realism in the theatre and abolish all the old-fashioned techniques. His designs for *The Song of the Nightingale* used geometric forms for strange plants and cubist forms for the 'marionettisation' of the costumes. They were too extreme even for Diaghilev, and were impractical because the production was still to be a ballet with dancers. So the designs were not used.

Diaghilev then approached Matisse. It was, again, an inspired choice of artist, even though Matisse had not worked for the theatre before. His designs have all the brilliant economy of line and colour which is so effective on stage and yet they retain that essential 'chinese' feeling. Matisse himself painted the lines and the colours onto the costumes.

But he was not happy working in the theatre. He was unused to and made uneasy by the many different elements and personalities involved in a stage production. Even when Balanchine restaged it in 1925 and Matisse invented, for Alicia Markova's costume, the 'all-over' tights which are now so often the standard 'uniform' of the dancer, the production was not really a success. It was many years before Matisse worked again for the theatre; then, with much greater success, on Massine's *Le Rouge et le Noir* in 1939.

First Performance 2 February 1920

Theatre:	Théâtre national de l'Opéra, Paris
Company:	Les Ballets Russes de Serge Diaghilev
Conductor:	Ernest Ansermet
Choreographer:	Leonide Massine
Scenery & Costumes:	Henri Matisse
Principal Cast:	Tamara Karsarvina (the Nightingale)
	Stanislas Idzikowski (the Mechanical Nightingale)
	Lydia Sokolova (Death)

Synopsis

Based on a story by Hans Andersen. The story of the ballet is the same as that of the opera, but without the first act.

The score was revised to exclude the vocal parts.

(From the programme of the revival with choreography by George Balanchine):

In the Emperor's Palace all are busily occupied in preparing for the Emperor's reception of the Nightingale. All the doors are open and the draughts agitate thousands of bells. The song of the Nightingale is heard as it makes its way to Court. Now the Emperor and his suite make their entrance. Then the Nightingale sings. When the song is ended there is an outburst of enthusiasm. But suddenly there arrive envoys from the Emperor of Japan, who has sent his powerful neighbour a mechanical Nightingale.

The Japanese Maestro causes this curious automaton to make itself heard. But the Emperor is taken ill. The real Nightingale has fled, and the new arrival is turned out of the Palace.

At their wit's end, the courtiers improvise with their arms a throne to carry the sick Emperor. They return to fetch the throne, and the Chamberlains draw the curtains of the Emperor's room. At his bedside Death holds vigil. Then the Nightingale returns. Death would drive it away, but it sings. Death is charmed into yielding, and departs, taking the Nightingale, who is slain.

The whole court believes the Emperor to be dead, and a procession approaches. But the Emperor's hand is seen to move. He rises, cured. The Court falls back, in ecstasy, overawed by the miracle.

94

wishing.

Markova
Russian Ballet
1928.

Alicia Markova as the Nightingale in the revival of the ballet in London, 1927.
Photo: Dame Alicia Markova.

Left: Costume of a mourner.
Right: Costume of a warrior.
Theatre Museum, V & A.

White is notoriously the most difficult colour to use on stage and yet Matisse, the painter with an incomparable sense of colour, uses it with startlingly successful effect.

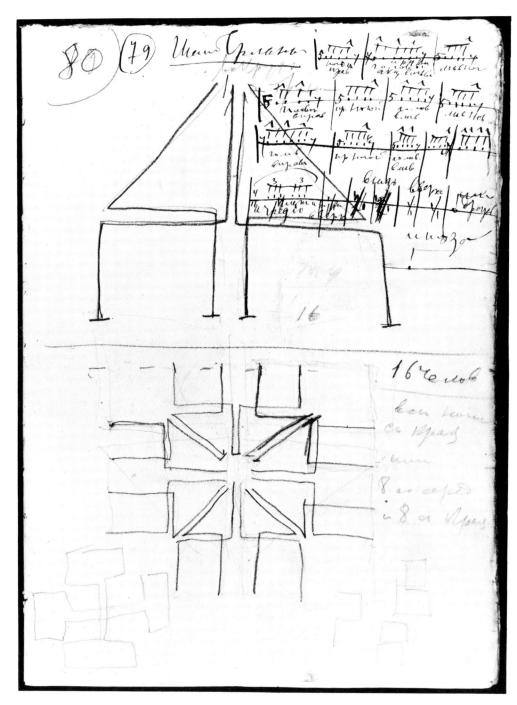

A page from Massine's choreographic notebook.   *Theatre Museum, V & A.*
Massine had his own system of working out his choreography, but one can see
how the patterns on the paper were transposed to the stage. The annotations in
Russian are as follows:
Heading: Chamberlain.
First line: Leg and right (arm)/hands and head to the left/with the left leg.
Second line: Head to the rght/ with the right leg/
            Head to the left/with the left leg.
Third line: Head to the right/with the right leg/Head to the left.
Fourth line: Allegro and arms up/down/up/shivers/and attitude.
Lower diagram: 16 men/all begin from the side/or
            8 from the centre/and 8 from the side.

Other Major Productions

16 July 1920 London, Royal Opera House

Company: Les Ballets Russes de Serge Diaghilev
Conductor: Ernest Ansermet
Choreographer: Leonide Massine
Scenery & Costumes: Henri Matisse
Principal Dancers: Tamara Karsavina (Nightingale),
Lydia Sokolova (Death), Serge Grigoriev (Emperor),
Stanislas Idzikowski (Mechanical Nightingale)

17 June 1925 Paris, Gaîté-Lyrique

Company: Les Ballets Russes de Serge Diaghilev
Conductor: Marc-César Scotto
Choreographer: Georges Balanchin*
Scenery & Costumes: Henri Matisse
Principal Dancer: Alicia Markova

*Later 'anglicised' as George Balanchine

18 July 1927 London, Princes

Company: Les Ballets Russes de Serge Diaghilev
Conductor: Roger Désormière
Choreographer: Georges Balanchin*
Scenery & Costumes: Henri Matisse
Principal Dancers: Alicia Markova (Nightingale), Lydia
Sokolova (Death), Serge Grigoriev (Emperor), Leon
Woizikowsky (Mechanical Nightingale)

1929 Berlin, Städtische Oper

Choreographer: Lizzie Maudrik
Scenery & Costumes: Prof. Dobrowen

1968 Munich, Bayerische Staatsoper

Choreographer: John Cranko

17 June 1972 Stuttgart, Württembergische Staatstheater

Company: Stuttgart Ballet
Choreographer: John Cranko
Scenery & Costumes: Dorothee Zippel

22 June 1972 New York, NY State Theatre

Company: New York City Ballet
Choreographer: John Taras
Scenery & Costumes: Rouben Ter-Arutunian
Principal Dancers: Gelsey Kirkland (Nightingale), Elise
Flagg (Mechanical Nightingale), Francisco Moncion
(Emperor), Penny Dudleston (Death)

Matisse's designs for make-up and head-dresses for a warrior and a minister.
Photo: Bibliothèque Nationale, fonds Kochno.

Pablo Picasso's design for the set. The final version of the design eliminated the stage boxes and the minstrels' gallery. *Photo: Musées Nationaux, Paris. © SPADEM.*

Souvenir programme cover of 1923 season reproducing scene design by Pablo Picasso. *Theatre Museum, V & A.*

Pulcinella

Based on scores by Giambattista Pergolesi
Libretto by Igor Stravinsky
40 minutes (EWW 46)

Leonide Massine had the first idea for this ballet – a work inspired by the *Commedia dell'Arte* and its traditional masked characters. Picasso, with characteristic energy, did a large number of designs both for the costumes and the scenery, developing his prolific ideas on paper. Always refining. Always simplifying. Until the final effect was just right. Charming but not sentimental. Picturesque but not untheatrical. But the ballet was a very complicated story and subsequent productions have tried to simplify it while keeping the spirit of the *Commedia dell'Arte*.

The designs by Eugene Berman for the version by the New York City Ballet in 1972 are the most recently successful because they kept the spirit meticulously. To strip the ballet of all its traditional Italian origins and flavour, as has recently been done in Paris, reduces it to nothing, whatever clever quasi-philosophical arguments may be used for such a staging.

The successful modernisation or reinterpretation of a work is not achieved by disregarding its original essence. The spirit of a work is its life, and to ignore the spirit is to kill the work.

But no doubt Pulcinella will be revived again.

First Performance 15 May 1920

Theatre:	Théâtre national de l'Opéra, Paris
Company:	Les Ballets Russes de Serge Diaghilev
Conductor:	Ernest Ansermet
Choreographer:	Leonide Massine
Scenery & Costumes:	Pablo Picasso
Principal Cast:	Leonide Massine (Pulcinella)
	Tamara Karsavina (Pimpinella)
	Lubov Tchernicheva (Prudenza)
	Vera Nemtchinova (Rosetta)
	Sigmund Novak (Furbo)
	Stanislas Idzikowski (Caviello)
	Nicolas Zverev (Florindo)
	Enrico Cecchetti (The Doctor)
	Stanislas Kostetsky (Tartaglia)
	Anatole Bourman, Okhimovsky,
	Mikolaichik, Leighton Lukine
	(Four little Pulcinellas)
Singers:	Mafalda de Voltri
	Angelo Masini Pieralli
	Zoia Rosovska
	Romanitza
	Aurelio Anglada
	Gino de Vecchi

Synopsis

The scene is Naples and the characters are taken from the *Commedia dell'Arte*.

Caviello and Florindo are courting Rosetta and Prudenza. Leaning out of a window the two girls pour water over the boys' heads. The Doctor arrives and chases the boys away. Pulcinella enters. He dances and attracts Prudenza, who tries to embrace him. Pulcinella rejects her. Rosetta appears chaperoned by her father Tartaglia. She tells him she loves Pulcinella. She dances for him and he gives her a kiss. Pimpinella, Pulcinella's mistress, discovers them and is jealous. He protests his innocence.

Pimpinella is placated. Caviello and Florindo, in disguise, are angered by Pulcinella's flirtations. Florindo stabs Pulcinella. As soon as Caviello and Florindo leave, Pulcinella cautiously gets up. Four little Pulcinellas enter carrying the body of Furbo disguised as another Pulcinella. They lay the body on the floor. The Doctor and Tartaglia come in with their daughters. The girls are horrified. The Doctor pronounces that Pulcinella is dead. A magician appears and assures the girls that he can revive the corpse. The body is revived and the girls again show their affection. The fathers cannot believe the miracle. The magician takes off his cloak to reveal that he is the real Pulcinella and that the revived corpse is his friend, Furbo. Pulcinella and Furbo trick the Doctor and Tartaglia into leaving. Pimpinella enters but is frightened by seeing two Pulcinellas. Then Florindo and Caviello return, also disguised as Pulcinellas, and renew their courtship of Prudenza and Rosetta. Pimpinella, Rosetta and Prudenza dance with three false Pulcinellas. The real Pulcinella kicks each of the three men. He unmasks Florindo and Caviello while Furbo dons the magician's cloak. The Doctor and Tartaglia return and are persuaded by Furbo, the magician, to allow their daughters to marry Florindo and Caviello. Finally the magician marries the two couples and Pulcinella and Pimpinella.

Pablo Picasso's drawing of Pulcinella and Harlequin.
Photo: Musées Nationaux, Paris. © *SPADEM.*

Pablo Picasso's costume design for Pimpinella with annotation: Karsavina.
Photo: Musées Nationaux, Paris. © SPADEM.

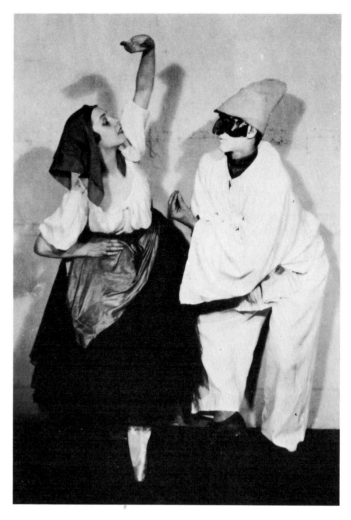

Lydia Lopokhova as Pimpinella and Leon Woizikowsky as Pulcinella in London, 1923.   *Photo: Sasha. Theatre Museum, V & A, London Archives of the Dance.*

Costume designs by Pablo Picasso for Pimpinella and Pulcinella reproduced in the souvenir programme of the Ballets Russes 1923 season. *Theatre Museum, V & A.*

Jerome Robbins and George Balanchine as Beggars in the New York City Ballet
production for the Stravinsky Festival, New York, June 1972.
Photo: Martha Swope.

104

Other Major Productions

10 June 1920 London, Royal Opera House

Company: Les Ballets Russes de Serge Diaghilev
Conductor: Ernest Ansermet
Choreographer: Leonide Massine
Scenery & Costumes: Pablo Picasso
Principal Dancers: Leonide Massine (Pulcinella),
Tamara Karsavina (Pimpinella), Lubov Tchernicheva
(Prudenza), Vera Nemtchinova (Rosetta), Leon
Woizikowsky (Furbo), Stanislas Idzikowski (Caviello),
Nicolas Zverev (Florindo), Enrico Cecchetti (Dottore),
Stanislas Kostetsky (Tartaglia), Bourman, Okhimovsky,
Mikolaichik, Lukine (Four little Pulcinellas)
Singers: Mafalda de Voltri, Aurelio Anglada, Gino de
Vecchi

16 May 1926 Petrograd, Maryinsky

Choreographer: Fedor Lopukhov
Scenery & Costumes: Vladimir Dimitriev
Principal Dancers: B.N.Komarov (Pulcinella),
E.P.Gerdt, T.A.Troyanovka

1926 Hanover, Landestheater

Choreographer: Yvonne Georgi
Scenery & Costumes: Georg Kirsta
Revived on 15 April 1963.

1927 Stockholm, Royal Opera

Choreographer: Lisa Steier
Scenery & Costumes: Isaac Grunewald

1928 Buenos Aires, Teatro Colon

Conductor: Aquiles Lietti
Choreographer: Boris Romanov
Scenery & Costumes: Rodolfo Franco
Singers: M.Trilla, R.Dominquez, J.Alsina
Principal Dancers: Helene Smirnova, Dora Del Grande,
Leticia de la Vega, Boris Romanov, Sinibaldo Cofone,
Raul Dall'Lago

1928 Gera, Duke of Reuss

Choreographer: Wiener

1929 Cologne, Opernhaus

Choreographer: Lasar Galpern
Scenery & Costumes: Hans Blanke

27 May 1931 London, Lyceum

Company: Ballet de l'Opéra Russe à Paris
Conductor: Eugene Goossens
Choreographer: Boris Romanov
Scenery & Costumes: Giorgio de Chirico
Principal Dancers: Boris Romanov (Pulcinella), Felia
Dubrovska (Pimpinella), Anatole Oboukhoff (Leandro),
Tatiana Lipkovskaya (Prudenza), L.Pavlova (Rosetta),
C.Pavlova (Carolina)
Singers: C.Jakovleva, Avseenko, S.Ritch

1932 Essen, Opernhaus

Company: Ballets Jooss
Choreographer: Kurt Jooss
Scenery & Costumes: Hein Heckroth

May 1933 Augsburg, Stadttheater

Choreographer: Aurel Milloss
Scenery & Costumes: Annie Strauss

1933 Riga, Latvian Opera & Ballet Theatre

Choreographer: Anatole Wiltzak
Scenery & Costumes: Romana Suta

1933 Chicago

Company: New York Music Guild
Choreographer: Laurent Novikov
Scenery & Costumes: Paepeke & Badger

12 April 1934 Hamburg, Staatstheater

Conductor: Richard Richter
Choreographer: Helga Swedlund
Scenery & Costumes: Gerd Richter

1935 London, Coliseum

Conductor: Anatole Fistoulari
Choreographer: Leon Woizikovsky
Principal Dancers: Leon Woizikovsky (Polichinelle),
Nina Raievska (Pimpinella), Valentina Blinova (Rosine),
Ruth Chanova (Constance), André Eglevsky (1st
cavalier), Igor Youskewitch (2nd cavalier)
Vocalist: Morgan Davies

As *Les Deux Polichinelles*.

1938 Rome, Teatro Quirinetta

Choreographer: Boris Romanov
Scenery & Costumes: Gino Severini

1940 Venice, La Fenice

Choreographer: Boris Romanov
Scenery & Costumes: Gino Severini

1942 Rome, Teatro Reale

Choreographer: Aurel Milloss
Scenery & Costumes: Nicola Benois

31 August 1952 Berlin, Deutsche Oper

Choreographers: Keith & Gustav Blank
Scenery & Costumes: Josef Fenneker

1 April 1956 Frankfurt, Städtische Bühnen

Conductor: Hans Drewanz
Choreographer: Herbert Freund
Scenery & Costumes: Hein Heckroth
Principal Dancers: Irene Mann, Herbert Freund

25 June 1957 Dartington, England, Barn

Company: Western Theatre Ballet
Choreographer: Elizabeth West
Scenery: Barry Kay
Costumes: Phyllida Law
Principal Dancers: Jeffery Taylor (Caviello), Brenda
Last (a boy), Erling Sunde (Florindo), Rudi Szigeti
(Capitano), Peter Darrell (Pulcinella), Suzanne Musitz
(Prudenza), Margaret Grey (Rosetta), Barry Salt
(Tartaglia), Anna Paskevska (Pimpinella), Oliver
Symons (Furbo), Desirée Jervis, Brenda Last, Jennifer
Leyland, Hazel Merry (Four little Pulcinellas)

This production performed in London, Arts Theatre, on
23 July 1957.

18 February 1958 Hamburg, Staatsoper

Conductor: Wilhelm Rüggeberg-Brückner
Choreographer: Gustav Blank
Scenery & Costumes: Ita Maximowna
Principal Dancers: Christa Kempf, Maria Litto

28 September 1961 Cologne, Bühnen der Stadt

Conductor: Hermin Esser
Choreographer: Aurel Milloss

27 October 1961 Brussels, Théâtre royal de la Monnaie

Choreographer: Maurice Béjart
Scenery & Costumes: Bernard Daydé
Principal Dancers: Paolo Bortoluzzi (Duke), Jaleh
Kerendi (Duchess), Maurice Béjart (Pulcinella), Dolores
Laga (Pulcinella's elder son)
Singers: Jean-Jacques Scheurs, Jules Bastin, Gia Baldi

First performed at Liège on 10 September 1957.

1965/66

Company: National Ballet of Canada
Choreographer: Grant Strate
Scenery & Costumes: Mack Negin

11 July 1968 New York, Metropolitan Opera House

Company: American Ballet Theatre
Choreographer: Michael Smuin
Scenery: Jack Brown
Costumes: Stanley Simmons
Principal Dancers: Susan Casey, Ellen Everett, Georgina
Vidal, Diana Weber, Ian Horvath, Terry Orr, Michael
Smuin, John Sowinski

As *Pulcinella Variations*.

10 December 1971 Milan, La Scala

Conductor: Bruno Maderna
Choreographer: Leonide Massine
Scenery & Costumes: Pablo Picasso
Principal Dancers: Aida Accolla (Rosetta), Jean Babilée (Pulcinella), Dario Brigo (Doctor), Fiorella Cova (Pimpinella), Paolo Podini (Florindo), Santambrogio (Tartaglia)

23 June 1972 New York, NY State Theatre

Company: New York City Ballet
Conductor: Robert Irving
Choreographers: Jerome Robbins & George Balanchine
Scenery & Costumes: Eugene Berman
Lighting: Ronald Bates
Principal Dancers: Edward Villella, Violette Verdy, Francisco Moncion, Michael Arshansky, Shaun O'Brien, George Balanchine, Jerome Robbins

19 July 1974 Düsseldorf, Deutsche Oper am Rhein

Choreographer: Erich Walter

9 October 1974 New York, City Center

Company: City Center Joffrey Ballet

1974 Lucerne, Opera

Choreographer: Riccardo Duse
Scenery & Costumes: Vaclav Elias

25 October 1975 Mannheim, Nationaltheater

Choreographer: Lothar Höfgen
Scenery: Paul Walter
Costumes: Winnie Schneider

9 October 1980 Geneva, Grand Theatre

Conductor: Jean-Marie Auberson
Choreographer: Oscar Araiz
Scenery & Costumes: Carlos Cytrynowski
Principal Dancers: Cristina Martinelli, Roger Shim, Laura Smeak, Cheryl Wrench, Robert Thomas, Raquel Rossetti, Jackie Planeix, Lucas Crandall, Tom Crocker

18 November 1980 Paris, Théâtre des Champs-Elysées

Conductor: Manuel Rosenthal
Choreographer: Douglas Dunn
Lighting: John Davis

13 June 1981 Kassel, Staatstheater

Choreographer: Ronald Ashton
Lighting & Costumes: Rita Seitz
Principal Dancers: Hans Wrona (Pulcinella), Lynette Blechta (Pimpinella)

To taped music of *Pulcinella Suite.*

17 June 1981 Osnabrück, Städtische Bühnen

Conductor: Alfred Eschwé
Choreographer: Hans-Henning Ende
Scenery: Edgar Ruth
Costumes: Marga Sommerkamp
Principal Dancers: Andrzej Kucharski (Pulcinella), Lisa Kohl (Pimpinella)

Michel Larionov: Drawing for the set dated 1921.
Theatre Museum, V & A.

Renard

A burlesque to be sung and played
Libretto by Igor Stravinsky
adapted from a Russian story
20 minutes (EWW 31)

This work, like *The Song of the Nightingale*, was first staged by one choreographer and then restaged by another soon afterwards, using the original
designs. In this case the designer was Michel Larionov. As with Benois' *Petrushka*
designs it is often impossible to say with definitive accuracy for which of the two
productions, 1922 or 1929, Larionov did his. Indeed he drew and painted many
pictures called 'Scene' or 'Costume design for Renard' which are not practical
designs but variations on the theme after the event.

Serge Lifar in his restaging in 1929 introduced acrobats pairing the main
characters. This circus element has been used in other interpretations, with the
Cock on a tightrope.

'As for the Fox,' said Maurice Béjart in a programme note, 'that legendary
character, that ambiguous creature ("Madame Fox" as the text has it), symbolising all the wiles of an ever-reborn femininity – surely the Fox is immortal? And
in this tale, half ballet and half cantata, is it the animals who copy human beings,
or the humans who are aping the animals?'

First Performance 18 May 1922

Theatre:	Théâtre national de l'Opéra, Paris
Company:	Les Ballets Russes de Serge Diaghilev
Conductor:	Ernest Ansermet
Choreographer:	Bronislava Nijinska
Scenery & Costumes:	Michel Larionov
Singers:	Fabert
	Dubois
	Narçon
	Mahieux
Principal Dancers:	Bronislava Nijinska (the Fox)
	Stanislas Idzikowski
	Jean Jasvinsky
	Michel Fedorov

Synopsis

Standing on his perch, the Cock gloomily describes his daily life. Enters Renard, disguised as a nun. He begs the Cock to come down and confess his sins. The Cock declares that he has no need to confess. 'Come, come,' says Renard, 'You not only have far too many wives, but you also treat them badly.' At this the Cock hops down from his perch, whereupon Renard grabs him by the tail. The Cock screeches for help from his friends, the Cat and the Goat. They rescue him, and all three dance triumphantly while Renard flees.

At the start of the second part, the cock complacently regains his perch and resumes his melancholy song. Renard enters again, this time without disguise. He tries once more to entice the Cock to the ground by flattery and bribery. At first the Cock is not fooled, but eventually is persuaded to jump down. Renard immediately pounces on him, and this time the Cock's friends are slow in coming to the rescue. Renard starts to pull out his feathers and the Cock begs for mercy. Realising that all is lost, he prays for the welfare of his surviving relatives and passes out. The Cat and the Goat appear at last and, feigning friendship, insinuate to Renard that his wife is unfaithful to him. He is caught off guard and they seize the opportunity to strangle him.

The Cat, the Goat and the Cock dance once more and beg for a token of gratitude from the audience if the tale has pleased them.

Michel Larionov: Costume design for the Fox.
Victoria and Albert Museum.

Jean Hoyer as the Cat, Boris
Lissanevitch as the Goat,
Nicolas Efimov as the Cock at
the Royal Opera House, Covent
Garden, 1929.
*Photo: Sasha. Theatre Museum,
V & A, London Archives of the
Dance.*

Scene at the Stanislavsky-
Nemirovitch Danchenko
Musical Theatre, Moscow,
designed by Marina Sokolova.
The evening also included a
performance of *Mavra* in the
same fanciful setting – an
artistically successful solution to
the problem of staging these two
works together.
Photo: N.Stepanova.

112

Other Major Productions

2 January 1927 Petrograd, Maryinsky

Conductor: Alexander Gauk
Choreographer: Fedor Lopukhov
Scenery & Costumes: Vladimir Dimitriev
Principal Dancers: K.V.Zuikov (Fox), A.V. Lopoukov
(Cock), B.N. Komarov (Cat), V.I.Vainonin (Ram)
Singers: I.V.Ershov (Fox), V.F.Tikhi (Cock), A.T. Fomin
(Cat), N.N. Butiagin (Ram)

21 May 1929 Paris, Sarah Bernhardt

Company: Les Ballets Russes de Serge Diaghilev
Conductor: Igor Stravinsky
Choreographer: Serge Lifar
Scenery & Costumes: Michel Larionov
Principal Dancers: Leon Woizikowsky (Fox), Nicolas
Efimov & Louis Agustino (Cock), Boris Lissanevitch &
Bernardo Agustino (Ram), Jean Hoyer & Adolph
Hierlinger (Cat)
Singers: Grégoire Raissoff, Michel Tkhorjewsky, Eugène
Maltzeff, Jan Nedra

15 July 1929 London, Royal Opera House

Company: Les Ballets Russes de Serge Diaghilev
Conductor: Roger Desormière
Choreographer: Serge Lifar
Scenery & Costumes: Michel Larionov
Principal Dancers: Leon Woizikowsky (Fox), Nicolas
Efimov & Louis Agustino (Cock), Boris Lissanevitch &
Bernardo Agustino (Goat), Jean Hoyer & Adolf
Hierlinger (Cat)
Singers: Grégoire Raissoff, Michel Tkhorjewsky, Eugène
Maltzeff, Jan Nedra

1941 Rome, Teatro delle Arti

Choreographer: Carletto Thieben
Scenery & Costumes: Enrico Prampolini

13 January 1947 New York, Hunter College Playhouse

Company: Ballet Society
Choreographer: George Balanchine
Scenery & Costumes: Esteban Francés
Principal Dancers: Todd Bolender (Fox), Lew
Christensen (Cock), Fred Danieli (Cat), John Taras
(Ram)

7 April 1954 Frankfurt, Städtische Bühnen

Conductor: Georg Solti
Choreographer: Herbert Freund
Scenery & Costumes: Teo Otto
Principal Dancers: Irene Mann, Marcel Luipart, Herbert
Freund

5 February 1955 Hamburg, Staatsoper

Conductor: Leopold Ludwig
Director: Günther Rennert
Scenery & Costumes: Teo Otto
Principal Dancers: Erica Lihn, Herbert Freund, Erich
Rohlf, Heinz Schmiedel
Singers: Fritz Lehnert, Kurt Marschner, Karl Otto,
Hermann Prey

May 1958 Florence, Pergola

Choreographer: Aurel Milloss
Scenery & Costumes: Emanuele Luzzati

4 September 1961 Edinburgh, Empire

Company: Western Theatre Ballet
Conductor: Alexander Gibson
Choreographer: Alfred Rodrigues
Scenery & Costumes: Arthur Boyd
Lighting: Richard Pilbrow
Principal Dancers: Dennis Griffith (Cock), Suzanne Musitz (Renard), Oliver Symons (Goat), Peter Cazalet (Cat)
Singers: Murray Dickie, Alfred Hallett, John Lawrenson, Trevor Anthony

1 August 1962 Santa Fe, New Mexico, Santa Fe Opera, Stravinsky Festival

Conductor: Robert Craft
Choreographer: Thomas Andrew
Scenery & Costumes: Henry Heymann
Principal Dancers: Ron Sequoio (Fox), Vincent Warren (Rooster), Lawrence Eddington (Cat), Howard Sayette (Goat)
Singers: Stanley Kolk, John McCollum, William Murphy, Donald Gramm

17 November 1962 Munich, Bayerische Staatsoper

Company: Munich Ballet
Conductor: Wilhelm Killmayer
Choreographer: Heinz Rosen
Scenery & Costumes: Rudolf Heinrich
Principal Dancers: Heino Hallhuber (Cock), Ronald Frazier (Fox), Svea Köller, Paul Bierck, Margot Werner, Hannes Winkler
Singers: Annelies Kupper, Gertrud Vordemfelde, Lorenz Fehenberger, Hans Günter Nöcker

1965 Paris, Théâtre national de l'Opéra

Company: Paris Opera Ballet
Conductor: Pierre Boulez
Choreographer: Maurice Béjart
Scenery & Costumes: Germinal Casado
Principal Dancers: Claire Motte, Attilio Labis, Lucien Duthoit, Franck

10 January 1969 London, Queen Elizabeth Hall

Company: Royal Ballet Choreographic Group
Conductor: David Atherton
Choreographer: David Drew
Scenery & Costumes: Ian Mackintosh & Vincent Cork
Principal Dancers: Deanne Bergsma, Alexander Grant, Stanley Holden, Wayne Sleep
Singers: Gerald English, Alexander Oliver, John Shirley Quirk, Joseph Rouleau

April 1972 Venice, La Fenice

Company: Ballet Théâtre Contemporain
Choreographer: Jacques Lecoq
Scenery & Costumes: Edouard Pignon
Principal Dancers: Jean-Claude Giorgini (Renard), Itchko Lazarov (Cock), Chantal Graf (Cat), Serge Chaufour (Goat)
Singers: Jean-Pierre Chevalier, Michel Hubert, George Jollis, Michel Llado

First performed at the Théâtre de la Ville, Paris on 14 June 1972.

9 February 1974 Brussels, Théâtre royal de la Monnaie

Company: Ballet du XXe siècle
Choreographer: Maurice Béjart
Scenery & Costumes: Germinal Casado
Lighting: Christian Boeckx
Principal Dancers: Jan Nuyts (Fox), Victor Ullate (Cock), Piotr Nardelli (Cat), Gérard Wilk (Goat)

13 December 1974 London, Queen Elizabeth Hall

Company: The Royal Ballet with London Sinfonietta
Conductor: David Atherton
Choreographer: Ashley Killar
Scenery & Costumes: Terence Emery
Principal Dancers: Margaret Barbieri, Stephen Jefferies, Graham Goodbody, Michael Harper
Singers: Gerald English, Peter Hall, Derek Hammond-Stroud, Joseph Rouleau

4 July 1974 Würzburg, Stadttheater

Choreographer: Klaus Meyer

19 July 1974 Duisberg, Theater der Stadt

Company: Deutsche Oper am Rhein
Choreographer: Gise Furtwängler

Mavra

Opera buffa in one act
Libretto by Boris Kochno
after Alexander Pushkin's poem
'The Little House in Kolomna'
25 minutes (EWW 50)

Diaghilev asked Leon Bakst to design the set for this opera, but when they could not agree about the fee Diaghilev approached Léopold Survage.

Although both the libretto by Boris Kochno and the music interpret Pushkin's poem, the opera is too small for a large house. It was almost crushed out of existence at its first performance by the overwhelming grandeur of the Paris Opera and took some time to recover.

The comparison between the productions at the Scala and the Piccola Scala shows exactly how wrong the large stage is for it and how right the small. It has been 'rediscovered' several times and, like the earlier opera *The Nightingale*, enjoys certain vogue periods. Although its length prevents it from being included easily into an opera company's repertoire it would make excellent television. Indeed, television, the medium now for mass entertainment, apparently hungers for new ideas but has not yet explored the possibilities of video-recording Stravinsky's experimental works, which seem ideally suited to it as they combine so many different elements of performance. To have singers, dancers, actors and musicians performing with equal excellence – a requirement of many of Stravinsky's works – is a serious administrative and financial problem for theatre companies but need not be for television companies. The works are also the right length for television.

First Performance 18 May 1922

Theatre: Théâtre de l'Opéra, Paris
Company: Les Ballets Russes de Serge Diaghilev
Conductor: Gregor Fitelberg
Director: Bronislava Nijinska
Scenery & Costumes: Léopold Survage
Cast: Oda Slovodskaya (Parasha)
Hélène Sadoven (the Neighbour)
Zoia Rosovska (the Mother)
Belina Skoupevsky (the Hussar)

Synopsis

Parasha has not seen her love for a whole week. Her love, Vassily the Hussar, returns. They arrange to meet again the following evening. The mother comes in and laments the cook's death. Parasha asks if she can help. The mother sends her out to look for a new cook. The mother again sings the praises of her dead cook – Thecla. A neighbour calls. They sing about the weather, the cost of living, clothes. Parasha returns with a new cook whose name is Mavra. It is Vassily, the Hussar, in disguise. The mother is delighted and asks Parasha to give instructions to the new cook while she gets ready to go out. Parasha and the cook, the Hussar, rejoice that they are together. Parasha and her mother go out. The cook is alone. He feels it's time to shave. He takes off his disguise. The mother returns, thinks he is a burglar, and faints. Parasha revives her mother. The neighbour comes in. The cook, Mavra, escapes. Parasha calls after him.

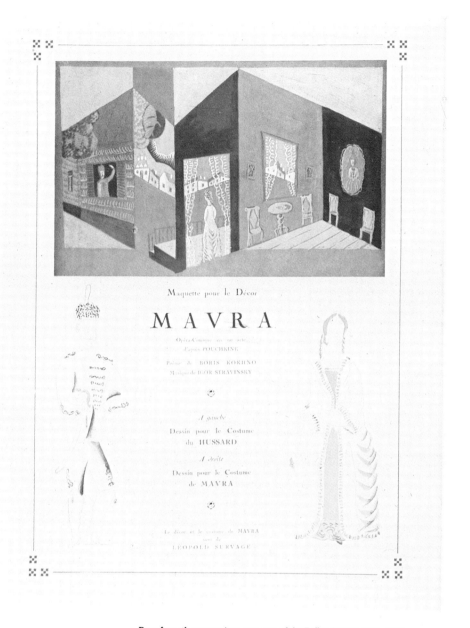

Maquette pour le Décor

MAVRA

Opéra-Comique en un acte
d'après POUCHKINE

Poème de BORIS KOCHNO
Musique de IGOR STRAVINSKY

❦

A gauche
Dessin pour le Costume
du HUSSARD

A droite
Dessin pour le Costume
de MAVRA

❦

Le décor et les costumes de MAVRA
sont de
LÉOPOLD SURVAGE

Page from the souvenir programme of the Ballets Russes, Paris, 1922, reproducing the designs by Léopold Survage for the set, and the costumes for the Hussar in uniform and when he is disguised as Mavra.
Theatre Museum, V & A.

117

The scene at the Teatro alla Scala, Milan, 1955 with Lucia Danieli as Parasha.
Photo: Erio Piccagliani. Harold Rosenthal Collection

The scene at the Piccola Scala, Milan, 1960 with, left to right, Edda Vincenzi as Parasha, Jolanda Gardino as the Neighbour, Luigi Pontiggia as the Hussar and Fiorenza Cossotto as the Mother.
Photo: Erio Piccagliani, Harold Rosenthal Collection.

The comparison between these two pictures shows how much more suited *Mavra* is to the smaller stage. Indeed, filling out the stage of the larger house with a double cast – one of singers and one of dancers – only harmed the work by trying to give it a scale which it does not have.

118

Other Major Productions

23 February 1928 Berlin, Krolloper

Conductor: Otto Klemperer
Director: Otto Klemperer
Scenery & Costumes: Ewald Dülberg
Principal Singers: Marie Schulz-Dornburg (Mother),
Else Ruziczka (Neighbour), Ellen Burger (Parasha),
Albert Peters (Hussar)

1928 Vienna, Staatsoper

Director: Lothar Wallerstein
Scenery & Costumes: Alfred Roller

28 December 1934 Philadelphia

Director: Herbert Graf
Scenery & Costumes: Serge Soudeikine

7 March 1942 Rome, Teatro dell'Opera

Choreographer: Aurel Milloss
Scenery & Costumes: G.Abkhasi

17 May 1945 Milan, La Scala

Conductor: Gianandrea Gavazzeni
Director: Giuseppe Marchioro
Scenery & Costumes: Vitrotto
Principal Mimes: Vanna Busolini (Neighbour), Ferni
Faraboni (Hussar), Ermanno Savaré (Mother), Wanda
Sciaccaluga (Parasha),
Singers: Elena Nicolai, Emilio Renzi, Ornella Rovero,
Giuseppina Sani

7 April 1954 Frankfurt, Städtische Bühnen

Conductor: Georg Solti
Director: Günther Rennert
Scenery & Costumes: Teo Otto

30 May 1955 Milan, La Scala

Conductor: Nino Sanzogno
Choreographer: Tatiana Gsovski
Scenery & Costumes: Sciltian
Principal Dancers: Giuliana Barabaschi (Mother), Tilde
Baroni (Neighbour), Luciana Novaro (Parasha), Mario
Pistoni (Hussar),
Singers: Lucia Danieli, Jolanda Gardino, Eugenia Ratti,
Aldo Bertocci

January 1956 Venice, La Fenice

Conductor: Ettore Gracis
Principal Dancers: Clara Betner, Barbara Gibson,
Amedeo Berdini

21 August 1956 Edinburgh, King's

Company: Hamburg State Opera
Director: Günther Rennert
Scenery & Costumes: Teo Otto
Principal Singers: Melitta Muszely (Parasha), Margarete
Ast (Neighbour), Gisela Litz (Mother), Jürgen Förster
(Hussar)
Performed at Hamburg on 23 September 1956.

1958 Berlin, Kongresshalle

Company: Studio der Städtischen Oper
Conductor: Hermann Scherchen
Principal Dancers: Theo Altmeyer (Hussar), Helga
Hildebrand (Parasha)

8 February 1960 Milan, Piccola Scala

Conductor: Nino Sanzogno
Director: Francesco Enriquez
Scenery & Costumes: Théodore Strawinsky
Principal Singers: Fiorenza Cossotto (Mother), Jolanda
Gardino (Neighbour), Pontiggia (Hussar), Edda Vicenzi
(Parasha)

1 August 1962 Santa Fe, New Mexico, Santa Fe Opera, Stravinsky Festival

Conductor: Robert Baustian
Director: Carolyn Lockwood
Scenery & Costumes: Henry Heymann
Principal Singers: Doris Yarick (Parasha), Mary Minott (Neighbour), Elaine Bonazzi (Mother), Paul Franke (Hussar)

15 September 1973 Dresden, Staatstheater

Director: Kupfer
Principal Singers: Horst Hiestermann (Hussar), Helga Termer (Parasha), Brigitte Pfetzschner (Mother), Barbara Gubisch (Neighbour)

6 March 1974 Brussels, Théâtre royal de la Monnaie

Company: L'Opéra-Studio en travail
Conductor: Augustin Kiss
Scenery & Costumes: Christelle Cormil
Principal Dancers: Mireille Capelle (Parasha), Cecile Leleux (Neighbour), Brigitte Giard (Mother), Joep Weys (Hussar)

28 January 1976 Florence, Teatro Comunale

Conductor: Pier Luigi Urbini
Director: Giampiero Calasso
Scenery & Costumes: Sando La Ferla
Principal Dancers: Fedora Barbieri (Mother), Gabrielle Ravazzi (Parasha), Rosina Cavicchiolo (Neighbour), Lajos Kozma (Hussar)

Leon Bakst's projected design for the set.
Victoria and Albert Museum.

Les Noces

Russian choreographic scenes
Libretto by Igor Stravinsky
35 minutes (EWW 37)

A Russian peasant wedding. The idea came to Stravinsky in 1912. He started to compose in 1914. He put it aside. He returned to it. He changed it. He finished the instrumental score a month before the first performance in 1923. And in between the starting and the finishing – the War and the Russian Revolution. Hope changed to disillusionment.

A Russian peasant wedding. Gontcharova first worked on some designs in 1915. Dancers dressed in gaily coloured folk costumes in her bright reds and yellows of *Coq d'Or*. She changed them. She searched for the right pattern, the right colours. She finished them, uniform brown and white, also a month before the first performance.

And Nijinska's choreography. The music, the text, the scenery and costumes, the dancing – Nijinska put them together and made the work into a synthesis of the ritual. She last choreographed the work for The Royal Ballet in 1966. Other choreographers while not imitating her have not ignored her influence.

121

First Performance 13 June 1923

Theatre:	Théâtre de la Gaîté-Lyrique, Paris
Company:	Les Ballets Russes de Serge Diaghilev
Conductor:	Ernest Ansermet
Director:	Bronislava Nijinska
Scenery & Costumes:	Natalia Gontcharova
Principal Dancers:	Felia Dubrovska (the Bride)
	Leon Woizikowsky (the Bridegroom)
Solo Singers:	Helen Smirnova
	Maria Davidova
	Michel d'Arial
	Georges Lanskoy
Pianists:	Hélène Léon
	Marcelle Meyer
	Georges Auric
	Edouard Flament

Synopsis

A cantata with dances showing an old Russian peasant wedding. Originally divided into four scenes: Blessing the Bride, Blessing the Bridegroom, the Bride's Departure and the Wedding, the Wedding Feast.

Natalia Gontcharova's choreographic costume design for three female dancers
(two versions).   *Victoria and Albert Museum.*

Natalia Gontcharova's design for the set, Scene IV. Because this design is not
colourful it has usually been reproduced in black and white, but the decision on
the final colour of the set and costumes was only made after a great deal of
painstaking experimentation, and was the crucial factor in the interpretation of
the work.   *Victoria and Albert Museum.*

The scene at the Royal Opera House, Covent Garden, 1966. In this production
for Covent Garden Bronislava Nijinska reproduced her original choreography.
Photo: Houston Rogers. Theatre Museum, V & A.

Svetlana Beriosova as the Bride,
Royal Opera House, Covent
Garden, 1966.
Photo: Houston Rogers.
Theatre Museum, V & A.

The Ballet du XXe siècle in
Maurice Béjart's version, at the
Théâtre royal de la Monnaie,
Brussels, 1962.
*Photo: Oscar. Théâtre royal de
la Monnaie.*

125

Other Major Productions

14 June 1926 London, His Majesty's

Company: Les Ballets Russes de Serge Diaghilev
Conductor: Eugene Goossens
Choreographer: Bronislava Nijinska
Scenery & Costumes: Natalia Gontcharova
Principal Dancers: Lubov Tchernicheva, Felia
Dubrovska, Alice Nikitina, Alexandra Danilova, Leon
Woizikowsky, Thadée Slavinsky, Serge Lifar, Nicolas
Kremnev
Singers: Anna Kerner, Hélène Sadoven, Grégoire
Raissoff, Georges Lanskoy
Pianists: Georges Auric, Francis Poulenc, Vittorio Rietti,
Vladimir Dukelsky

1926 Buenos Aires, Teatro Colon

Conductor: Aquiles Lietti
Choreographer: Bronislava Nijinska
Scenery & Costumes: Natalia Gontcharova
Principal Dancers: Anatole Wiltzak, Ludmilla Schollar
Singers: Tina Di Bari, Christina Salas Molina, Carlos
Rodriguez, Gregorio Svetloff

25 April 1929 New York, Metropolitan Opera House

Company: League of Composers
Choreographer: Elizaveta Anderson-Ivantzova
Director: Victor Andoga
Scenery & Costumes: Serge Soudeikine

1929 Königsberg, Städtisches Theater

Choreographer: Marion Hermann
Scenery & Costumes: Fritz Jakobs

21 May 1942 Rome, Teatro delle Arti

Choreographer: Alice Alanova
Scenery & Costumes: Enrico Prampolini

1948 Zurich, Stadttheater

Choreographer: Hans Macke
Scenery & Costumes: Teo Otto

1953 Stuttgart, Württembergische Staatstheater

Choreographer: Robert Mayer
Scenery & Costumes: Leni Bauer-Ecsy

28 January 1954 Milan, La Scala

Conductor: Carlo Maria Giulini
Choreographer: Tatiana Gsovski
Scenery & Costumes: Nicola Benois
Principal Dancers: Tilde Baroni (Bridegroom's mother),
Luciana Novaro (Bride), Angelo Pietri (Bride's mother),
Mario Pistoni (Bridegroom)
Singers: Amedeo Berdini, Cloe Elmo, Magda Laszlo,
Ivan Sardi

1956, Montreal

Choreographer: Ludmilla Chiriaeff
Scenery: Alexis Chiriaeff
Costumes: Claudette Picard

24 July 1962 Aix en Provence, Archbishop's Courtyard

Choreographer: George Skibine

31 October 1962 Brussels, Théâtre royal de la Monnaie

Company: Ballet du XXe siècle
Choreographer: Maurice Béjart
Scenery & Costumes: Joëlle Roustan and Roger Bernard
Principal Dancers: Nicole Raes (Bride), Duska Sifnios (the vision of her thoughts), Daniel Lambo (Bridegroom), Jorg Lanner (The vision of his thoughts), Nicole Floris, Blanche Aubrée (Mothers), Antonio Cano (Fathers)
Singers: Raymonde Serverius, Marie-José De Mattos, Louis Devos, Jules Bastin
Pianists: Robert Leuridan, Jacques Genty, Lysette Leveque, Marcel Druart

Performed at the Théâtre national de l'Opéra, Paris for the first time on 23 April 1965 with Jean-Pierre Bonnefous and Martine Parmain.

17 November 1962 Munich, Bayerische Staatsoper

Conductor: Wilhelm Killmayer
Choreographer: Heinz Rosen
Scenery: Rudolph Heinrich
Costumes: Charlotte Fleming
Principal Dancers: Natasha Trofimova (Bride), Winfried Krisch (Bridegroom), Margot Werner, Paul Bierck, Inge Bertl, Ronald Frazier

30 March 1965 New York, NY State Theatre

Company: American Ballet Theatre
Choreographer: Jerome Robbins
Scenery: Oliver Smith
Costumes: Patricia Zipprodt
Principal Dancers: Erin Martin (Bride), William Glassman (Bridegroom)

23 March 1966 London, Royal Opera House

Company: The Royal Ballet
Conductor: John Lanchberry
Choreographer: Bronislava Nijinska
Scenery & Costumes: Natalia Gontcharova
Principal Dancers: Svetlana Beriosova (Bride), Robert Mead (Bridegroom), Gerd Larsen, Romayne Grigorova, Leslie Edwards, Ray Roberts (Parents)
Singers: Roxolana Roslak, Elizabeth Bainbridge, Jack Irons, Jules Bruyère
Pianists: Richard Rodney Bennett, John Gardner, Edmund Rubbra, Malcolm Williamson

6 May 1966 Milan, Piccola Scala

Conductor: Armando Gatto
Choreographer: Leonide Massine
Scenery & Costumes: Natalia Gontcharova
Principal Dancers: Aida Accolla (Bridegroom's mother), Alfredo Caporilli (Bridegroom), Elettra Morini (Bride), Dora Ricci (Bride's mother),
Singers: Bianca Bortoluzzi, Walter Gullino, Paolo Montarsolo, Giuliana Tavolaccini

10 May 1975 Lyon, Opéra

Conductor: André Vandernoot
Choreographer: Vittorio Biagi
Scenery & Costumes: Roger Bernard

10 May 1975 Florence, Pergola

Company: Royal Opera Ballet, Stockholm
Conductor: Björn Hallman
Choreographer: Jerome Robbins
Scenery & Costumes: Sean Kenny
Principal Dancers: Kerstin Lindstrom (Bride), Klas Richman (Bridegroom)

Performed in 1971 at the Théâtre des Champs-Elysées, Paris.

3 September 1976 New York, Delacorte Theatre

Company: Lar Lubovitch Dance Company
Choreographer & Costumes: Lar Lubovitch
Lighting: Craig Miller
Principal Dancers: Susan Weber, Bob Besserer

12 September 1976 Hamburg, Staatsoper

Conductor: Kazuhiro Koizumi
Choreographer: Jerome Robbins
Scenery: Oliver Smith
Costumes: Patricia Zipprodt
Principal Dancers: Lynne Charles (Bride), Magali Messac (Bride's mother), Tanju Tüzer (Bride's father), Richard Gibbs (Bridegroom), Beatrice Cordua (Bridegroom's mother), Michael Steele (Bridegroom's father)
Singers: Yoko Kawahara, Elisabeth Steiner, Frieder Stricker, Ernst Wiemann
Pianists: Klaus Arp, Hisako Yoshiyama, Lienhard Krüger, Udo Bartels

23 January 1977 Venice, La Fenice

Conductor: Karl Martin
Choreographer: Ugo Dall'Ara
Scenery & Costumes: Alberto Gianquinto
Principal Dancers: Taina Beryll (Bride), Rocco
(Bridegroom), Sandra Fontolan, Elena Roncaglio
(Mothers),
Singers: Marjorie Wright, Giovanna Fioroni, Antonio
Bevacqua, Alfredo Mariotti
Pianists: Duo Gorini-Bagnoli, Anna Barutti, Ezio
Lazzarini

18 February 1978 Florence, Teatro Comunale

Conductor: Roberto Gabbiani
Choreographer: Maurice Béjart
Scenery & Costumes: Roger Bernard and Joëlle Roustan
Principal Dancers: Marga Nativo (vision of the Bride),
Jorge Donn (vision of the Bridegroom), Anna Berardi
(Bride), Francesco Bruno (Bridegroom)
Singers: Laura Musella, Giovanna Fioroni, Giuseppe
Baratti, Nicola Pigliucci
Pianists: Maria-Concetta Balducci, Gianfranco Cosmi,
Marcello Guerini, Francesco Novelli

Ewald Dülberg's design for the set and (opposite) the ground plan for the
Krolloper, Berlin, production of *Oedipus Rex*, 1928.

Oedipus Rex

Opera-oratorio in two acts
Libretto by Jean Cocteau after Sophocles
translated into Latin by Jean Daniélou

52 minutes (EWW 56)

As at the first public performance *Oedipus Rex* is still more often done as an oratorio than as an opera. But it is an opera. The myth as ritual. Unrealistic, almost abstract, but not unreal. Theatrical alienation is not achieved by principals and chorus in dinner jackets surrounded by an orchestra even if they are singing in Latin. Nor is the reality achieved by conventional staging which neglects the ritual. Ritual is real when it is stylised, and the full effect and power of the opera only comes across when it is performed in a full set with all the singers costumed and masked.

Although Vienna staged the opera two days before Berlin, it was Klemperer's production there which made the real impact. The Krolloper in Berlin was a shortlived (only four years, 1927-1931) but enormously influential experiment. Otto Klemperer was the founder and the artistic director. He gathered round him a team of designers who shared his aspirations for finding new ways of staging operas, and in particular new operas. The first of two Stravinsky evenings was on 25 February 1928 with *Oedipus Rex*, *Mavra* and *Petrushka* in the programme. The second evening was on 11 October 1928 when *Oedipus Rex* was repeated with *Histoire du Soldat*.

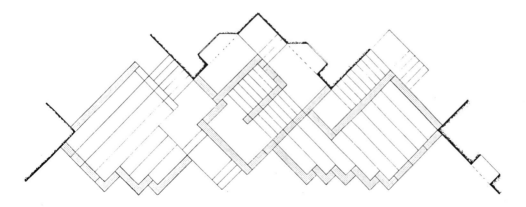

First Performance as an Oratorio 30 May 1927

Theatre: Théâtre Sarah Bernhardt, Paris
Company: Les Ballets Russes de Serge Diaghilev
Conductor: Igor Stravinsky
Cast: Pierre Brasseur (Narrator)
Hélène Sadoven (Jocasta)
Stephan Balina-Skupievsky (Oedipus)
Georges Lanskoy (Creon)
Kapitan Zaporojetz (Tiresias)
Michel d'Arial (Shepherd)

First Performance as an Opera 23 February 1928

Theatre: Staatsoper, Vienna
Conductor: Lothar Wallerstein
Scenery & Costumes: Alfred Roller

Synopsis

Thebes is ravaged by the plague. The people ask Oedipus, their King, to save them. Creon, the King's brother-in-law, returns from the oracle at Delphi. He has been told that the city will be saved only when the murderer of the previous King, Laius, is discovered and condemned.

Tiresias, the blind soothsayer, reveals that the murderer of the King is a King himself. Oedipus is angered by the implication and accuses Creon of conspiring with Tiresias to depose him. Jocasta, widow of Laius and now married to Oedipus, calms the people by declaring that the oracle has been wrong before. It had said that Laius would be killed by his own son, whereas he had been killed by robbers at a crossroads. Her declaration disturbs Oedipus for he remembers killing a stranger at the crossroads. A messenger arrives to announce the death of Polybus, the supposed father of Oedipus. He also reveals that Oedipus was only his adopted son. A shepherd describes how he found Oedipus abandoned in the mountains. Jocasta and Oedipus now guess the terrible truth; that he has murdered his father and married his mother. The oracle had been right. Jocasta kills herself. Oedipus blinds himself with her gold pin. The men of Thebes sing a last farewell to him before he leaves the city.

The collaboration between Stravinsky and Cocteau in creating *Oedipus Rex* extended, in 1952, to performing it together with Stravinsky as conductor and Cocteau as Narrator and designer of the *tableaux vivants*.

Scene of the second tableau, 'The Sorrow of Athens', designed by Jean Cocteau, Paris, 1952.
Photo: Serge Lido. Harold Rosenthal Collection.

Jean Cocteau's design for a mask, *c* 1952.
Theatre Museum, V & A.

131

The scene at the Sadler's Wells Theatre, 1960, designed by Abd' elkader Farrah.
Theatre Museum, V & A.

The scene at the Opera House, Warsaw, 1962, designed by Jan Kosinski.
Photo: Franciszek Myszkowski. Harold Rosenthal Collection.

William Marshall as the Speaker, Donald Gramm as Creon, Lyric Opera, Chicago, 1968.
Harold Rosenthal Collection.

These scenes demonstrate the essentially static nature of the work, but the monumental quality of the productions in London and Warsaw are more effective than the attempt at a certain realism in Chicago.

Other Major Productions

25 February 1928 Berlin, Krolloper

Director & Conductor: Otto Klemperer
Scenery & Costumes: Ewald Dülberg
Principal Singers: Caspar Koch (Oedipus), Sabine Kalter (Jocasta), Oskar Kalman (Creon), Emanuel List (Tiresias), Bernard Bötel (Shepherd), Martin Abendroth (Messenger), Heinrich Schnitzler (Narrator)

1928 Düsseldorf, Stadttheater

Director: Schram

1928 Essen, Opernhaus

Director: Marie Schulz-Dornburg
Scenery & Costumes: Caspar Neher

1930 Essen, Staatsoper

Director: Fritz Cohen
Scenery & Costumes: Hein Heckroth

21 April 1931 New York, Metropolitan Opera House

Company: League of Composers
Conductor: Leopold Stokowski
Performers: Remo Bufano's Puppets & Chorus

11 August 1931 Buenos Aires, Teatro Colon

Scenery & Costumes: Ewald Dülberg

1934 Zurich, Stadttheater

Director: Zimmerman
Scenery & Costumes: Roman Clemens

22 May 1937 Florence, Teatro Comunale

Conductor: Bernardino Molinari
Director: Celestino Celestini
Scenery & Costumes: Antonio Valente
Principal Singers: Giovanni Malpiero (Oedipus), Gilda Alfano (Jocasta), Armando Dado (Creon), Bruno Sbalchiero (Tiresias), Valerio Degli Abbati (Narrator)

1942 Buenos Aires, Teatro Colon

Scenery & Costumes: Hector Basaldua

24 April 1948 Milan, La Scala

Conductor: Nino Sanzogno
Director: Savinio & Giuseppe Marchioro
Scenery & Costumes: Alberto Savinio
Principal Singers: Ettore Bastianini (Tiresias), Suzanne Danco (Jocasta), Demetz (Oedipus), Mario Petri (Creon)

1949 New York

Choreographer: Fritz Cohen
Scenery & Costumes: Kiesler

19 May 1952 Paris, Théâtre des Champs-Elysées

Conductor: Igor Stravinsky
Scenery & Costumes: Jean Cocteau
Principal Singers: Léopold Simoneau (Oedipus), Eugenia Zareska (Jocasta), Jean Cocteau (Narrator)

Presented as seven *tableaux vivants*.

1953 Buenos Aires, Teatro Colon

Conductor: Karl Böhm
Principal Singers: Anton Dermota, Ruzena Horakova, Marko Rothmuller, Felipe Romito, Kurt Böhme

7 April 1954 Frankfurt, Städtische Bühnen

Conductor: Georg Solti
Director: Günther Rennert
Scenery & Costumes: Teo Otto

5 February 1955 Hamburg, Staatsoper

Conductor: Leopold Ludwig
Director: Günther Rennert
Scenery & Costumes: Teo Otto
Principal Singers: Maria von Ilosvay (Jocasta), Fritz Lehnert (Shepherd), Helmut Melchert (Oedipus), Arnold van Mill (Tiresias), James Pease (Creon)

Performed at the King's Theatre Edinburgh on 21 August 1956 with the same principals (first stage performance in Great Britain).

1958 Vienna, Staatsoper

Conductor: Herbert von Karajan
Director: Oscar Fritz Schuh
Principal Singers: Martha Mödl, Waldemar Kmentt, Kurt Böhme, Gottlob Frick, Oskar Czerwenka, Murray Dickie, Jean Cocteau (Narrator)

22 October 1959 Brussels, Théâtre royal de la Monnaie

Conductor: André Vandernoot

1959 New York, City Center

Conductor: Leopold Stokowski
Director: Paul Sylbert
Principal Singers: Richard Cassily (Oedipus), Claramae Turner (Jocasta), Arnold Voketaitis (Creon), Joshua Hecht (Tiresias), Wesly Addy (Narrator)

15 January 1960 London, Sadler's Wells

Company: Sadler's Wells Opera
Conductor: Colin Davis
Director: Michel St Denis
Scenery & Costumes: Abd'elkader Farrah
Principal Singers: Ronald Dowd (Oedipus), Monica Sinclair (Jocasta), Raimund Herincx (Creon), David Ward (Tiresias), Alberto Remedios (Shepherd), Raimund Herincx (Messenger), Michael Hordern (Narrator)

12 July 1960 Santa Fe, New Mexico, Santa Fe Opera

Conductor: Igor Stravinsky
Director: Hans Busch
Scenery: Henry Heymann
Costumes: Tanya Moiseiwitsch
Masks: Jacqueline Cundall
Principal Singers: Paule Franke (Oedipus), Mary MacKenzie (Jocasta), Gimi Beni (Creon), Andrew Foldi (Tiresias), Rolf Sander (Shepherd), Therman Bailey (Messenger), Paul Horgan (Narrator)

10 January 1962 Warsaw, Opera House

Conductor: Bohdan Wodiczko
Director: Konrad Swinarski
Scenery & Costumes: Jan Kosinski
Principal Singers: Bogdan Paprocki (Oedipus), Krystyna Szczepanska (Jocasta)

8 August 1962 Santa Fe, New Mexico, Santa Fe Opera

Conductor & Director: John Crosby
Scenery & Costumes: Henry Heymann
Principal Singers: George Shirley (Oedipus), Helen Vanni (Jocasta), Theodor Uppman (Creon), Donald Gramm (Tiresias), Loren Driscoll (Shepherd), Therman Bailey (Messenger), Winfield T.Scott (Narrator)

24 June 1963 Milan, La Scala

Conductor: Igor Stravinsky
Director: Günther Rennert
Scenery & Costumes: Teo Otto
Principal Singers: Boese (Jocasta), Fliether (Creon), Josef Greindl (Tiresias), Helmut Melchert (Oedipus), Carlo d'Angelo (Narrator)

20 October 1967 Frankfurt, Städtische Bühnen

Conductor: Theodore Bloomfield
Director: Kurt Horres
Scenery & Costumes: Hein Heckroth
Principal Singers: George Maran (Oedipus), Joann Grillo (Jocasta), Leonardo Wolovsky (Creon), Franz Crass (Tiresias)

5 November 1967 Copenhagen, Det Kongelige Teater

Conductor: Poul Jorgensen
Director, Scenery & Costumes: Lars Runsten

13 November 1968 Chicago, Lyric Opera

Conductor: Jean Fournet
Directors: Luigi Squarzina & Giampiero Calasso
Scenery & Costumes: Giacomo Manzù
Principal Singers: Mirto Picchi (Oedipus), Oralia Dominguez (Jocasta), Donald Gramm (Creon & Messenger), Paolo Washington (Tiresias), William Marshall (Narrator)

13 March 1969 Milan, La Scala

Conductor: Claudio Abbado
Director: Giorgio De Lullo
Scenery & Costumes: Pier Luigi Pizzi
Principal Singers: Lajos Kozma (Oedipus), Marilyn Horne (Jocasta), Giovanni Foiani (Creon), Luigi Roni (Tiresias), Piero De Palma (Shepherd), Alfredo Giacometti (Messenger)

26 July 1970 Munich, Nationaltheater

Conductor: Michael Gielen
Director: Hans Hartleb
Scenery & Costumes: Ekkehard Grübler
Principal Singers: Hertha Töpper (Jocasta), Sven Olaf Eliasson (Oedipus), Hans Günther Nöcker (Creon), Keith Engen (Tiresias), Willi Brokmeier (Shepherd), Karl Christian Kohn (Messenger), Michael Degen (Narrator)

29 November 1971 Rome, Teatro dell'Opera

Conductor: Pier Luigi Urbini
Directors: Luigi Squarzina & Giampiero Calasso
Scenery & Costumes: Giacomo Manzù
Principal Singers: Giorgio Casellato Lamberti (Oedipus), Fedora Barbieri (Jocasta), Mario Petri (Creon), Carlo Cava (Tiresias), Giorgio Albertazzi (Narrator)

16 December 1971 Venice, La Fenice

Conductor: Ettore Gracis
Director: Roberto Guicciardini
Scenery & Costumes: Lorenzo Ghilia
Principal Singers: Mirto Picchi (Oedipus), Ruth Hesse (Jocasta), Mario Basiola (Creon), Stefan Elenkov (Tiresias), Carlo Gaifa (Shepherd)

10 April 1973 Berlin, Deutsche Oper

Conductor: Heinrich Hollreiser
Director: Oscar Fritz Schuh
Scenery & Costumes: Wilhelm Reinking
Principal Singers: Donald Grobe (Oedipus), Patricia Johnson (Jocasta), Hans Günther Nöcker (Creon), Ivan Sardi (Messenger), Bengt Rundgren (Tiresias), Helmut Krebs (Shepherd), Peter Matic (Narrator)

6 March 1974 Oslo, Norske Opera

Conductor: Per Åke Anderson
Director: Kenneth Tillson
Scenery & Costumes: William Dudley
Principal Singers: Sven Olaf Eliasson (Oedipus), Thørbjorn Lindjem (Creon), Vessa Hanssen (Jocasta), Almar Heggen (Tiresias), Svein Carlesen (Messenger)

12 March 1978 Cologne, Oper der Stadt

Conductor: John Pritchard
Director: Michael Hampe
Scenery & Costumes: John Bury
Principal Singers: William Lewis (Oedipus), Hans Günther Nöcker (Creon), Franz Mazura (Tiresias), Hermann Winkler (Shepherd), Thomas Thomaschke (Messenger), Hans Schulze (Narrator)

24 March 1981 Leeds, Grand Theatre

Company: English National Opera North
Conductor: David Lloyd-Jones
Director: Patrick Libby
Scenery & Costumes: Stefanos Lazaridis
Principal Singers: Robert Ferguson (Oedipus), Hugh-Nigel Sheehan (Creon & Messenger), John Tranter (Tiresias), Josephine Veasey (Jocasta), Justin Lavender (Shepherd), Barry Stanton (Narrator)

13 October 1981 Geneva, Grand Theatre

Conductor: Horst Stein
Director: Jorge Lavelli
Scenery & Costumes: Max Bignens
Principal Singers: Kenneth Riegel (Oedipus), Dunja Vejzovic (Jocasta), Siegmund Nimsgern (Creon), Peter Meven (Tiresias), Robert Dumé (Shepherd), Peter Meven (Messenger), Genevieve Page (Narrator)
Production created at the Opéra, Paris, May 1979.

3 December 1981 New York, Metropolitan Opera House

Conductor: James Levine
Director: John Dexter
Scenery & Costumes: David Hockney
Principal Singers: Tatiana Troyanos, Richard Cassilly, Franz Mazura, John Macurdy, Anthony Dowell (Narrator)

Serge Lifar as Apollo in the first revival by the Ballets Russes, 12 June 1928. *Theatre Museum, V & A.*

Adolf Bolm as Apollo in the first production, 27 April 1928, at the Library of Congress, Washington DC. *Theatre Museum, V & A.*

No comment on the comparison between these first two Apollos!

136

Apollo

(Apollon Musagète)
Ballet in two scenes
30 minutes (EWW 57)

A frequent problem with Stravinsky is what to perform with what. It is a mistake to combine him with another composer in the same programme, but the wrong combinations of his own works can also make unsatisfactory evenings. The 'compare and contrast' kind of programming never works as well as the 'compare and develop'.

So *Apollo* should be seen as the first part of a triptych evening, with *Orpheus* second and *Agon* third. This is not just because that is the chronological order of composition, but because it is the natural order in the development of Stravinsky's ideas about music for 'classical' ballets on Greek mythology.

Although it was first performed and choreographed by Adolf Bolm it was quickly offered to Diaghilev, who then asked George Balanchine to do the choreography. Balanchine had worked with Stravinsky before on the restaging of *The Song of the Nightingale*, but *Apollo* was the first time they collaborated together. It was the beginning of an artistic partnership which revived traditions of classical ballet and then developed them into pure dance.

Every dancer, every choreographer, particularly in the United States and in Germany, has learnt from this partnership.

First Performance 27 April 1928

Theatre:	Library of Congress, Washington DC
Choreographer:	Adolf Bolm
Scenery & Costumes:	Nicholas Remisov
Principal Dancers:	Adolf Bolm (Apollo)
	Ruth Page, Elise Reiman
	Berenice Holmes (the Muses)

Commissioned by the Elizabeth Sprague Coolidge Foundation.

First Revival 12 June 1928

Theatre:	Théâtre Sarah Bernhardt, Paris
Company:	Les Ballets Russes de Serge Diaghilev
Conductor:	Igor Stravinsky
Choreographer:	George Balanchine
Scenery & Costumes:	André Bauchant
Scenery executed by:	Prince A.Schervachidze
Principal Dancers:	Serge Lifar (Apollo)
	Alice Nikitina (Terpsichore)
	Lubov Tchernicheva (Calliope)
	Felia Dubrovska (Polyhymnia)

Synopsis

Scene I: Leto gives birth to the god Apollo. Attendant handmaidens dance to him and bring him a lute.

Scene II: The three Muses, Calliope (poetry), Polyhymnia (acting) and Terpsichore (singing and dancing) pay homage to Apollo who gives them gifts, symbols of their art. Apollo leads the Muses in a procession up towards Parnassus.

The final moment in the first production by the Ballets Russes, 1928, with Serge Lifar as Apollo, Alice Nikitina as Terpsichore, Lubov Tchernicheva as Calliope and Felia Dubrovska as Polyhymnia.
Theatre Museum, V & A.

The same scene at the Royal Opera House, Covent Garden, 1966, with Donald MacLeary as Apollo, Svetlana Beriosova as Terpsichore, Monica Mason as Polyhymnia and Georgina Parkinson as Calliope.
Photo: Houston Rogers.
Theatre Museum, V & A.

Other Major Productions

25 June 1928 London, His Majesty's

Company: Les Ballets Russes de Serge Diaghilev
Conductor: Igor Stravinsky
Choreographer: George Balanchine
Scenery & Costumes: André Bauchant
Principal Dancers: Serge Lifar (Apollo), Alice Nikitina, Lubov Tchernicheva, Felia Doubrovska

Presented as *Apollo-Musagetes.*

18 January 1931 Copenhagen, Det Kongelige Teater

Choreographer: George Balanchine
Scenery & Costumes: Kjeld Abell

Revived 9 January 1957.

27 April 1937 New York, Metropolitan Opera House

Company: American Ballet
Choreographer: George Balanchine
Scenery & Costumes: Stewart Chaney
Principal Dancers: Lew Christensen (Apollo), Elise Reiman, Holly Howard, Daphne Vane, Kyra Blank, Rabana Hasburgh, Jane Burkhalter

Production performed at Teatro Municipal, Lima, Peru, September, 1941.

1941 Rio de Janeiro

Company: American Ballet
Choreographer: George Balanchine
Scenery & Costumes: Tomás Santa Rosa

1941 Rome, Teatro delle Arti

Choreographer: Aurel Milloss
Scenery & Costumes: Enrico Prampolini

1942 Buenos Aires, Teatro Colon

Conductor: Juan José Castro
Choreographer: George Balanchine
Scenery & Costumes: Pavel Tchelitchev
Principal Dancer: Michel Borovsky

25 April 1943 New York, Metropolitan Opera House

Company: American Ballet Theatre
Choreographer: George Balanchine
Scenery: Dunkel Studios
Costumes: Barbara Karinska
Principal Dancers: André Eglevsky (Apollo), Vera Zorina (Terpsichore), Nora Kaye (Polyhymnia), Rosella Hightower (Calliope), Miriam Golden, Shirley Eckl, June Morris

21 May 1947 Paris, Théâtre national de l'Opéra

Choreographer: George Balanchine
Scenery: André Delfau
Costumes: Gabrielle Chanel
Principal Dancers: Michel Renault (Apollo), Maria Tallchief (Terpsichore), Paulette Dynalix (Calliope), Jacqueline Moreau (Polyhymnia)

1951 Strasbourg

Choreographer: Françoise Adret

10 March 1956 Milan, Piccola Scala

Conductor: Antonino Votto
Choreographer: Serge Lifar
Scenery & Costumes: Giorgio de Chirico
Principal Dancers: Youly Algaroff (Apollo), Claire Sombert (Polyhymnia), Spear (Calliope), Nina Vyroubova (Terpsichore)

4 November 1956 Wuppertal, Opernhaus

Choreographer: Erich Walter
Scenery: Heinrich Wendel
Costumes: Günther Kappel

24 September 1958 Berlin, Städtische Oper

Choreographer: Tatiana Gsovski
Scenery & Costumes: Stanislas Lepri

17 April 1959 Brussels, Théâtre royal de la Monnaie

Choreographer: André Leclair

19 June 1959 Hamburg, Staatsoper

Conductor: Albert Bittner
Choreographer: Werner Ulbrich
Scenery & Costumes: Alfred Siercke

15 November 1966 London, Royal Opera House

Company: The Royal Ballet
Conductor: John Lanchberry
Choreographer: George Balanchine, staged by John Taras
Scenery & Costumes: John Craxton
Lighting: William Bundy
Principal Dancers: Donald MacLeary (Apollo), Svetlana Beriosova (Terpsichore), Monica Mason (Polyhymnia), Georgina Parkinson (Calliope)

12 February 1967 Stuttgart, Württembergische Staatstheater

Company: Stuttgart Ballet
Choreographer: George Balanchine

31 October 1969 Berlin, Deutsche Oper

Conductor: Ashley Lawrence
Choreographer: George Balanchine, staged by John Taras
Principal Dancers: Jean-Pierre Bonnefous (Apollo), Kay Mazzo (Terpsichore), Karin von Aroldingen (Polyhymnia), Lynn Seymour (Calliope)

9 November 1970 Nottingham, Theatre Royal

Company: Royal Ballet Touring Company
Choreographer: George Balanchine, staged by John Taras
Scenery: Elisabeth Dalton
Costumes: John Craxton
Principal Dancers: Keith Rosson (Apollo), Svetlana Beriosova (Terpsichore), Patricia Ruanne (Polyhymnia), Sandra Conley (Calliope)

11 October 1973 Geneva, Grand Theatre

Conductor: Jean Meylan
Choreographer: George Balanchine, staged by Patricia Neary
Principal Dancers: Peter Breuer (Apollo), Eva Evdokimova (Terpsichore), Aniko Csisky (Polyhymnia), Maria Galeazzo (Calliope)

18 October 1973 Oslo, Norske Opera

Conductor: Per Åke Anderson
Choreographer: George Balanchine
Scenery & Costumes: Thor Sutowski
Principal Dancers: Rudolf Nureyev (Apollo), Leoni Leahy (Terpsichore), Inger-Johanne Rütter (Calliope), Anne Merete Sundberg (Polyhymnia)

First performed in Oslo, 7 October 1966.

13 November 1974 Paris, Théâtre national de l'Opéra

Conductor: Marius Constant
Choreographer: George Balanchine
Principal Dancer: Michel Denard (Apollo)

26 December 1974 New York, Uris

Company: Nureyev and Friends
Conductor: Jacques Beaudry
Choreographer: George Balanchine, staged by John Taras
Principal Dancers: Rudolf Nureyev (Apollo), Merle Park (Terpsichore), Lynda Yourth (Polyhymnia), Lisa Bradley (Calliope)

30 October 1977 Vienna, Staatsoper

Company: Ballett der Wiener Staatsoper
Conductor: Stefan Soltesz
Choreographer: George Balanchine, staged by Patricia Neary
Principal Dancers: Rudolf Nureyev (Apollo), Lilly Scheuermann (Terpsichore), Judith Gerber (Polyhymnia), Gisela Cech (Calliope)

141

Margot Fonteyn as the Fiancée, Vic Wells Ballet, 1935.
*Photo: J.W. Debenham. Theatre Museum, V & A,
London Archives of the Dance.*

Le Baiser de la Fée

(The Fairy's Kiss)
Allegorical ballet in four scenes
inspired by the music of Tchaikovsky
from the story 'The Ice Maiden' by Hans Andersen
45 minutes (EWW 58)

Commissioned by Ida Rubinstein and performed by her company, *Le Baiser de la Fée* killed the friendship between Stravinsky and Diaghilev. Perhaps Diaghilev gloated over the fact that it was not a success.

Stravinsky agreed to the commission because it was the thirty-fifth anniversary of Tchaikovsky's death, and he wanted to commemorate his work.

In the title of the ballet Stravinsky acknowledges that his composition was inspired by the Muse of Tchaikovsky. He also thought that the story by Hans Christian Andersen was 'particularly appropriate as an allegory'. The fairy who gives the child the magic but fatal kiss is the muse which also marks Tchaikovsky. As Stravinsky himself says in his autobiography: 'The magic imprint has made itself felt in all the muscial creations of this great artist.' Stravinsky continues: 'Although I gave full liberty to painter and choreographer in the staging of my composition, my innermost desire was that it should be presented in classical form, after the manner of *Apollo*. I pictured all the fantastic roles as danced in white ballet skirts, and the rustic scenes as taking place in a Swiss landscape, with some of the performers dressed in the manner of early tourists and mingling with the friendly villagers in the good old theatre tradition.'

By trying to fulfil Stravinsky's 'innermost desire' it becomes a difficult ballet to make comprehensible, and has not been produced many times. The 'pretty' classicism of Benois' and Halicka's designs obscured the allegory. The Vic-Wells production of 1935 is also now only remembered because in it Margot Fonteyn created her first role and began her important partnership with the choreographer, Frederick Ashton. Using excerpts from the *Divertimento* version, Balanchine, in 1972, broke through the choreographic barrier which the original score persistently seemed to impose upon him. Nancy Goldner wrote on that occasion: 'If Fokine was the prototype for Balanchine, Balanchine's solo as performed by Tomasson is now the prototype for the future.'

'Allegory' is the crucial word for the choreographer Oscar Araiz. 'This allegory lets us glimpse the conflict experienced by the artist, who draws his inspiration from human life, while yet remaining as it were on the side-lines.'

The allegory makes the ballet comprehensible.

First Performance 27 November 1928

Theatre: Théâtre national de l'Opéra, Paris
Company: Ballets d'Ida Rubinstein
Conductor: Igor Stravinsky
Director: Bronislava Nijinska
Scenery & Costumes: Alexandre Benois
Principal Dancers: Ida Rubinstein (the Fairy)
Anatole Wiltzak (Rudi)
Ludmilla Schollar (Babette)

Synopsis

The score has the *Argument:* A fairy marks a young man with her mysterious kiss while he is still a child. She withdraws him from his mother's arms. She withdraws him from life on the day of his greatest happiness, in order to possess him and preserve this happiness for ever. She marks him once more with her kiss.

Alice Halicka's design for the third scene, Théâtre national de l'Opéra, Paris, 1947. Alice Halicka had already designed this ballet for the production at the Metropolitan Opera House, New York, 1937, which also had choreography by George Balanchine.

"Le Baiser de la fée."
Alternative Winds.

Kenneth Rowell's costume design for the Winds, for the production at the Royal
Opera House, Covent Garden, 1960.
Theatre Museum, V & A, Arts Council of Great Britain Collection.

146

Other Major Productions

1933 Buenos Aires, Teatro Colon

Conductor: Aquiles Lietti
Choreographer: Bronislava Nijinska
Scenery & Costumes: Hector Basaldua
Principal Dancers: Lida Martinoli (Fairy), Maria
Ruanova, Dora Del Grande, Anatole Wiltzak, Michel
Borovsky

26 November 1935 London, Sadler's Wells

Company: Vic-Wells Ballet
Conductor: Constant Lambert
Choreographer: Frederick Ashton
Scenery & Costumes: Sophie Fedorovitch
Principal Dancers: Pearl Argyle (Fairy), Harold Turner
(Young Man), Margot Fonteyn (Fiancée), Ursula
Moreton (Mother)

27 April 1937 New York, Metropolitan Opera House

Company: American Ballet
Choreographer: George Balanchine
Scenery & Costumes: Alice Halicka
Principal Dancers: Kathryn Mullowney (Fairy), William
Dollar (Young Man), Gisella Caccialanza (Fiancée),
Rabana Hasburgh (Shadow), Annabelle Lyon (Mother)

10 April 1940 New York, Metropolitan Opera House

Company: Ballet Russe de Monte Carlo
Choreographer: George Balanchine
Scenery & Costumes: Alice Halicka
Principal Dancers: Mia Slavenska (Fairy), André
Eglevsky (Young Man), Alexandra Danilova (Fiancée)

17 February 1946 New York, City Center

Company: Ballet Russe de Monte Carlo
Choreographer: George Balanchine
Scenery & Costumes: Alice Halicka
Principal Dancers: Alexandra Danilova, Frederic
Franklin, Maria Tallchief

2 July 1947 Paris, Théâtre national de l'Opéra

Choreographer: George Balanchine
Scenery & Costumes: Alice Halicka
Principal Dancers: Alexandre Kalioujny (Young Man),
Tamara Toumanova (Fiancée), Maria Tallchief (Fairy)

4 April 1953 Milan, La Scala

Conductor: Nino Verchi
Choreographer: George Balanchine
Scenery: Horace Armistead
Costumes: Barbara Karinska
Principal Dancers: Luciana Novaro (Fairy), Giulio
Perugini (Young Man), Tanaquil Le Clercq (Fiancée)

8 September 1958 Stuttgart, Württembergische
Staatstheater

Company: Stuttgart Ballet
Choreographer: Nicholas Beriosoff
Scenery & Costumes: Helmut Koniarsky

12 April 1960 London, Royal Opera House

Company: The Royal Ballet
Conductor: Colin Davis
Choreographer: Kenneth MacMillan
Scenery & Costumes: Kenneth Rowell
Lighting: William Bundy
Principal Dancers: Svetlana Beriosova (Fairy), Donald
MacLeary (Young Man), Lynn Seymour (Fiancée),
Meriel Evans (Mother)

5 December 1960 Mannheim, Nationaltheater

Choreographer: Heino Heiden
Scenery: Paul Walter
Costumes: Gerda Schulte

16 December 1968 Amsterdam, Stadsschouwburg

Company: Netherlands National Ballet
Choreographer: Ronald Hynd
Scenery & Costumes: John Hubbard

2 January 1972 Frankfurt, Städtische Bühnen

Company: Frankfurt Opera Ballet
Choreographer: John Neumeier
Scenery & Costumes: Jürgen Rose
Principal Dancers: Maximo Barra, Stephen Maurer, Marianne Kruuse, Persephone Samaropoulo

This version, also using Tchaikowsky's *Feuillet d'Album* Op.19 No 3 and *None but the lonely heart* Op.6 No 6, has a different scenario with flashbacks.

18 July 1974 New York, NY State Theatre

Company: American Ballet Theatre
Choreographer: John Neumeier
Scenery & Costumes: Jürgen Rose
Principal Dancers: Ivan Nagy, Jonas Kage, Zhandra Rodriguez, Cynthia Gregory (Fairy)

3 April 1975 Milan, La Scala

Conductor: Pier Luigi Urbini
Choreographer: Loris Gai
Scenery & Costumes: Anna Anni
Principal Dancers: Carla Fracci (Fairy), Paolo Bortoluzzi (Young Man), Anna Razzi (Fiancée)

20 February 1981 Geneva, Grand Theatre

Conductor: Jean-Marie Auberson
Choreographer: Oscar Araiz
Scenery: Carlos Cytrynowski
Costumes: Renata Schussheim
Principal Dancers: Iracity Cardoso, Frédéric Gafner, Cheryl Wrench, Tom Crocker, Bonnie Wyckoff

Presented as *Le Baiser.*

Lynn Seymour and Donald MacLeary at the Royal Opera House, Covent Garden, 1960.   *Photo: Houston Rogers. Theatre Museum, V & A.*

Perséphone

Melodrama in three scenes
Text by André Gide
56 minutes (EWW 64)

Stravinsky's next work for the stage was also commissioned by Ida Rubinstein.

However, as L.Franc Scheuer wrote of her in *The Dancing Times*, 1934, 'If she is an incomparable Maecenas, a patroness of the Arts, she is not so successful as interpretess. But often the faults pass by unnoticed for Mme Rubinstein's presence on stage is purely negative. It leaves a tremendous space where the *ballerina* should have been.'

There were many arguments before the first production. Gide never appeared. Stravinsky wanted his son, Théodore, to be the designer. Copeau had already chosen Barsacq. Only Jooss's choreography met with the composer's approval. The production ran for only three performances.

As with so many of Stravinsky's works, *Perséphone* contains a number of different theatrical elements, which makes it unappealing to conventional managements and producers. Therefore it has only rarely been staged.

In 1961 The Royal Ballet was able to fill that 'tremendous space' with the incomparable ballerina, Svetlana Beriosova, who could also act the part and declaim the French text.

Usually, however, it is given concert performances, although, for full effect, it certainly needs to be staged. Stravinsky knew what he was doing.

First Performance 30 April 1934

Theatre:	Théâtre national de l'Opéra, Paris
Company:	Ballets d'Ida Rubinstein
Conductor:	Igor Stravinsky
Director:	Jacques Copeau
Choreographer:	Kurt Jooss
Scenery & Costumes:	André Barsacq
Principal Performers:	Ida Rubinstein (Persephone)
	René Maison (Eumolpus)
	Anatole Wiltzak (Mercury)
	Natalie Krassovska (Demeter)
	Keith Lester (Triptolemus)

Synopsis

Scene I: The Abduction of Persephone. Eumolpus sings to Demeter, goddess of fertility and mother of Persephone. Persephone is warned by the Nymphs not to pick the narcissus, for its scent gives a vision of Hades. But Persephone ignores the warning and, as she smells the flower, sees the Shades of the Underworld. She has pity on them. Eumolpus tells her that if she goes to the Underworld she will relieve them of their misery, and they will lead her to Pluto to be his bride. Persephone agrees to go.

Scene II: Persephone in the Underworld. Pluto has banished spring from the earth, and Persephone is Queen of the Underworld. Mercury brings her a pomegranate, and when she tastes it she remembers the earth above and longs for it even though she only sees endless winter. Eumolpus tells her that winter will not last for ever and that Demeter will bring salvation by teaching men to till the earth. Persephone is reborn and rejoins her mother and her earthly husband.

Scene III: Persephone reborn. Spring returns to earth. But, having restored the seasons, Persephone realises that it is her destiny to rejoin the Shades. She takes the torch which Mercury offers her to light the way back into the dark.

André Barsacq's design for the set and
his costume design for Persephone.
© *SPADEM.*

André Barsacq's costume
designs.   © *SPADEM.*

Triptolemus.

Opposite: Svetlana Beriosova
as Persephone, the Royal Opera
House, Covent Garden, 1961.
Photo: Houston Rogers.
Theatre Museum, V & A.

A Dancer.

Demeter.

152

Other Major Productions

1938 Brunswick, Landestheater

Director: Heinz Arnold

21 May 1939 Florence, Teatro Comunale

Conductor: Igor Stravinsky
Soloists: Victoria Ocampo, Federico Anspach

Presented in concert form with *Petrushka* by the Ballet de Monte Carlo, choreography by Fokine, scenery and costumes by Alexandre Benois

1948 Zurich, Stadttheater

Choreographer: Hans Macke
Scenery & Costumes: Teo Otto

6 February 1956 Palermo, Massimo

Conductor: Tulio Serafin
Choreographer: Janine Charrat
Scenery & Costumes: Toti Scialoja
Principal Performers: Edmonda Aldini (Persephone), Allessandro Ziliani (Eumolpus), Helene Trailine (Demeter), Esteban Cerda (Pluto), Wladimir Ouktomsky (Triptolemus), Walter Scherer (Mercury), Carlo Faraboni (Angel of Death)

April 1956 Rome, Teatro dell'Opera

Conductor: Santini
Choreographer: Margherita Wallmann
Scenery & Costumes: Colasanti and Moore
Principal Dancers: Ludmilla Tcherina (Persephone), Giacinto Prandelli (Eumolpus)

31 May 1960 Wuppertal, Opernhaus

Conductor: Hans Georg Ratjen
Directors: Erich Walter & Heinrich Wendel
Costumes: Günther Kappel
Principals: Adrian de Peyer (Eumolpus), Ingrid Emde (Demeter), Denise Laumer (Persephone), Joachim König (Triptolemus)

15 July 1961 Santa Fe, New Mexico, Santa Fe Opera

Conductor: Robert Craft – Igor Stravinsky on 19 July 1961
Director: Hans Busch
Choreographer: Thomas Andrew
Scenery: Henry Heymann
Costumes: Henry Heymann, after Vera Stravinsky
Principals: Vera Zorina (Persephone), Loren Driscoll (Eumolpus), Thomas Andrew (Mercury)

12 December 1961 London, Royal Opera House

Company: The Royal Ballet
Conductor: John Lanchberry
Choreographer: Frederick Ashton
Scenery & Costumes: Nico Ghika
Lighting: William Bundy
Principal Dancers: Svetlana Beriosova (Persephone), Alexander Grant (Mercury), Keith Rosson (Pluto), Gerd Larsen (Demeter), Derek Rencher (Demaphoon), André Turp (Eumolpus)

8 August 1962 Santa Fe, New Mexico, Santa Fe Opera, Stravinsky Festival

Conductor: John Crosby
Director: Thomas Andrew
Scenery: Henry Heymann
Costumes: Henry Heymann, after Vera Stravinsky
Principals: Vera Zorina (Persephone), Loren Driscoll (Eumolpus), Thomas Andrew (Mercury), Ron Sequoio (Pluto)

10 March 1966 Milan, La Scala

Conductor: Nino Sanzogno
Choreographer: Margherita Wallmann
Scenery & Costumes: Enrico D'Assia
Principal Performers: Annie Giardot (Persephone), Merighi (Eumolpus), Jozo Borcic (Pluto), Roberto Fascilla (Mercury), Bruno Telloli (Triptolemus), Valerio (Demeter)

The final scene at the Royal Opera House, Covent Garden, 1961.
Photo: Houston Rogers. Theatre Museum, V & A.

14 August 1968 Santa Fe, New Mexico, Santa Fe Opera

Conductor: Robert Baustian
Director & Choreographer: Vera Zorina
Scenery & Costumes: Rouben Ter-Arutunian
Principals: Anastasios Vrenios (Eumolpus), Vera Zorina (Persephone), Clive Thompson (Pluto), James de Bolt (Mercury)

1970 Florence, Teatro Comunale

Choreographer: Aurel Milloss
Scenery & Costumes: Corrado Cagli

21 February 1978 Ulm, Stadttheater

Choreographer: Günther Pick

A page from a magazine, showing Annabelle Lyon as the Queen of Hearts, Leda Anchutina as the Queen of Spades, and William Dollar as the Joker in the first production, Metropolitan Opera House, New York, 1937. This photo-montage in colour has been used to illustrate the first production because the original designs by Irene Sharaff no longer exist. *Photo: Anton Bruehl. Theatre Museum, V & A.*

The scene at the Bayerische Staatsoper, Munich, first performed on 10 November 1975. This production, with choreography by John Cranko and scenery and costumes by Dorothee Zippel, was first performed in Stuttgart in 1965 and has been regularly produced since then, particularly in Germany. *Photo: Sabine Toepffer.*

Jeu de Cartes

Ballet in three deals
by Igor Stravinsky and N.Malaieff
21 minutes (EWW 67)

Commissioned by Lincoln Kirstein for the American Ballet, this was the first collaboration between Balanchine and Stravinsky in the United States.

Balanchine asked Stravinsky for a 'classical ballet'. Stravinsky returned to music for dancing, without words, without theatrical complications, a simple, easily understandable, entertaining story based on his favourite card game – poker.

Subtler meanings than Stravinsky had intended were inevitably given to the work – the Joker is the spirit of evil who tries to dominate others but is defeated in the end; parallels were made with previous works – Kashchei against the Firebird, the Moor against Petruskha, the Devil against the Soldier. But critics, confined within traditional aesthetic boundaries, will always seek to circumscribe works of art with influences, comparisons, definitions, and often deny them simple originality. Great artists – Picasso, Matisse, Nijinsky, Balanchine, collaborators of Stravinsky, and Stravinsky himself – are never bound by tradition but spring out of it. (They know the grammar but break the rules.) Sometimes they stumble but usually they land on their feet – to the consternation of the critics.

First Performance 27 April 1937

Theatre:	Metropolitan Opera House, New York
Company:	The American Ballet
Conductor:	Igor Stravinsky
Choreographer:	George Balanchine
Scenery & Costumes:	Irene Sharaff
Principal Dancers:	William Dollar (the Joker)
	Ann Campbell, Jane Burkhalter,
	Lillian Moore, Vera Volkenau (Aces)
	Lew Christensen, Joseph Lane,
	Douglas Coudy, Erick Hawkins (Kings)
	Annabelle Lyon, Leda Anchutina,
	Ariel Lang, Hortense Kahrklin (Queens)
	Charles Laskey, Joseph Levinoff,
	Eugene Loring, Serge Temoff (Jacks)

Synopsis

The dancers are cards in a game of poker, with the Joker directing the game. In the first deal, one of the three players is beaten, while the other two remain with even 'straights'. In the second deal the Joker is victorious because of four Aces who defeat four Queens. In the third deal, the Joker is finally beaten by three flushes.

Other Major Productions

1937 Dresden, Staatsoper

Conductor: Carl Böhm
Choreographer, Scenery & Costumes: Valeria Kratina
Principal Dancer: Vera Mahlke (Queen of Hearts)

1938 Zurich, Stadttheater
Choreographers: Pia & Pino Mlakar
Scenery & Costumes: Roman Clemens

14 October 1940 New York, 51st Street Theatre

Company: Ballet Russe de Monte Carlo
Choreographer: George Balanchine
Scenery & Costumes: Irene Sharaff
Principal Dancers: Frederic Franklin (Joker), Alexandra Danilova, Nathalie Krassovska, Alicia Markova, André Eglevsky, Igor Youskevitch

12 October 1945 Paris, Théâtre des Champs-Elysées

Company: Ballets des Champs-Elysées
Choreographer: Janine Charrat
Scenery & Costumes: Pierre Roy
Principal Dancers: Jean Babilée (Joker)
Performed at the Adelphi London, on 9 April 1946.

22 March 1948 Belgrade, State Opera House

Choreographer: Janine Charrat
Scenery & Costumes: Gustav Oláh
Principal Dancer: Janine Charrat

1948 Buenos Aires, Teatro Colon

Choreographer: Margherita Wallmann
Scenery & Costumes: Hector Basaldua

1948 Rome, Teatro dell'Opera

Choreographer: Aurel Milloss
Scenery & Costumes: Renato Guttuso

1953 Munich, Bayerische Staatsoper

Choreographer: Pia & Pino Mlakar
Scenery & Costumes: Ludwig Hornsteiner

7 March 1959 Milan, La Scala

Conductor: Luciano Rosada
Choreographer: Luciana Novaro
Scenery & Costumes: Dino Buzzati
Principal Dancers: Vera Colombo (Queen of Diamonds), Roberto Fascilla (Knave of Clubs), Carla Fracci (Queen of Clubs), Elettra Moroni (Queen of Hearts), Mario Pistoni (Knave of Hearts), Carmen Puthod (Queen of Spades), Aldo Santambrogio (Knave of Spades), Walter Venditti (Knave of Diamonds)

22 June 1960 Hamburg, Staatsoper

Conductor: Albert Bittner
Choreographer: Gustav Blank
Scenery & Costumes: Alfred Siercke
Principal Dancers: Uta Graf, Christa Kempf, Christel Teelen, Heinz Clauss, Joachim Weinberg

27 October 1961 Brussels, Théâtre royal de la Monnaie

Choreographer: Janine Charrat
Scenery & Costumes: Germinal Casado
Principal Dancers: André Leclair (Joker), Andrée Marlière (Queen of Hearts), Dolores Laga (Queen of Spades), Jeanine Renquet (Queen of Diamonds), Louba Dobrievitch (Queen of Clubs), Germinal Casado (Knave of Hearts), Pierre Dobrievitch (Knave of Spades), Franco Romano (Knave of Diamonds), Jacques Sausin (Knave of Clubs)

22 January 1965 Stuttgart, Württembergische Staatstheater

Company: Stuttgart Ballet
Choreographer: John Cranko
Scenery & Costumes: Dorothee Zippel
Lighting: Gilbert V.Hemsley

18 February 1966 London, Royal Opera House

Company: The Royal Ballet
Conductor: John Lanchberry
Choreographer: John Cranko
Scenery & Costumes: Dorothee Zippel
Principal Dancers: Christopher Gable (Joker), Annette Page (Queen of Hearts), Lynn Seymour (Two of Diamonds)

23 October 1966 Copenhagen, Det Kongelige Teater

Choreographer: John Cranko
Scenery & Costumes: Dorothee Zippel

2 March 1973 Pittsburgh, Heinz Hall

Choreographer: Nicholas Petrov
Scenery & Costumes: Henry Heymann

3 October 1973 London, Sadler's Wells

Company: The Royal Ballet Touring Company
Conductor: David Taylor
Choreographer: John Cranko
Scenery & Costumes: Dorothee Zippel
Principal Dancers: Stephen Jefferies (Joker), Vyvyan Lorrayne (Queen of Hearts), Margaret Barbieri (Two of Diamonds)

18 October 1973 Oslo, Norske Opera

Choreographer: John Cranko
Scenery & Costumes: Dorothee Zippell
Dancers: Stefan Petterson (Joker), Peter Lewis, Alan Watson, Alan Mugglestone, Anderej Ludwicki, Antony Geeves, Frederic Konrad, Raymond Bertrand, Terje Solberg, Bernard Hourseau, Sissel Westnes, Mona Pettersen, Grete Kleivdal, Wayne McKnight, Bjorn Berg, Ellen Kiellberg

26 January 1974 Karlsruhe, Badisches Staatsoper

Conductor: Winfried Petzold
Choreographer: Peter Köhler
Scenery: Waldemar Mayer-Zick
Costumes: Helmi Henssler
Principal Dancers: Ivan Buzga (Joker), Janice White (Queen of Hearts), Karin Zinner (Queen of Clubs), Renate Hejlova (Queen of Spades), Marjorie Auburtin (Queen of Diamonds)

February 1975 Chicago, Auditorium Theatre

Company: Joffrey Ballet
Choreographer: John Cranko
Scenery & Costumes: Dorothee Zippel

25 October 1975 New York, City Center

Company: Joffrey Ballet
Conductor: Sung Kwak
Choreographer: John Cranko, staged by Georgette Tsinguirides & restaged by Hiller Huhn
Scenery & Costumes: Dorothee Zippel
Principal Dancer: Gary Chryst (Joker)

1977 Lübeck, Stadttheater

Choreographer: John Grant

160

Circus Polka

For a young elephant
4 minutes (EWW 74)

Ringling Brothers, with good circus flair for the right publicity, commissioned
Balanchine to choreograph an elephant act. Balanchine asked Stravinsky to
compose the music. He agreed when Balanchine assured him that the elephants
were very young.
' . . .Newest and biggest of the spectacles is the "Ballet of the Elephants" staged
by Balanchine and danced last night by his screen star wife. In this, what seemed
like several thousand girls in brief red costumes spun and hung from the maze of
ropes above the arena, while the mastodons cavorted below to the music of
Merle Evans's swell circus band which was doing a Town Hall job with the Igor
Stravinsky music.' *Daily News*, 10 April 1942.

The elephants performed the act 425 times, but elephants in tutus are absurd.
Little girls in tutus are delightful, and performed Jerome Robbins's revival for
the Stravinsky Festival twice, once as an encore, forming themselves, at the end,
into the initials 'IS'.

First Performance 9 April 1942

Theatre: Madison Square Garden, New York
Company: Ringling Brothers of the
                    Barnum and Bailey Circus
Conductor: Merle Evans
Choreographer: George Balanchine
Elephant Trainer: Walter McLain
Costumes: Norman Bel Geddes

Revival 21 June 1972

Theatre: New York State Theatre
Company: New York City Ballet
Conductor: Robert Irving
Choreographer: Jerome Robbins
Lighting: Ronald Bates
Dancers: 48 children
Ringmaster: Jerome Robbins

In the programme of the third evening of the Stravinsky Festival.

Synopsis

'*The Ballet of the Elephants*. Fifty Elephants and Fifty Beautiful Girls in an Original Choreographic Tour de Force' – Description of act in programme.

The act featured Modoc, the elephant known as Bessie, as the 'première [sic] ballerina', with Vera Zorina, Balanchine's wife, on its back.

162

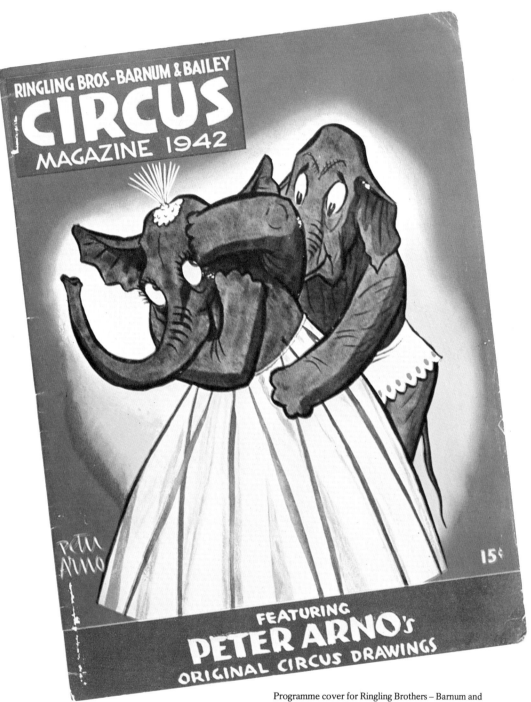

Programme cover for Ringling Brothers – Barnum and
Bailey Circus, 1942.
Circus World Museum, Baraboo, Wisconsin.

Other Major Productions

9 February 1974 Brussels, Théâtre royal de la Monnaie

Company: Ballet du XXe siècle
Choreographer: Paul Mejia
Costumes: Germinal Casado
Dancers: Anouchka Babkine, Kyra Kharkevitch, Brigitte Kher, Claudia Minne, Martine Detournay, Rita Lussi, Beatrice Berger, Axelle Arnouts (Horses), Orie Ohara, Michelle Mottet, Lise Pinet (Pierrettes)

Jerome Robbins as the Ringmaster in his revival for the Stravinsky Festival at the New York State Theatre, June 1972, with some of the 48 children.   *Photo: Martha Swope.*

13 March 1974 Paris, Théâtre national de l'Opéra

Conductor: Manuel Rosenthal
Choreographer: Jerome Robbins
Dancers: Jerome Robbins (Ringmaster), Pupils of the École de Danse de l'Opéra

29 April 1980 Dresden, Staatstheater

Choreographer: Harald Wandtke
Dancers: Dietmar Jacob, Akef Megahed, Hannes-Detlef Vogel

To taped music.

164

Danses Concertantes

20 minutes (EWW 73)

The Werner Janssen Orchestra of Los Angeles commissioned and first performed *Danses Concertantes* on 8 February 1942, conducted by Stravinsky.

Perhaps therefore this work should not really be included in this part of the book, but it is clear, even apart from the title, that Stravinsky did have a ballet in mind and, according to George Balanchine, 'had conceived the work with the choreographer and had intended his score to be used in the theatre'. Robert Craft has added 'I conclude that the piece was intended to be staged for the reasons that the music is so specifically for ballet and that Stravinsky wanted to compose a ballet at the time; his correspondence does mention this much.'

Balanchine has made two versions, with 28 years between them. He gives a most revealing insight into the way he thinks and works when he says: 'How in the world is it possible – really for me, it is not – to create a ballet first done many years ago, with young dancers who are very different. Writers think with words; I think with bodies and the ballets I work on necessarily have a great deal to do with the here and now, not a recollection or a notation of someone's idea of accuracy of the past . . . I am too busy making for now. I think ballet is now.'

Too much in ballet elsewhere has become mummified.

First Performance 10 September 1944

Theatre: New York City Center
Company: Ballet Russe de Monte Carlo
Choreographer: George Balanchine
Scenery & Costumes: Eugene Berman
Principal Dancers: Alexandra Danilova
                        Leon Danielian
                        Maria Tallchief
                        Ruthanne Boris
                        Mary Ellen Moylan

Synopsis

Although not specifically written for the stage, the score is a suite of dances:
1. Marche – Introduction
2. Pas d'Action Con moto
3. Thème varié Lento
   Variation 1 Allegretto
   Variation 2 Scherzando
   Variation 3 Andantino
   Variation 4 (Coda) Tempo giusto
4. Pas de Deux Risoluto
   Andante sostenuto
5. Marche – Conclusion

166

Alexandra Danilova and
Frederic Franklin in the
original production, 1944.
*Photo: Constantine. Theatre
Museum, V & A.*

Colleen Neary, Francis Sackett,
Renée Estopinal, the New York
City Ballet, the Stravinsky
Festival, June 1972, in the
original setting by Eugene
Berman.
Photo: Martha Swope.

Nicholas Georgiadis' design for the
Royal Ballet production, 1955.
*Theatre Museum, V & A, Arts
Council of Great Britain Collection.*

Doreen Wells (centre) in the Royal
Ballet production.
*Photo: Houston Rogers. Theatre
Museum, V & A.*

168

Other Major Productions

18 January 1955 London, Sadler's Wells

Conductor: John Lanchberry
Choreographer: Kenneth MacMillan
Scenery & Costumes: Nicholas Georgiadis
Principal Dancers: Maryon Lane, Donald Britton, David Poole, Sara Neil, Gilbert Vernon, Annette Page, Donald MacLeary, Bryan Lawrence, Pauline Barnes, Shirley Bishop, Brenda Bolton, Yvonne English, Yvonne Lakier, Margaret Lee

13 March 1959 London, Royal Opera House

Company: The Royal Ballet
Conductor: Hugo Rignold
Choreographer: Kenneth MacMillan
Scenery & Costumes: Nicholas Georgiadis
Principal Dancers: Maryon Lane, Desmond Doyle, Pirmin Trecu, Doreen Wells, Merle Park

13 October 1959 San Francisco, Opera

Company: San Francisco Ballet
Choreographer: Lew Christensen
Scenery & Costumes: Tony Duquette

16 December 1961 Copenhagen, Det Kongelige Teater

Choreographer: Kenneth MacMillan
Scenery & Costumes: Nicholas Georgiadis

9 July 1964 Cologne, Opernhaus

Choreographer: Todd Bolender
Costumes: Ed Wittstein

7 November 1965 Stuttgart, Württembergische Staatstheater

Company: Stuttgart Ballet
Choreographer: Kenneth MacMillan
Scenery & Costumes: Nicholas Georgiadis

29 November 1971 London, Sadler's Wells

Company: Ballet-Théâtre Contemporain
Conductor: Diego Masson
Choreographer: Félix Blaska
Scenery & Costumes: Sonia Delaunay
Principal Dancers: Thérèse Thoreux, Dominique Mercey, Chantal Graf, Jean-Claude Giorgini

1 December 1971 Berlin, Deutsche Oper

Choreographer: John Taras

20 June 1972 New York, NY State Theatre

Company: New York City Ballet
Conductor: Robert Irving
Choreographer: George Balanchine
Scenery & Costumes: Eugene Berman
Principal Dancers: Lynda Yourth, John Gifford

3 May 1981 Pforzheim, Stadttheater

Choreographer: Ingrid Burmeister

Scènes de ballet

Three projects for the set design, by André Beaurepaire.
Theatre Museum, V & A, Gift of Richard Buckle.

The final design, as can be seen from the photograph below, was very different from these projects: the designer having started with a realistic set finished with almost an abstract one. This was even refined further, because almost immediately after the first performance the central arch was removed.

Moira Shearer and John Hart in the first version at the Royal Opera House, Covent Garden, 1948.   *Photo: Roger Wood. Theatre Museum, V & A.*

170

Scènes de Ballet

18 minutes (EWW 79)

Commissioned by Billy Rose for an act in a revue called at first *The Lively Arts* and, later, *The Seven Lively Arts*, it was to some extent swamped by the rest of the programme and not appreciated for its own sake.

Anton Dolin had sent Stravinsky a telegram before the New York opening: 'Ballet great success...can the *pas de deux* be orchestrated with the strings carrying the melody this is most important to insure greater success...' But Stravinsky telegraphed back 'Satisfied great success'.

The greater success, without tampering with the score, came in London when *Scènes de Ballet* was done by Frederick Ashton in 1948. It was the first ballet by Stravinsky to be performed by the Royal Ballet at Covent Garden after the war. Although the original setting was too cumbersome and was simplified early on, the ballet has been in the repertoire ever since.

There is nothing like success for more than a slight case of mummification.

First Performance 24 November 1944

Theatre: Forrest Theatre, Philadelphia
Conductor: Maurice Abravanel
Choreographer: Anton Dolin
Scenery: Norman Bel Geddes
Costumes: Paul Dupont
Principal Dancers: Alicia Markova
                      Anton Dolin

Presented as part of the revue, *The Seven Lively Arts*, which was subsequently performed at the Ziegfeld Theatre, New York from 7 December 1944 to 12 May 1945.

First Performance of new version 11 February 1948

Theatre: Royal Opera House, London
Company: Sadler's Wells Ballet
Choreographer: Frederick Ashton
Scenery & Costumes: André Beaurepaire
Principal Dancers: Margot Fonteyn
                         Michael Somes
                         Alexander Grant
                         John Field
                         Donald Britton
                         Philip Chatfield

Synopsis

Plotless ballet after forms of classical dance for two soloists and a *corps de ballet* of four boys and twelve girls.

Opposite: Patricia McBride, the New York City Ballet, the Stravinsky Festival, New York State Theatre, June 1972. Most of the illustrations have been chosen to show the scene on the full stage, but here a shot of a single dancer – who could be poised in any ballet – has been included because it so perfectly illustrates the movement, the tension and the joy of dancing.   *Photo: Martha Swope.*

Other Major Productions

1951 Berlin, Städtische Oper

Choreographer: Gustav Blank
Scenery & Costumes: Josef Fenneker

1952 Stuttgart, Württembergische Staatstheater

Choreographer: Robert Mayer
Scenery & Costumes: Gerd Richter

6 October 1954 The Hague, Gebouw voor Kunsten en Wetenschappen

Company: Het Nederlands Ballet
Choreographer: John Taras
Scenery & Costumes: Charles Roelofsz

18 February 1958 Hamburg, Staatsoper

Conductor: Wilhelm Rüggeberg-Brückner
Choreographer: Gustav Blank
Scenery & Costumes: Günther Schneider-Siemssen
Principal Dancers: Uta Graf, Erica Lihn, Christel Teelen, Richard Bernwinkler, Heinz Schmiedel, Gerd Schneidereit

20 January 1962 Hamburg, Staatsoper

Choreographer: Peter Van Dijk

14 February 1962 Kassel, Staatstheater

Conductor: Paul Schmitz
Choreographer: Robert Mayer
Scenery & Costumes: Ekkehard Grübler

10 June 1962 Stuttgart, Württembergische Staatstheater

Company: Stuttgart Ballet
Choreographer: John Cranko

11 March 1968 Berlin, Deutsche Oper

Conductor: Ashley Lawrence
Choreographer: Frederick Ashton
Scenery & Costumes: André Beaurepaire
Principal Dancers: Silvia Kesselheim, Klaus Beelitz

22 June 1972 New York, NY State Theatre

Company: New York City Ballet
Conductor: Robert Irving
Choreographer: John Taras
Costumes: Barbara Karinska
Principal Dancers: Patricia McBride, Jean-Pierre Bonnefous

Orpheus

Ballet in three scenes
30 minutes (EWW 86)

The middle part of a trilogy – *Apollo*, *Orpheus*, *Agon* – so it should be seen. So it was given at the New York City Ballet's Stravinsky Festival in 1972.

Orpheus was commissioned by Lincoln Kirstein, the American Diaghilev, for the Ballet Society, and afterwards the New York City Ballet was formed. George Balanchine worked very closely with Stravinsky throughout the preparation of the score. Isamu Noguchi was the third choice of designer (Pavel Tchelitchew and Esteban Frances having been rejected), and he created, in the words of Lincoln Kirstein, 'a timeless climate in which three-dimensional movement would be enhanced by the formal solidarity of hand-hewn ritual appurtenances – masks, bones, flames, lyres, shaped as independent sculptured objects.'

Ballet as ritual. Part two of the ritual. The penultimate act of collaboration between Stravinsky and Balanchine. But before the final act came Stravinsky's longest work for the theatre.

First Performance 28 April 1948

Theatre:	New York City Center
Company:	Ballet Society
Conductor:	Igor Stravinsky
Choreographer:	George Balanchine
Scenery & Costumes:	Isamu Noguchi
Lighting:	Jean Rosenthal
Principal Dancers:	Nicholas Magallanes (Orpheus)
	Maria Tallchief (Eurydice)
	Francisco Moncion (Dark Angel)
	Beatrice Tompkins (Leader of the Furies)
	Tanaquil Le Clercq (Leader of the Bacchantes)
	Herbert Bliss (Apollo)
	Edward Bigelow (Pluto)
	Job Sanders (Satyr)

Synopsis

A modern version of the Orpheus myth.

Scene I: At the grave of Eurydice. Orpheus, with his lyre, mourns the death of his wife, Eurydice. The Angel of Death appears, takes the lyre, covers Orpheus's face with a golden mask which he must not take off until the end of the journey, and begins to lead him on the long journey across the river Styx back to Eurydice.

Scene II: In Hades. Orpheus and the Angel of Death are met by the Furies. The Angel gives Orpheus the lyre. Orpheus begins to play and the Furies are calmed. Pluto appears with Eurydice. The Furies bring Orpheus to Eurydice. Pluto joins their hands. Orpheus and Eurydice begin their tormented journey back to earth. Orpheus tries to hold on to Eurydice but she slips and falls, and he loses contact with her. He cannot find her hand. In desperation he tears the mask off his face and, instantly, Eurydice dies. Orpheus is alone. He tries to reach his lyre but, just as he is about to touch it, it disappears. He crawls off in search of it. The Bacchantes enter and surround Orpheus when he returns carrying his mask. They seize the mask. Orpheus cannot escape. They attack him savagely. The leader cuts off his right arm, then his left arm, and finally his head.

Scene III: Apotheosis of Orpheus. Apollo comes to the grave of Orpheus and holds up the golden mask invoking the spirit of Orpheus as the God of Music. But the sound is only a weak imitation. Apollo puts down the mask and stands in front of the grave. As he raises his arm, so the lyre, garlanded with flowers, rises from the tomb, symbolising the tenderness and power of music.

Isamu Noguchi's costume design for the original production by the New York
City Ballet, 1948.   *Photo: Courtesy the artist.*

Nicholas Magallanes as Orpheus and Tanaquil LeClercq as Leader of the
Bacchantes, the New York City Ballet, 1948.
Photo: George Platt Lynes. Theatre Museum, V & A.

178

Other Major Productions

9 September 1948 Venice, La Fenice

Company: Rome Opera Company
Choreographer: Aurel Milloss
Scenery & Costumes: Fabrizio Clerici

16 November 1948 Paris, Théâtre des Champs-Elysées

Choreographer: David Lichine
Scenery & Costumes: Mayo

1949 Buenos Aires, Teatro Colon

Choreographer: Aurel Milloss
Principal Dancers: E.Lommi (Orpheus), E.Agoglia
(Eurydice), V. Moreno, A.Truyol

1952 Santiago, Chile, Teatro Municipal

Company: Ballet Nacional Chileno
Choreographer: Heinz Poll
Scenery & Costumes: Guenther Raushch

1954 Wuppertal, Opernhaus

Choreographer: Erich Walter
Scenery: Heinrich Wendel
Costumes: Günther Kappel

November 1955 Hanover, Landestheater

Choreographer: Yvonne Georgi
Scenery & Costumes: Rudolf Schulz

12 November 1961 Frankfurt, Opernhaus

Conductor: Wolfgang Rennert
Choreographer: Tatiana Gsovski
Scenery & Costumes: Hein Heckroth

14 February 1962 Kassel, Staatstheater

Conductor: Paul Schmitz
Choreographer: Robert Mayer
Scenery & Costumes: Ekkehard Grübler

26 March 1962 Leningrad, Maly

Choreographer: Konstantin Boyarski
Principal Dancers: Valery Panov, Larissa Klimova

6 June 1970 Stuttgart, Württemburgische Staatsoper

Company: Stuttgart Ballet
Choreographer: John Cranko
Principal Dancers: Birgit Keil, Heinz Clauss

13 March 1974 Paris, Théâtre national de l'Opéra

Conductor: Manuel Rosenthal
Choreographer: George Balanchine
Scenery & Costumes: after Isamu Noguchi
Principal Dancers: Jean-Pierre Bonnefous (Orpheus),
Alain Bogreau (Apollo)

15 March 1974 Vienna, Staatsoper

Conductor: Stefan Soltesz
Choreographer: Aurel Milloss
Scenery & Costumes: Pantelis Dessyllas
Principal Dancers: Michael Birkmeyer (Orpheus), Lilly
Scheuermann (Eurydice)

26 March 1974 London, Sadler's Wells

Company: Dutch National Ballet
Conductor: André Presser
Choreographer: Rudi van Dantzig
Scenery & Costumes: Toer van Schayk
Principal Dancers: Maria Aradi, Zoltan Peter

First performed 21 February 1974 in Holland.

1 November 1974 Gothenburg, Stora Teatern

Choreographer: Ulf Gadd

Jean-Pierre Bonnefous as Orpheus, the New York City Ballet, the Stravinsky Festival at the New York State Theatre, 1972. *Photo: Martha Swope.*

12 September 1976 Hamburg, Staatsoper

Conductor: Kazuhiro Koizumi
Choreographer: Fred Howald
Scenery & Costumes: Marco Arturo Marelli
Principal Dancers: François Klaus (Orpheus), Silvia Winterhalder (Eurydice)

The Rake's Progress

Opera in three acts
Fable by W.H.Auden and Chester Kallman
2 hours 30 minutes (EWW 88)

Stravinsky's first full length opera, an opera in English, his longest composition for the stage, work begun in 1947 with W.H.Auden, finished a few weeks before the first performance.

Stravinsky himself describes the work: '*The Rake's Progress* is, emphatically, an opera – an opera of arias and recitatives, choruses and ensembles. Its musical structure, the conception of the use of these forms, even to the relations of tonalities, is in the line of the classical tradition.'

Stravinsky had wisely chosen to have *The Rake's Progress* produced at the Fenice, a fairly small house, instead of one of the bigger houses like the Metropolitan, New York or the Scala, Milan but three weeks was not enough preparation. The first night, therefore, was a *succès d'estime* rather than a *succès fou*. Nevertheless, it quickly began to be performed in all the opera houses of America and Europe, both big and small, and maintains a consistent popularity.

The inspiration for the opera had come to Stravinsky after he had visited a Hogarth exhibition, and yet only the Collettivo di Brera for an Italian tour and David Hockney for Glyndebourne have recognised this inspiration in their designs. They also looked back to Hogarth, but without being slavish, and created entirely appropriate yet 'modern' sets.

While it is true that the opera is most suited to intimate opera houses such as Glyndebourne, it cannot be ignored just because it is a 'classical', small scale, work. Mozart's operas are not swamped by the grandiose surroundings of the Royal Opera House, Covent Garden, nor was *The Rake's Progress* when it was belatedly produced there in 1979 and a wider audience at last had the opportunity to appreciate the greatness of the work.

First performance 11 September 1951

Theatre:	La Fenice, Venice
Conductor:	Igor Stravinsky
Producer:	Carl Ebert
Scenery & Costumes:	Gianni Ratto
Chorus and Orchestra:	La Scala, Milan
Cast:	Raffaele Arié (Trulove), bass
	Elisabeth Schwarzkopf (Anne, his daughter), soprano
	Robert Rounseville (Tom Rakewell, her sweetheart), tenor
	Otakar Kraus (Nick Shadow), baritone
	Nell Tangeman (Mother Goose, a brothel keeper), mezzosoprano
	Jennie Tourel (Baba the Turk, a bearded lady), mezzosoprano
	Hugues Cuénod (Sellem, the auctioneer), tenor
	Emanuel Menkes (Keeper of the Madhouse), bass

Synopsis

The action takes place in England in the eighteenth century

Act I, Scene 1: Tom and Anne are engaged. All is love and happiness between them in the idyllic setting of her father's country garden, but Trulove has misgivings about his future son-in-law's prospects and offers him a secure position in the City. Tom declines, for his plans are more ambitious. All he wants is money. A stranger, Nick Shadow, suddenly appears with news for Tom of a large inheritance from an unknown uncle. Nick was his servant and will now serve Tom. Anne, Tom and Trulove rejoice in this unexpected good fortune, but Nick persuades Tom to leave immediately for London. Nick's wages will be settled after a year and a day have passed, when Nick will ask for his due.

Scene 2: Tom is drinking with Nick and Mother Goose in her brothel in London. Under Nick's guidance Tom has become a cynic. His new motto is 'my duty to myself to do'. Only the word 'love' seems to elicit any emotion from him. He tries to leave his drinking companions, but Nick tricks him into staying by resorting to magic. Tom entertains the company with a song, and Mother Goose selects him as her partner for the night.

Scene 3: Anne has had no news of Tom since he left several months ago. She feels he needs her, and decides to desert her father and join Tom in London.

Act II, Scene 1: Tom has not found happiness in London. His words 'I wish I were happy' seem to bring forth the arrival of Nick Shadow with a poster advertising a grotesque bearded lady, Baba the Turk, who appears at freak shows. Nick suggests that Tom should marry her and thus 'be free of the twin tyrants of appetite and conscience'. The idea is so preposterous that Tom bursts out laughing and agrees.

Scene 2: Tom, returning to his house in a sedan chair, is distressed to find Anne

182

waiting for him. As he sends her away, Baba reveals her presence, and Tom has to tell Anne that he is married.

Scene 3: Baba has filled Tom's house with a fantastic collection of bric-a-brac and chatters endlessly about her possessions. Tom is so exasperated that he slaps his wig on her head and shuts her up in mid song. He is too unhappy even to weep, his only refuge is sleep. While he sleeps, Nick wheels in a fantastic machine which, by means of a crude kind of false bottom, gives the illusion of turning stones into bread. Tom, who wakes up having dreamt of just such a machine, thinks his dream has come true. Nick assures him that his miraculous invention will make him rich, and suggests that he should tell his wife; but Tom answers 'I have no wife, I have buried her.'

Act III, Scene I: Several months later. Everything in the house is covered in dust and cobwebs. Baba is still sitting with the wig over her head. The contents of the house are to be auctioned. Sellem, the auctioneer, prepares to auction Baba and snatches the wig off her face, whereupon she comes to life and resumes her singing where it was interrupted. Anne is searching for Tom, and Baba suggests that she should take care of him as he still loves her. Baba decides to go back to the stage.

Scene 2: Nick has led Tom to a churchyard and claims his wages: he wants Tom's soul. Tom begs for mercy and Nick seems to relent; he proposes a game of cards and if Tom wins, he is free, but if he loses he must kill himself and be damned. Tom wins the game, but this so enrages Nick that he condemns him to insanity. Tom loses his mind and imagines himself to be Adonis.

Scene 3: Tom in Bedlam, still taking himself for Adonis, tells the other madmen to prepare for his wedding to Venus. Anne comes to visit him and he welcomes her as Venus; she humours him. He is overcome by exhaustion and has to lie down while Anne sings him to sleep. Anne's father comes to take her away. When Tom wakes up, his Venus has disappeared and he dies of a broken heart.

Epilogue: The four main characters unite to sing the moral of the story: 'For idle hands and hearts and minds the devil finds a work to do, a work, dear Sir, fair Madam, for you – and you!'

Scene at the first performance at the Fenice, Venice, with Elisabeth Schwartzkopf as Anne and Robert Rounseville as Tom Rakewell.
Photo: Eric Piccagliani. Harold Rosenthal Collection.

Scene at the first production in Germany, at Stuttgart, 1951, with Gustav Niedlinge, Lore Wissmann, Richard Holm and Walter Hagner. German opera houses were quick to produce this new work: Stuttgart on 4 November was followed by Hamburg on the 14th. The ultra-economical settings, however, were not in sympathy with Stravinsky's intentions.
Harold Rosenthal Collection.

Finale of Act II at the Staatsoper, Hamburg, 1951, with Hedy Gura as Trulove, Kathe Maas as Anne, and Rudolf Schock as the Keeper of the Madhouse.
Photo: Hamburgische Staatsoper Archiv. Harold Rosenthal Collection.

From the Glyndebourne
souvenir programme, 1954,
reproducing Osbert Lancaster's
design for the Street Scene in
front of Rakewell's house, Act I,
Scene 5.
Theatre Museum, V & A.

David Hockney's model of the
stage design: the Street in front
of Rakewell's house, Act I,
Scene 5, for the Glyndebourne
revival, 1975.
© *David Hockney 1974*
Courtesy Petersburg Press.

Glyndebourne was the first English company to produce the work. Not
only was the theatre ideally suited to it, but the designs by Osbert
Lancaster, well known for his architectural drawing, exactly caught the
period and the 'Englishness' of the opera. Hockney returned, as
Stravinsky had done, to the paintings of Hogarth for his inspiration, but
gave them his own original interpretation from a deep understanding of
the opera.

David Hockney's sketch of Three Men in Costume. This crayon drawing, giving an accurate impression of the costumes, was made soon after the first production at Glyndebourne. © *David Hockney 1975. Courtesy Petersburg Press.*

David Hockney's model of the stage design: Bedlam, Act II, Scene 4.
© *David Hockney 1974.*
Courtesy Petersburg Press.

The actual scene in Bedlam at Glyndebourne, 1975, with Leo Goeke as Tom Rakewell, and chorus.
Photo: Guy Gravett.
Glyndebourne Festival Opera.

The scene in the famous production at the Royal Opera House, Stockholm, 1966, directed by Ingmar Bergman with Margareta Hallin as Anne and Ragnar Ulfung as Tom Rakewell.
Harold Rosenthal Collection.

The scene in the Scottish Opera production at the Edinburgh Festival, 1967, with Alexander Young as Tom Rakewell, Peter van der Bilt as Nick Shadow and Sona Cervena as Baba the Turk. The rather 'gimmicky' setting designed by Ralph Koltai was not really appropriate.
Photo: Bob Anderson. Harold Rosenthal Collection.

Other Major Productions

4 November 1951 Stuttgart, Staatstheater

Conductor: Ferdinand Leitner
Director: Kurt Puhlmann
Scenery & Costumes: Leni Bauer-Ecsy
Singers: Gustav Neidlinger, Lore Wissmann, Richard Holm, Walter Hagner

14 November 1951 Hamburg, Staatsoper

Conductor: Wilhelm Schleuning
Director: Günther Rennert
Scenery: Arnold Fiedler
Singers: Sigmund Roth (Trulove), Kathe Maas (Anne), Rudolf Schock (Tom Rakewell), Toni Blankenheim (Nick Shadow), Elfriede Wasserlthal (Mother Goose), Hedy Gura (Baba the Turk), Fritz Göllnitz (Sellem), Karl Otto (Keeper of the Madhouse)

8 December 1951 Milan, La Scala

Conductor: Ferdinand Leitner
Director: Carl Ebert
Scenery: Gianni Ratto
Costumes: Ebe Colciaghi
Principal Singers: Giuseppe Modesti (Trulove), Elisabeth Schwarzkopf (Anne), Mirto Picchi (Tom Rakewell), Otakar Kraus (Nick Shadow), Galmio (Mother Goose), Cleo Elmo (Baba the Turk), Hugues Cuénod (Sellem), Emanuel Menkes (Keeper of the Madhouse)

25 April 1952 Vienna, Staatsoper

Conductor: Heinrich Hollreiser
Director: Günther Rennert
Principal Singers: Erna Berger (Anne), Rudolf Schock (Tom Rakewell), Alfred Jerger (Nick Shadow), Elisabeth Höngen (Baba the Turk)

December 1952 Strasbourg, Théâtre Municipal

Conductor: Ernest Bour
Director: Roger Lalande
Singers: Marthe Luccioni, George Genin, Heinz Rehfuss, Joseph Peyron, André Pactat

14 February 1953 New York, Metropolitan Opera

Conductor: Fritz Reiner
Director: George Balanchine
Scenery & Costumes: Horace Armistead
Principal Singers: Norman Scott (Trulove), Hilde Güden (Anne), Eugene Conley (Tom Rakewell), Mack Harrell (Nick Shadow), Martha Lipton (Mother Goose), Blanche Thebom (Baba the Turk), Paul Franke (Sellem), Lawrence Davidson (Keeper of the Madhouse)

18 June 1953 Paris, Opéra Comique

Director: André Cluytens
Scenery & Costumes: Georges Wakhevitch
Principal Singers: Janine Micheau (Anne), Léopold Simoneau (Tom Rakewell), Xavier Depraz (Nick Shadow), Simone Couderc (Baba the Turk)

25 August 1953 Edinburgh, King's

Company: Glyndebourne Opera Company
Conductor: Alfred Wallenstein
Director: Carl Ebert
Choreography: Pauline Grant
Scenery & Costumes: Osbert Lancaster
Principal Singers: Hervey Alan (Trulove), Elsie Morison (Anne), Richard Lewis (Tom Rakewell), Jerome Hines (Nick Shadow), Mary Jarred (Mother Goose), Nan Merriman (Baba the Turk), Murray Dickie (Sellem), Dennis Wicks (Keeper of the Madhouse)

1953 Munich, Theater am Gärtenplatz

Conductor: Robert Heger
Director: Hans Zimmerman
Principal Singers: Erika Köth (Anne), Richard Holm (Tom Rakewell), Albrecht Peter (Nick Shadow), Imgard Barth (Baba the Turk)

1953 Boston, University Opera Workshop

Conductor: Igor Stravinsky
Director: Sarah Caldwell assisted by Robert Craft

27 February 1957 Cologne, Bühnen der Stadt

Conductor: Wolfgang von der Nahmer
Principal Singers: Käthe Möller-Siepermann (Anne), Albert Weikenemeir (Tom Rakewell)

17 June 1957 The Hague, Holland Festival

Conductor: Erich Leinsdorf
Director: Peter Potter
Principal Singers: Ge Smith (Trulove), Graziella Sciutti (Anne), Eugene Conley (Tom Rakewell), Otakar Kraus (Nick Shadow), Mimi Aarden (Baba the Turk), Frans Vroons (Sellem)

18 July 1957 Santa Fe, New Mexico, Santa Fe Opera

Conductor: Robert Craft
Director: Bliss Hebert
Scenery & Costumes: Patton Campbell
Principal Singers: Marguerite Willauer (Anne), Loren Driscoll (Tom Rakewell), Spelios Constantine (Trulove), Robert Rue (Nick Shadow), Mary McMurray (Mother Goose), Regina Sarfaty (Baba the Turk), William McGrath (Sellem), Leonard Potter (Keeper of the Madhouse)

The first performance was rained off. The first complete performance was on 19 July 1957.

22 July 1957 London, Sadler's Wells

Company: New Opera Company
Conductor: Leon Lovett
Director: Brian Trowell
Scenery: Lionel March
Principal Singers: George Prangnell (Trulove), Doreen Murray (Anne), Kenneth Bowen (Tom Rakewell), Raymond Hayter (Nick Shadow), Johanna Peters (Mother Goose), Thetis Blacker (Baba the Turk), Alan Mayall (Sellem),Peter Hemmings (Keeper of the Madhouse)

This production was first performed by Cambridge University Opera Group on 19 November 1956 in Cambridge.

?1957 Ulm, Staatstheater

Conductor: Harald von Goertz
Director: Bruno Voges
Principal Singers: Claus Hennecke, Elisabeth Roon, Richard Owens, Gertrud Probst

10 December 1958 Frankfurt, Opernhaus

Conductor: Hermann Scherchen
Director: Harry Buckwitz
Scenery & Costumes: Hein Heckroth

28 July 1959 London, Sadler's Wells

Company: New Oxford Company
Conductor: Leon Lovett
Director: Brian Trowell
Scenery & Costumes: Lionel March
Principal Singers: Leon Greene (Trulove), Heather Harper (Anne), Kenneth Bowen (Tom Rakewell), Raymond Hayter (Nick Shadow), Brenda Scaife (Mother Goose), Monica Sinclair (Baba the Turk), Kevin Miller (Sellem), James Atkins (Keeper of the Madhouse)

Summer 1959 Buenos Aires, Teatro Colon

Conductor: J.E.Martini
Singers: Victor de Narke (Trulove), Maria Altamura (Anne), Marco Cubas (Tom Rakewell), Angelo Mattiello (Nick Shadow), Louisa Bartoletti (Baba the Turk)
Sung in Italian.

23 July 1960 Santa Fe, New Mexico, Santa Fe Opera

Conductor: Robert Craft
Director: Bliss Hebert
Scenery: Henry Heymann
Costumes: Patton Campbell
Principal Singers: Mildred Allen (Anne), Gimi Beni (Trulove), Loren Driscoll (Tom Rakewell), John Reardon (Nick Shadow), Sylvia Anderson (Mother Goose), Elaine Bonazzi (Baba the Turk), Paul Franke (Sellem), Therman Bailey (Keeper of the Madhouse)

22 April 1961 Stockholm, Royal Opera

Conductor: Michael Gielen
Director: Ingmar Bergman
Scenery: Berger Bergling
Costumes: Kerstin Hedeby
Principal Singers: Arne Tyren (Trulove), Margarete Hallin (Anne), Ragnar Ulfung (Tom Rakewell), Erik Saeden (Nick Shadow), Barbro Ericson (Mother Goose), Kirstin Meyer (Baba the Turk), Olle Sivall (Sellem), Erik Sundqvist (Keeper of the Madhouse)

2 February 1962 London, Sadler's Wells

Conductor: Colin Davis
Director: Glen Byam Shaw
Scenery & Costumes: Motley
Principal Singers: Don Garrard (Trulove), Elsie Morison (Anne), Alexander Young (Tom Rakewell), Raimund Herincx (Nick Shadow), Edith Coates (Mother Goose), Ann Robson (Baba the Turk), Kevin Miller (Sellem), Robert Ivan Foster (Keeper of the Madhouse)

15 August 1962 Santa Fe, New Mexico, Santa Fe Opera, Stravinsky Festival

Conductor: Robert Craft
Director: Bliss Hebert
Scenery: Henry Heymann
Costumes: Patton Campbell
Principal Singers: Doris Yarick (Anne), Therman Bailey (Trulove), Loren Driscoll (Tom Rakewell), John Reardon (Nick Shadow), Jacquiline Rohrbacker (Mother Goose), Elaine Bonazzi (Baba the Turk), Paul Franke (Sellem), William Wiederanders (Keeper of the Madhouse)

19 October 1962 San Francisco, Opera House

Conductor: Leopold Ludwig
Scenery: Wolfram Skalicki & Thomas L.Colangelo Jr
Principal Singers: Richard Lewis, Mary Costa, Thomas Tipton, Kirstin Meyer

20 November 1962 New York

Company: American Opera Society
Conductor: Robert Craft
Principal Singers: Judith Raskin (Anne), Alexander Young (Tom Rakewell), John Reardon (Nick Shadow), Betty Allen (Baba the Turk), Justino Diaz (Keeper of the Madhouse)

30 November 1962 Munich, Cuvilliés

Conductor: Heinrich Hollreiser
Director: Günther Rennert
Scenery: Helmut Jürgens
Costumes: Liselotte Erler
Principal Singers: Max Proebstl (Trulove), Lotte Schadle (Anne), Gerhard Stolze (Tom Rakewell), Benno Kusche (Nick Shadow), Annelie Waas (Mother Goose), Lilian Benningsen (Baba the Turk), Ferry Gruber (Sellem), Hans Hermann Nissen (Keeper of the Madhouse)

2 August 1963 Glyndebourne

Conductor: Paul Sacher
Director: Peter Ebert, after Carl Ebert
Scenery & Costumes: Osbert Lancaster
Principal Singers: Dennis Wicks (Trulove), Heather Harper (Anne), Richard Lewis (Tom Rakewell), Delme Bryn-Jones (Nick Shadow), Tamara Chumakova (Mother Goose), Gloria Lane (Baba the Turk), Hugues Cuénod (Sellem), Derick Davies (Keeper of the Madhouse)

23 November 1963 Zurich, Stadttheater

Conductor: Christian Vöchting
Director: Werner Düggelin
Principal Singers: Vera Schlosser (Anne), Kurt Wehofschitz (Tom Rakewell), John Modenos (Nick Shadow), Annemarie Bessel (Baba the Turk), Leonhard Päckl (Sellem)

1964/65 Season Oslo, Norske Opera

Conductor: Bryden Thomson
Principal Singers: Astri Herseth (Anne), Ragnar Ulfung (Tom Rakewell), Jonas Brunvoli (Nick Shadow), Marit Isene (Baba the Turk)

14 March 1965 Vienna, Staatsoper

Conductor: Oscar Danon
Director: Otto Schenk
Scenery: Günther Schneider-Siemssen
Costumes: Hill Reihs-Gromes
Principal Singers: Annelise Rothenberger (Anne), Waldemar Kmentt, Eberhard Waechter, Frederick Guthrie, Vera Little, Hilde Konetzni, Herbert Prikopa

27 July 1966 Santa Fe, New Mexico, Santa Fe Opera

Conductor: Robert Craft
Director: Bliss Hebert
Scenery: John Wright Stevens
Costumes: Patton Campbell
Principal Singers: Doris Yarick (Anne), Ragnar Ulfung (Tom Rakewell), Gimi Beni (Trulove), Donald Gramm (Nick Shadow), Jean Kraft (Mother Goose), Elaine Bonazzi (Baba the Turk), Paul Franke (Sellem), Leon Petrus (Keeper of the Madhouse)

191

23 March 1967 Hamburg, Staatsoper

Conductor: Charles Mackerras
Director: Gian-Carlo Menotti
Scenery: Mario Chiari
Principal Singers: Hans Sotin (Trulove), Arlene
Saunders (Anne), Loren Driscoll (Tom Rakewell), Tom
Krause (Nick Shadow), Edith Lang (Mother Goose),
Tatiana Troyanos (Baba the Turk), Erwin Wohlfart
(Sellem), Carl Schultz (Keeper of the Madhouse)

26 May 1967 Berlin, Deutsche Oper

Conductor: Heinrich Hollreiser
Director: Carl Ebert
Scenery: Wilhelm Reinking
Costumes: Christel Raeder
Principal Singers: Victor von Halem (Trulove), Erika
Köth (Anne), Donald Grobe (Tom Rakewell), William
Dooley (Nick Shadow), Sieglinde Wagner (Mother
Goose), Vera Little (Baba the Turk), Karl-Ernst Mercker
(Sellem)

May 1967 Basle, City Theatre

Conductor: Hans Lowlein
Director: Lars Runsten
Scenery: Anelies Corrodi
Principal Singers: Margarita Kyriaki (Anne), Nigel
Douglas (Tom Rakewell), Ladislas Anderko (Nick
Shadow), Eva Gilhofer (Baba the Turk)

21 August 1967 Edinburgh, King's

Company: Scottish Opera
Conductor: Alexander Gibson
Director: Peter Ebert
Scenery & Costumes: Ralph Koltai
Lighting: Charles Bristow
Principal Singers: David Kelly (Trulove), Elizabeth
Robson (Anne), Alexander Young (Tom Rakewell),
Peter van der Bilt (Nick Shadow), Johanna Peters
(Mother Goose), Sona Cervena (Baba the Turk), Francis
Egerton (Sellem), Ronald Morrison (Keeper of the
Madhouse)

7 August 1970 Santa Fe, New Mexico, Santa Fe Opera

Conductor: John Moriarty
Director: Bliss Hebert
Scenery: Allen Klein
Costumes: Suzanne Mess
Principal Singers: Gimi Beni (Trulove), Joanna Bruno
(Anne), Loren Driscoll (Tom Rakewell), Donald Gramm
(Nick Shadow), Jean Kraft (Mother Goose), Joy
Davidson (Baba the Turk), Douglas Perry (Sellem),
Howard Chadwick (Keeper of the Madhouse)

12 January 1971 Lyon, Opéra

Conductor: Serge Bando
Director: Louis Erlo
Scenery & Costumes: Jacques Rapp
Principal Singers: Louis Hagen-William (Trulove),
Anne-Marie Blanzat (Anne), Nolan Van Way (Tom
Rakewell), Frantz Petri (Nick Shadow), Emmy Gregor
(Mother Goose), Regina Sarfaty (Baba the Turk), Jose
Denisty (Sellem), Christos Grigoriou (Keeper of the
Madhouse)

14 November 1971 San Francisco, Opera House

Conductor: Günther Schuller
Director: Paul Hager
Principal Singers: Clifford Grant (Trulove), Jane Marsh
(Anne), Gregory Dempsey (Tom Rakewell), William
Dooley (Nick Shadow), Sylvia Anderson (Baba the
Turk)

6 February 1972 Lisbon, São Carlos

Director: Louis Erlo
Principal Singers: Anne Marie Blanzat (Anne), Nolan
Van Way (Tom Rakewell), Jean Brun (Nick Shadow),
Emmy Gregor (Baba the Turk)

11 March 1972 Turin, Teatro Nuovo

Conductor: Gianfranco Rivoli
Director: Franco Enriquez
Scenery: Emanuele Luzzati
Principal Singers: Franco Calabrese (Trulove), Claudia
Parada (Anne), Mirto Picchi (Tom Rakewell), Mario
Basiola (Nick Shadow), Gina Martinez (Mother Goose),
Anna-Maria Rota (Baba the Turk), Ferrando Ferrari
(Sellem)

March 1972 Amsterdam

Company: Netherlands Opera
Conductor: Edo de Waart
Director: David Pountney
Scenery: Ralph Koltai
Principal Singers: Simon Estes (Trulove), Joanna Bruno
(Anne), David Hillman (Tom Rakewell), Peter van der
Bilt (Nick Shadow), Cora Canne-Meijer (Baba the Turk)

16 May 1972 Düsseldorf, Opernhaus

Conductor: Kizimierz Kord
Director: Georg Reinhardt
Scenery, Costumes & Lighting: Heinrich Wendel &
Liselotte Erler
Principal Singers: Rachel Yakar (Anne), Werner Gotz
(Tom Rakewell), Leif Roar (Nick Shadow), Gwynn
Cornell (Baba the Turk)

192

18 May 1972 Copenhagen, Det Kongelige Teater

Conductor: Poul Jorgensen
Director: Sam Besekow assisted by Niels Brincker, after Lars Runsten's production
Scenery: Annalies Corrodi
Costumes: Marlene Brod

2 June 1972 Prague, Tyl Theatre

Conductor: Albert Rosen
Director: Karel Jernek
Scenery: Josef Svoboda
Costumes: Olga Filippi
Principal Singers: Nada Sormova (Anne), Ivor Zidek (Tom Rakewell), Karel Berman (Nick Shadow), Ivana Mixova (Baba the Turk)

23 November 1972 Trieste, Teatro Verdi

Conductor: Gianfranco Rivoli
Director: Roberto Guicciardini
Principal Singers: Leonardo Monreale (Trulove), Fulvia Ciano (Anne), Lajos Kozma (Tom Rakewell), Mario Basiola (Nick Shadow), Rosamaria de Rive (Baba the Turk)

1972/73 Frankfurt

Conductor: Peter Schroffner
Director: Peter Lehmann
Scenery, Costumes & Lighting: Ekkehard Grubler
Principal Singers: June Card (Anne), Josef Hopferwiesser (Tom Rakewell), Richard Cross (Nick Shadow), Sona Cervena (Baba the Turk)

25 January 1973 Florence, Teatro Comunale

Conductor: Ettore Gracis
Director: Virginio Puecher
Scenery & Costumes: Collettivo dell'Accademia di Brera
Principal Singers: Nicola Pigliucci (Trulove), Lella Cuberli (Anne), Frank Little (Tom Rakewell), Claudio Desderi (Nick Shadow), Miciko Ara (Mother Goose), Katia Kolceva (Baba the Turk), Vincenzo Manno (Sellem), Manlio Mecheli (Keeper of the Madhouse)

Production first performed on 31 August 1972 at the Teatro dei Rinnuovati, Siena.

4 February 1973 Washington, DC, Kennedy Center

Company: The Opera Society
Conductor: Alexander Gibson
Director: Ian Strasfogel
Costumes: Carrie Robbins
Principal Singers: Willard White (Trulove), Evelyn Mandac (Anne), George Shirley (Tom Rakewell), Lenus Carlson (Nick Shadow), Dana Krueger (Mother Goose), Gwendolyn Killbrew (Baba the Turk), Alan Crowfoot (Sellem)

2 March 1973 Catania, Teatro Bellini

Conductor: Gianfranco Rivoli
Director: Filippo Crivelli
Principal Dancers: Nicola Pigliucci (Trulove), Claudia Parada (Anne), Mirto Picchi (Tom Rakewell), Mario Basiola (Nick Shadow), Laura Zanini (Baba the Turk)

18 January 1975 Como, Teatro Sociale

Conductor: Riccardo Chailly
Director: Virginio Puecher
Principal Singers: Leonida Bergamonti (Trulove), Romana Righetti (Anne), William McKinney (Tom Rakewell), Claudio Desderi (Nick Shadow), Laura Bocca (Baba the Turk)

Also performed on 26 January 1975 at the Teatro Sociale, Mantua.

21 June 1975 Glyndebourne

Conductor: Bernard Haitink
Director: John Cox
Scenery & Costumes: David Hockney
Principal Singers: Don Garrard (Trulove), Jill Gomez (Anne), Leo Goeke (Tom Rakewell), Donald Gramm (Nick Shadow), Thetis Blacker (Mother Goose), Rosalind Elias (Baba the Turk), John Fryatt (Sellem)

14 August 1975 Glen Falls, NY, Lake George Opera Festival Auditorium

Conductor: Michael Charry
Director: Adelaide Bishop
Choreographer: Dorothy Danner
Scenery & Costumes: Kristine Haugan
Lighting: Patricia Collins
Principal Singers: John West (Trulove), Diana Soviero (Anne), Robert Johnson (Tom Rakewell), Ronald Hedlund (Nick Shadow), Annie Lynn Bornstein & Judith Wood (Mother Goose), Nancy Williams (Baba the Turk), Harry Danner (Sellem), Eric Halfvarson (Keeper of the Madhouse)

17 April 1976 Venice, La Fenice

Conductor: Ettore Gracis
Director: Virginio Puecher
Scenery & Costumes: Collettivo di Brera
Principal Singers: Graziano del Vivo (Trulove), Lella Cuberli (Anne), Lajos Kosma (Tom Rakewell), Claudio Desderi (Nick Shadow), Rosetta Arena (Mother Goose), Rosa Laghezza (Baba the Turk), Oslavio di Credico (Sellem), Giovanni Antonini (Keeper of the Madhouse)

21 August 1977 Buenos Aires, Teatro Colon

Conductor: Antoniello
Director: Oscar Fugera
Scenery, Costumes & Lighting: Hugo de Ana
Principal Singers: Giorgio Algorta (Trulove), Diana Lopez Esponda (Anne), Garry Glaze (Tom Rakewell), Renato Cesari (Nick Shadow), Adriana Cantelli (Baba the Turk)

19 November 1977 Paris, Opéra Comique

Conductor: Sylvain Cambreling
Director: Louis Erlo
Principal Singers: Francine Laurent (Anne), Ian Caley (Tom Rakewell), Jean-Philippe Lafont (Nick Shadow), Jocelyne Taillon (Baba the Turk), Marcel Quillevere (Sellem)

2 April 1978 Dortmund, Städtische Bühnen

Conductor: Hiroshi Wakasugi
Director: Paul Hager
Scenery & Costumes: Lore Haas & Hans Schavernoch
Principal Singers: Gunther Wewel (Trulove), Jacqueline Benson (Anne), William Reeder (Tom Rakewell), Dieter Behlendorf (Nick Shadow), Elisabeth Glauser (Mother Goose), Linda Karen (Baba the Turk), Helmut Bohm (Sellem), Andreas Becker (Keeper of the Madhouse)

13 January 1979 Berlin, Komische Oper

Conductor: Jin Belohlavek
Director: Friedo Solter
Scenery: Lothar Scharsich
Costumes: Eleanore Kleiber
Principal Singers: Herbert Rosslers (Trulove), Jana Smitkova (Anne), John Moulson (Tom Rakewell), George Ionescu (Nick Shadow), Ruth Schob-Lipkas (Mother Goose), Nelly Boschkova (Baba the Turk), Hans Nöcker (Sellem), Alfred Wroblewski (Keeper of the Madhouse)

1979 Moscow, Chamber Musical Theatre

Principal Singers: L.M.Trofimova (Anne), N.V.Kurpe (Tom Rakewell), E.S.Akimov (Nick Shadow), L.F.Gavrilyuk (Mother Goose), E.N.Pruzhenkova (Baba the Turk)

Casts here are doubled and trebled.

10 May 1979 Milan, La Scala

Conductor: Riccardo Chailly
Director: John Cox
Scenery & Costumes: David Hockney
Principal Singers: Federico Davia (Trulove), Yasuko Hayashi (Anne), Philip Langridge (Tom Rakewell), Claudio Desderi (Nick Shadow), Laura Zanini (Mother Goose), Eleanora Jankovic (Baba the Turk), Walter Gullino (Sellem), Giuseppe Zecchillo (Keeper of the Madhouse)

18 June 1979 London, Royal Opera House

Conductor: Colin Davis
Scenery & Costumes: Timothy O'Brien & Tazeena Firth
Lighting: Nick Chelton
Principal Singers: Robert Lloyd (Trulove), Helen Donath (Anne), Robert Tear (Tom Rakewell), Donald Gramm (Nick Shadow), Patricia Payne (Mother Goose), Patricia Johnson (Baba the Turk), John Dobson (Sellem), Roderick Kennedy (Keeper of the Madhouse)

2 May 1980 Budapest, Opera House

Conductor: Andras Mihaly
Director: Andras Miko
Scenery: Gabar Forray
Principal Singers: Adrienne Csengery (Anne), Denes Guylas (Tom Rakewell), Istvan Gati (Nick Shadow), Katalin Seregelly (Baba the Turk)

25 July 1981 Santa Fe, New Mexico, Santa Fe Opera

Conductor: Raymond Leppard
Director: Bliss Hebert
Scenery & Costumes: Allen Charles Klein
Principal Singers: Joseph McKee (Trulove), Elizabeth Hynes (Anne), Jon Garrison (Tom Rakewell), James Morris (Nick Shadow), Carolyne James (Mother Goose), Rosalind Elias (Baba the Turk), Ragnar Ulfung (Sellem)

30 November 1981 Washington, DC, Kennedy Center

Conductor: John Manceri
Director: Francis Rizzo
Scenery & Costumes: Jack Brown
Principal Singers: Sheri Greenwald, Janice Meyerson, Jerry Hadley, William Dansby

Agon

Ballet for twelve dancers
20 minutes (EWW 95)

Agon – Greek for 'contest'.

Ballet as ballet, pure dance, no trappings, no effects except those achieved by the bodies of dancers dancing. The final part, but separate part, of the trilogy – *Apollo, Orpheus, Agon*. The final collaboration between Balanchine and Stravinsky. A picture of them both. And Lincoln Kirstein the genie again: '*Agon* is contest without competition, a hymn to endless, tireless struggle; opposition, tension; release; stops, starts; conciliation, mutual consideration, in chancy but designed encounters.'

Balanchine made the ballet so much his own that it is illustrated only by a picture of his interpreters. Ballet for now. But ballet is for the future. *'Agon'* – Greek for 'contest'. As if to say: 'Top that if you can . . .'

Other choreographers began to take up the challenge of Stravinsky's works – Maurice Béjart in 1959 with *Le Sacre du Printemps*. Other designers, other dancers, other singers. The second generation.

The contest continues. But not against Stravinsky. He is always on the side of his interpreters.

First Performance 27 November 1957

Theatre:	New York City Center
Company:	New York City Ballet
Choreographer:	George Balanchine
Lighting:	Nananne Porcher
Dancers:	Diana Adams
	Melissa Hayden
	Roberta Lubell
	Barbara Millberg
	Francia Russell
	Dido Sayers
	Ruth Sobotka
	Barbara Walczak
	Todd Bolender
	Arthur Mitchell
	Roy Tobias
	Jonathan Watts

Synopsis

Abstract ballet for twelve dancers dressed in practice clothes.

As George Balanchine said, 'It has no story except the dancing itself . . . . *Agon* was invented for dancing.'

Opposite: Allegra Kent and Arthur Mitchell, the New York City Ballet, the Stravinsky Festival at the New York State Theatre, June 1972. George Balanchine has made *Agon* very much his own ballet. This single telling illustration shows the essence of Balanchine's choreographic art. *Photo: Martha Swope.*

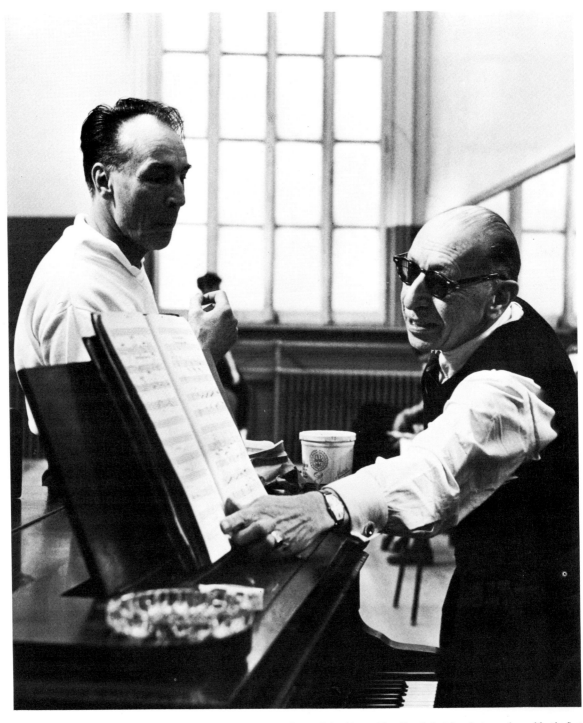

George Balanchine and Igor Stravinsky taken during a rehearsal for the first production.
Photo: Martha Swope.

198

Other Major Productions

27 January 1958 Düsseldorf, Deutsche Oper am Rhein

Choreographer: Otto Krüger
Costumes: Dominik Hartmann

3 May 1958 Berlin, Städtische Oper

Choreographer: Tatiana Gsovski
Scenery & Costumes: Jean-Pierre Ponnelle
Principal Dancers: Ivan Sertic, Rose Roth, Manon Vitzthum

21 May 1958 Hanover, Landestheater

Choreographer: Yvonne Georgi

20 August 1958 London, Royal Opera House

Company: The Royal Ballet
Conductor: Hugo Rignold
Choreographer: Kenneth MacMillan
Scenery & Costumes: Nicholas Georgiadis
Principal Dancers: Anya Linden, David Blair, Annette Page, Pirmin Trecu, Shirley Graham, Graham Usher, Maryon Lane, John Stevens, Deirdre Dixon, Ronald Hynd, Judith Sinclair, Georgina Parkinson, Antoinette Sibley, Doreen Wells

24 March 1959 Vienna, Staatsoper

Choreographer: Yvonne Georgi
Costumes: Marcel Escoffier
Principal Dancers: Christle Zimmerl, Karl Musil, Richard Adams, Edeltraude Brexner

30 November 1959 Frankfurt, Opernhaus

Conductor: Felix Prohaska
Choreographer: Tatiana Gsovski
Scenery & Costumes: Hein Heckroth

5 April 1962 Mannheim, Nationaltheater

Choreographer: Heino Heiden
Scenery: Paul Walter
Costumes: Gerda Schulte

24 June 1962 Hamburg, Staatsoper

Conductor: Robert Craft
Choreographer: George Balanchine
Principal Dancers: Melissa Hayden, Allegra Kent, Patricia McBride, Patricia Neary, Arthur Mitchell, Richard Rapp, Edward Villella, Jonathan Watts

28 January 1967 Copenhagen, Det Kongelige Teater

Choreographer: Eske Holm
Scenery & Costumes: Boye Willumsen

6 June 1970 Stuttgart, Württembergische Staatsoper

Company: Stuttgart Ballet
Choreographer: George Balanchine

25 January 1973 London, Royal Opera House

Company: The Royal Ballet
Conductor: Ashley Lawrence
Choreographer: George Balanchine, staged by Patricia Neary
Principal Dancers: Vergie Derman, Laura Connor, Anthony Dowell, David Wall, Wendy Ellis, Alfreda Thorogood, David Ashmole, Wayne Eagling, Jacqueline Elliott, Wendy Groombridge, Jacqui Tallis, Heather Walker

13 March 1974 Paris, Théâtre national de l'Opéra

Conductor: Manuel Rosenthal
Choreographer: George Balanchine
Principal Dancers: Jean Guizerix, Georges Piletta, Wilfride Piollet

28 March 1974 Geneva, Grand Theatre

Choreographer: George Balanchine, staged by Patricia Neary
Principal Dancers: Michael Denard, Peter Heubi, Pierre Polliaind, Steven Wistrich, Ghislaine Thesmer, Christl Siesz, Becky Ross, Aniko Csisky, Eva Baenen, Susan Freedman, Jillian Hessel, Suzanne Kay, Denise Capt, Dominique Charlier, Chantal Lambert

16 June 1974 Amsterdam, Stadsschouwburg

Company: Dutch National Ballet
Conductor: André Presser
Choreographer: George Balanchine

5 August 1974 London, Sadler's Wells

Company: Dance Theatre of Harlem
Choreographer: George Balanchine
Principal Dancers: Lydia Abarca, Virginia Johnson, Ronald Perry, Derek Williams, Gayle McKinney, Susan Lovelle, Homer Bryant, Paul Russell, Roslyn Sampson, Yvonne Hall, Ronda Sampson, Melva Murray-White

12 September 1976 Hamburg, Staatsoper

Conductor: Kazuhiro Koizumi
Choreographer: George Balanchine, staged by Patricia Neary
Principal Dancers: Magali Messac, Lynne Charles, Tanju Tüzer, Kevin Haigen, Dörte Rüter, Giselle Roberge, Eugen Ivanics, Michael Steele, Anne Drower, Gabrielle Günthard, Patricia Machette, Robyn White

5 November 1977 Berlin, Deutsche Oper

Choreographer: George Balanchine, staged by Patricia Neary
Principal Dancers: Eva Evdokima, Vladimir Gelvan, Felicitas Binder, Charlotte Butler, David Roland, Heidrun Schwaarz, Igor Kosak, Bernard Hourseau, Maria Holtz, Henriette Evelein, Sara Rendall, Cheryl Bernardi

Productions from other compositions

These ballets, made from compositions which were not originally intended for the stage, are given in alphabetical order of title of the performed work, and, wherever possible, the title of the original composition has been identified and given the EWW number. Over 50 of Stravinsky's compositions have inspired choreographers in Europe and America to make over 100 new ballets. Some compositions have been used many times, others only once, as is shown by the cross-referencing in the list below.

During one week, in June 1972, the New York City Ballet performed fifteen new ballets created from these compositions for their Stravinsky Festival. This was planned to be a celebration of Stravinsky's ninetieth birthday but, sadly, he did not live to see it.

This list also includes the sound and light show, *Feu d'Artifice*, with a set by the Italian futurist painter Giacomo Balla, the theatrical experiment presented by Diaghilev in 1917, and the composition for television *Noah and the Flood* first broadcast by CBS in 1962.

The compilation has been made from a number of sources, but again, wherever possible, from the theatre programme itself. It is curious that although it is always the music of Stravinsky that has provided the initial inspiration for the creation of a particular work, the title of the composition is only too frequently not identified by the programme editor. Nor, often, is the conductor. The music itself and those who perform it become relegated to anonymity. Yet, without the music there would be no performance. At least Stravinsky is credited as having been the composer of all these works.

Les Abeilles from *Scherzo Fantastique* (EWW 12)
16 minutes

10 January 1917, Paris, Théâtre national de l'Opéra
Company: Paris Opera Ballet
Choreographer: Leo Staats; *Scenery:* Maxime Dethomas

See also *Scherzo Fantastique*

Afterthoughts from *Two Suites for Small Orchestra* (EWW 32A and 32B)

1946, New York, NCASF
Choreographer & Scenery: Jerome Robbins

See also *Les Baladins; Capricci; Cous, Coudes, Corps & Coeurs; Deux Petites Suites; Eccentrique; Petites Suites*

Agrismene from *Octet for Wind Instruments* (EWW 51)
16 minutes

21 April 1958, New York, Phoenix Theatre
Company: Ballet Workshop Theatre
Choreographer: William Dollar; *Principal Dancers:* Lupe Serrano, Royes Fernandez

See also *Octet; Octuor*

The Antagonists from *Three Pieces for String Quartet* (EWW 25) and *Concertino for String Quartet* (EWW 47)
14 minutes

20 August 1955, Connecticut, Palmer Auditorium, Connecticut College
Choreographer: Ruth Currier; *Scenery:* Thomas De Gaetani; *Costumes:* Lavina Nielsen; *Dancers:* Ruth Currier (Zealot), Betty Jones (Victim)

See also *The Time Before the Time After*

Arcade from *Concerto for Piano and Wind Instruments* (EWW 52) 20 minutes

28 March 1963, New York, City Center
Company: New York City Ballet
Choreographer: John Taras; *Scenery:* David Hays; *Costumes:* Ruth Sobotka; *Dancers:* Robert Rodham, Ramon Segara, Earle Sieveling, Denis Lamont, Anthony Blum, Arthur Mitchell, Richard Rapp, William Weslow, Michael Steele, Frank Ohman, Kent Stowell, James De Bolt, Suzanne Farrell

See also *Concerto for Piano and Winds; 13 Stühle*

Arena unidentified selections from various compositions

8 December 1967, New York, Theatre 80 St Marks
Company: Manhattan Festival Ballet
Choreographer: James Waring

Attis und die Nymphe from *Concerto in D for String Orchestra* (EWW 84) 12 minutes

15 May 1959, Stuttgart, Württembergische Staatstheater
Choreographer: Werner Ulbrich; *Scenery & Costumes:* Helmut Koniarsky

See also *The Cage; Concerto in D; Kill What I Love; Tilt*

Les Baladins from Two Suites for Small Orchestra (EWW 32A and 32B)

1958, Paris, Opéra Comique
Choreographer: Michel Descombey

See also *Afterthoughts; Capricci; Cous, Coudes, Corps & Coeurs; Deux Petites Suites; Eccentrique; Petites Suites*

Balkan Sobranie from an unidentified work, with music also by Jean Françaix and Kazuo Fukushima

28 June 1972, Glasgow, Close Theatre
Company: Scottish Theatre Ballet
Choreographer: Richard Alston; *Scenery:* Myra Visser; *Dancers:* Anne Allan, Kit Lethby, Marian St Claire, Bruce Steivel

Balustrade from *Concerto in D for Violin and Orchestra* (EWW 61) 22 minutes

22 January 1941, New York, 51st Street Theater
Company: Original Ballet Russe
Choreographer: George Balanchine; *Scenery & Costumes:* Pavel Tchelitchev; *Principal Dancers:* Tamara Toumanova, Paul Petrov, Roman Jasinsky

See also *Violin Concerto*

The Cage from *Concerto in D for String Orchestra* (EWW 84) 12 minutes

14 June 1951, New York, City Center
Company: New York City Ballet
Choreographer: Jerome Robbins; *Costumes:* Ruth Sobotka; *Lighting:* Jean Rosenthal; *Principal Dancers:* Nora Kaye (Novice), Yvonne Mounsey (Queen), Nicholas Magallanes, Michael Maule (Intruders)

See also *Attis und die Nymphe; Concerto in D; Kill What I Love; Tilt*

Capricci from *Two Suites for Small Orchestra* (EWW 32A and 32B) 12 minutes

April 1943, Rome, Teatro delle Arte
Choreographer: Aurel Milloss; *Scenery:* Toti Scialoja

See also *Afterthoughts; les Baladins; Cous, Coudes, Corps & Coeurs; Deux Petites Suites; Eccentrique; Petites Suites*

Capriccio (EWW 59) 20 minutes

24 April 1948, Milan, La Scala
Company: La Scala Opera Ballet
Conductor: Nino Sanzogno; *Choreographer:* Leonide
Massine; *Scenery & Costumes:* Nicola Benois; *Principal
Dancers:* Olga Amati, Wanda Milly Clerici, Vera
Colombo, Ugo Dell' Ara, Giuseppe Pessina

28 August 1957, Munich, Prinzregententheater
Company: Bavarian State Opera
Choreographer, Scenery & Costumes: Alan Carter;
Principal Dancers: Annette Chappell, Heino Hallhuber

See also *Jewels*; *Stravinsky Capriccio for Piano and
Orchestra*

Chorale Variations on Bach's 'Vom Himmel hoch'
(EWW X) 10½ minutes

25 June 1972, New York, NY State Theatre
Company: New York City Ballet
Conductor: Robert Irving; *Choreographer:* George
Balanchine; *Scenery:* Rouben Ter-Arutunian; *Lighting:*
Ronald Bates; *Principal Dancers:* Karin von Aroldingen,
Melissa Hayden, Sara Leland, Violette Verdy, Anthony
Blum, Peter Martins

Circa '56 from *Ebony Concerto* (EWW 83) 11 minutes

21 April 1956, New York, Kaufman Auditorium
Company: Valerie Bettis and Company
Choreographer: Valerie Bettis; *Principal Dancers:*
Valerie Bettis, Duncan Noble

See also *Ebony Concerto*; *Jazz Concert*

Concerto for Piano and Winds (EWW 52) 20 minutes

20 June 1972, New York, NY State Theatre
Company: New York City Ballet
Conductor: Robert Irving; *Pianist:* Gordon Boelzner;
Choreographer: John Taras; *Costumes:* Rouben Ter-
Arutunian; *Lighting:* Ronald Bates; *Principal Dancers:*
Bruce Wells, Robert Maiorano, Frank Ohman, Tracy
Bennett, Victor Castelli, Peter Naumann

See also *Arcade*; *13 Stühle*

Concerto for Two Solo Pianos (EWW 66) 20 minutes

21 January 1971, New York, NY State Theatre
Company: New York City Ballet
Choreographer: Richard Tanner; *Costumes:* Stanley
Simmons; *Principal Dancers:* Gelsey Kirkland, John
Clifford, Colleen Neary, James Bogan, David
Richardson

See also *Concerto für zwei Klaviere*; *Rapid Transit*

Concerto für zwei Klaviere (EWW 66)

18 April 1960, Hamburg, Staatsoper
Company: Staatsoper Ballet
Choreographer: Gustav Blank
Costumes: Alfred Siercke; *Principal Dancers:* Christa
Kempf, Heinz Clauss

See also: *Concerto for Two Solo Pianos*; *Rapid Transit*

Concerto in D (EWW 84) known as *Vision*

18 February 1950, Hamburg, Staatsoper
Conductor: Wilhelm Rüggeberg-Brückner;
Choreographer: Dore Hoyer; *Scenery & Costumes:*
Alfred Siercke

See also *Attis und die Nymphe*; *The Cage*; *Kill What I
Love*; *Tilt*

Cous, Coudes, Corps & Coeurs from *Two Suites for
Small Orchestra* (EWW 32A and 32B) 12 minutes

17 June 1970, Stuttgart, Württemburgische
Staatstheater
Company: Stuttgart Ballet
Choreographer: John Cranko

See also *Afterthoughts*; *les Baladins*; *Capricci*; *Deux
Petites Suites*; *Eccentrique*; *Petites Suites*

Dance for Five Women from *Suite Italienne*
transcription from *Pulcinella* (EWW 46)

17 July 1976, Manchester, Vermont, Southern Vermont
Art Center
Company: Manhattan School of Dance
Choreographer: Edward Henkel

See also *Pulcinella* in Works Composed for the Stage

A Dancer Prepares from an unidentified work

8 November 1959, New York, YM-YWHA
Choreographer & Principal Dancer: Daniel Nagrin

Das Duell from *Fireworks* (EWW 13)

26 January 1980, Berlin, Deutsche Staatsoper
Choreographer: Hermann Rudolph; *Scenery:* Wilfried
Werz; *Costumes:* Christine Stromberg; *Dancers:*
Monika Lubitz, Bernd Dreyer

See also *Fireworks*

Deux Petites Suites from *Two Suites for Small Orchestra*
(EWW 32A & 32B)

1929, Düsseldorf, Stadttheater
Choreographer: Ruth Loeser; *Scenery:* Hellmut Jurgens

See also *Afterthoughts*; *les Baladins*; *Capricci*; *Cous,
Coudes, Corps et Coeurs*; *Deux Petites Suites*;
Eccentrique

Divertimento from 'Le Baiser de la Fée' (EWW 58A)
20 minutes

21 June 1972, New York, NY State Theatre
Company: New York City Ballet
Conductor: Robert Irving; *Choreographer:* George
Balanchine; *Lighting:* Ronald Bates; *Principal Dancers:*
Patricia McBride, Helgi Tomasson, Bettijanne Sills,
Carol Sumner

See also *Le Baiser de la Fée* in Works Composed for the
Stage

Dumbarton Oaks from *Concerto in E Flat* (EWW 70)
12 minutes

23 June 1972, New York, NY State Theatre
Company: New York City Ballet
Conductor: Robert Craft; *Choreographer:* Jerome
Robbins; *Costumes:* Patricia Zipprodt; *Lighting:* Ronald
Bates; *Principal Dancers:* Allegra Kent, Anthony Blum

See also *Rhyme Nor Reason*

Duo Concertant (EWW 62) 16 minutes

22 June 1972, New York, NY State Theatre
Company: New York City Ballet
Violinist: Lamar Alsop; *Pianist:* Gordon Boelzner;
Choreographer: George Balanchine; *Lighting:* Ronald
Bates; *Dancers:* Kay Mazzo, Peter Martins

Ebony Concerto (EWW 83) 11 minutes

29 December 1970, Stuttgart, Württembergische
Staatstheater
Company: Stuttgart Ballet
Choreographer: John Cranko; *Costumes:* Silvia
Strahammer

See also *Circa '56*; *Jazz Concert*

Eccentrique from *Four Studies for Orchestra* (EWW
38A) and *Suites for Small Orchestra No 1 and No 2*
(EWW 32A and 32B) 24 minutes

18 January 1972, New York, City Center
Company: American Ballet Theatre
Choreographer: Eliot Feld; *Scenery:* Oliver Smith;
Costumes: Frank Thompson; *Lighting:* Jennifer Tipton;
Principal Dancers: Elizabeth Lee, Christie Sarry, John
Sowinski

See also *Afterthoughts*; *les Baladins*; *Capricci*; *Cous,
Coudes, Corpes et Coeurs*; *Deux Petites Suites*; *Petites
Suites*

Elégie (EWW 81) 4½ minutes

5 November 1945, New York, Carnegie Hall
Company: Advanced Students of the School of
American Ballet
Choreographer: George Balanchine

First professional performance:

28 April 1948, New York, City Center
Company: Ballet Society
Choreographer: George Balanchine; *Dancers:* Tanaquil
Le Clercq, Patricia McBride

Feu d'Artifice (Fireworks) (EWW 13) 4 minutes

12 April 1917, Rome, Teatro Costanzi
Conductor: Ernest Ansermet; *Director:* Serge
Diaghilev; *Scenery & Lighting:* Giacomo Balla

See also *Feuilleton*; *Fireworks*

Feuilleton from 1. *Circus Polka* (EWW 74), 2. *Ode*
(EWW 76), 3. *Feu d'Artifice* (EWW 13), 4. *Ebony
Concerto* (EWW 83) 27 minutes

28 August 1957, Munich, Prinzregententheater
Company: Bavarian State Opera
Choreographer, Scenery & Costumes: Alan Carter;
Dancers: 1. Children of the Ballet School; 2. Hilde
Stadler, Inge Bertl; 3. Elizabeth Schuppen, Paul
Wünsch, Margot Werner; 4. Annette Chappell, Heino
Hallhuber, Franz Baur

Fireworks (EWW 13) 4 minutes

September 1956, Oxford, New Theatre
Choreographer: Kenneth MacMillan; *Dancers:* Nadia
Nerina, Alexis Rassine

See also *Feu d'Artifice*; *Feuilleton*

The Flood (EWW 102) 24 minutes

30 April 1963, Hamburg, Staatsoper
Conductor: Robert Craft; *Choreographer:* Peter Van
Dijk; *Director:* Günther Rennert; *Scenery & Costumes:*
Teo Otto; *Principal Singers:* Helga Pilarczyk, Heinz
Ehrhardt, Heinz Klevenow, Helmut Melchert, Vladimir
Ruzdak, Ernst Wiemann

See also *Noah and the Flood*

Four Against the Gods from an unidentified work

8 February 1976, New York, Theatre of the Riverside
Church
Company: Danscompany
Choreographer: Joyce Trisler

The Game of Noah from a number of short works

1 July 1965, The Hague, Holland Festival
Company: Nederlands Dans Theater
Choreographer: Glen Tetley; *Scenery:* Willa Kim;
Dancers: Alexander Radins, Hans Ebbelaar

Games from *Pulcinella Suite* (EWW 46)

8 June 1958, Spoleto, Teatro Nuovo
Company: Ballets USA
Choreographer: Todd Bolender; *Scenery & Costumes:*
Lucia Vernarelli; *Dancers:* Beryl Towbin, Joan van
Orden, Erin Martin, James Moore, Gwen Lewis, John
Mandia

New revision of *Commedia Balletica* given by the
Ballets Russes de Monte Carlo, 17 September 1945

See also *Pulcinella* in Works Composed for the Stage
and *Pulcinella Variations*

The Gentlemen from Cracow selection from *Le Sacre du Printemps* (EWW 21)

5 December 1955, New York, Madison Square Garden
Company: Sophie Maslow Company
Choreographer: Sophie Maslow

See also *Le Sacre du Printemps* in Works Composed for
the Stage

Gezeiten from *Symphony in Three Movements* (EWW 82) *c* 24 minutes.

4 January 1960, Cologne, Opernhaus
Company: Ballet der Bühnen der Stadt Köln
Conductor: Miltiades Caridis; *Choreographer:* Aurel
Milloss

Also known as *Par Flux et Marée*

See also *Olympiad; Symphonie in drei Sätzen;
Symphony in Three Movements*

Herr Orpheus from *Orpheus* (EWW 86) 30 minutes

28 August 1957, Munich, Prinzregententheater
Company: Bavarian State Opera
Choreographer & Costumes: Alan Carter; *Principal
Dancers:* Natascha Trofimova, Franz Baur, Will
Spindler

See also *Orpheus* in Works Composed for the Stage

I Never Saw Another Butterfly from a selection of music
by Igor Stravinsky, Henry Cowell and Irvin Srul Glick

14 April 1977, New York, Kaufman Auditorium
Company: Pearl Lang and Dance Company
Choreographer: Pearl Lang; *Scenery:* Don Jensen;
Costumes: Christiana Giannini; *Lighting:* Jeffrey
Schissler

Jazz Concert from *Ragtime* (EWW 42), *Ebony Concerto*
(EWW 83) and also *Les Biches* by Francis Poulenc and
Creation of the World by Darius Milhaud

7 December 1960, New York, City Center
Company: New York City Ballet
Choreographers: George Balanchine (*Ragtime*) and
John Taras (*Ebony Concerto*); *Scenery & Costumes:*
David Hays; *Dancers:* (*Ragtime*): Diana Adams, Bill
Carter; (*Ebony Concerto*): Patricia McBride, Arthur
Mitchell

See also *Ebony Concerto; Ragtime*

Jewels in three parts: for Emeralds from Gustav Fauré's
Pélléas et Mélisande and *Shylock*, for Rubies from Igor
Stravinsky's *Capriccio* (EWW 59), for Diamonds from
Piotr Tchaikovsky's *Symphony No 3 in D major* 20
minutes

13 April 1967, New York, NY State Theatre
Company: New York City Ballet
Choreographer: George Balanchine; *Scenery:* Peter
Harvey; *Costumes:* Barbara Karinska; *Principal
Dancers:* Patricia McBride, Edward Villella, Marnee
Morris, Stephen Caras, Richard Dryden, Denis Lamont,
Robert Weiss

See also *Capriccio; Stravinsky Capriccio for Piano and
Orchestra*

Kill What I Love from *Ode* (EWW 76) and *Concerto in D*
(EWW 84)

16 November 1973, Angers, Théâtre d'Angers
Company: Ballet Théâtre Contemporain
Choreographer: John Butler; *Scenery:* Tal Coat;
Principal Dancers: Martine Parmain, Jean-Claude
Giorgini, Muriel Belmondo, Jacques Garnier, André
Lafonta

See also *Attis und die Nymphe; The Cage; Concerto
in D; Ode; Tilt*

The Least Flycatcher from *Piano-Rag-Music* (EWW 44)
3 minutes

14 January 1961, New York, Hunter College Playhouse
Company: Paul Taylor Dance Company
Choreographer: Paul Taylor; *Costumes:* Robert
Rauschenberg; *Principal Dancer:* Paul Taylor

Originally performed on 6 May 1956 to sounds devised
by Robert Rauschenberg on magnetic tape.

See also *Piano-Rag-Music*

The Lottery from *Le Sacre du Printemps* in revised orchestration by Robert Rudolph

16 April 1974, New York, Harkness Theatre
Company: Harkness Ballet
Libretto: Based on a short story by Shirley Jackson;
Choreographer: Brian Macdonald; *Scenery:* Robert Mitchell; *Costumes:* François Barbeau

Mark of Cain from an unidentified work

1 February 1964, New York, 92nd Street 'Y'
Company: Don Redlich Company
Choreographer: Don Redlich

Memoir original title *Chrysalis* from an unidentified work

2 August 1957, Steamboat Springs, Colorado, Perry Mansfield Theater
Choreographer: Helen Tamiris; *Scenery:* Stuart P.Murphy; *Costumes:* Frankie Bliesner

Mini-Strawinni from *Four Norwegian Moods* (EWW 75), *Eight Instrumental Miniatures* (EWW 49A), *Ragtime* (EWW 42), *Tango* (EWW 72) & *Circus Polka* (EWW 74)

30 April 1977, Kassel, Staatstheater
Conductor: Michael Lloyd; *Choreographer:* Joel Schnee; *Scenery & Costumes:* Walter Perdacher

Moments from an unidentified work

17 December 1976, Turin, Teatro Regio
Choreographer: Paolo Bortoluzzi

Monumentum pro Gesualdo (EWW XII) 7 minutes

16 November 1960, New York, City Center
Company: New York City Ballet
Choreographer: George Balanchine; *Scenery:* David Hays; *Principal Dancers:* Diana Adams, Conrad Ludlow

Since 1963 performed as the first part of a ballet called *Movements*, the second part being *Movements for Piano and Orchestra*.

See also *Movements*; *Movements for Piano and Orchestra*

Movements

Title of ballet in two parts as performed by the New York City Ballet since 1963.
Part 1: *Monumentum pro Gesualdo*,
Part 2: *Movements for Piano and Orchestra*

See also *Monumentum pro Gesualdo*; *Movements for Piano and Orchestra*

Movements for Piano and Orchestra (EWW 97)
10 minutes

9 April 1963, New York, City Center
Company: New York City Ballet
Choreographer: George Balanchine; *Scenery:* David Hays; *Lighting:* Peter Harvey; *Principal Dancers:* Jacques D'Amboise, Suzanne Farrell

Since 1963 performed as the second part of a ballet called *Movements*, the first part being *Monumentum pro Gesualdo*.

See also *Monumentum pro Gesualdo; Movements*

Myth from *Symphonies of Wind Instruments* (EWW 48) 12 minutes

15 December 1971, New York, City Center
Company: Alvin Ailey Dance Theatre
Choreographer: Alvin Ailey; *Costumes:* Christiana Giannini; *Dancer:* Consuelo Atlas

See also *Symphonies d'Instruments à Vent*

The Nightingale and the Emperor of China *Le Rossignol et l'Empereur de Chine*

1959, First performance on French TV
Choreographer: Juan Corelli

Noah and the Flood from *The Flood* (EWW 102) Ballet-oratorio for television 24 minutes

14 June 1962, CBS-TV
Choreographer: George Balanchine; *Director:* Kirk Browning; *Scenery & Costumes:* Rouben Ter-Arutunian; *Voices:* Laurence Harvey (Narrator) Sebastian Cabot (Noah), Elsa Lanchester (Mrs Noah), Paul Tripp (Caller); *Dancers:* Jacques D'Amboise (Adam/Lucifer), Edward Villella (Satan), Jillana (Eve), Ramon Segara (Noah), Joysanne Sidimus (Mrs Noah), and artists of the New York City Ballet

A specially commissioned dance drama derived from the Book of Genesis and the York and Chester cycles of Mystery Plays.

See also *The Flood*

Octet *Octet for Wind Instruments* (EWW 51) 16 minutes

2 December 1958, New York, City Center
Company: New York City Ballet
Choreographer: William Christiansen; *Dancers:* Edward Villella, Barbara Walczak, William Weslow, Dido Sayers, Richard Rapp, Judith Green, Robert Lindgren, Roberta Lubell

See also *Agrismene, Octuor*

Octuor *Octet for Wind Instuments* (EWW 51)
16 minutes

21 June 1972, New York, NY State Theatre
Company: New York City Ballet
Conductor: Robert Irving; *Choreographer:* Richard
Tanner; *Lighting:* Ronald Bates; *Dancers:* Elise Flagg,
Deborah Flomime, Delia Peters, Lisa de Ribere, Tracy
Bennett, James Bogan, Daniel Duell, Jean-Pierre
Frohlich

See also *Agrismene, Octet*

Ode (EWW 76) 8 minutes

22 May 1961, Guildford, Guildford Theatre
Company: Western Theatre Ballet
Choreographer: Peter Darrell; *Scenery & Costumes:*
Pauline Whitehouse

1964, Brussels, Théâtre royal de la Monnaie
Company: Ballet du XXe siècle
Choreographer: André Leclair

23 June 1972, New York, NY State Theatre
Company: New York City Ballet
Conductor: Robert Craft; *Choreographer:* Lorca
Massine; *Lighting:* Ronald Bates; *Principal Dancers:*
Christine Redpath, Colleen Neary, Robert Maiorano,
Earle Sieveling

See also *Feuilleton*

Olympiad from *Symphony in Three Movements* (EWW
82) 24 minutes

11 March 1968, Berlin, Deutsche Oper
Company: Deutsche Oper Ballet
Choreographer: Kenneth MacMillan; *Principal
Dancers:* Lynn Seymour, Hannelore Peters, Karin
Jahnke, Klaus Beelitz, Rudolf Holz, Falco Kapuste,
André Doutreval, Gerhard Bohner, Frank Frey, Ralf
Harster

21 February 1969, London, Royal Opera House
Company: The Royal Ballet
Choreographer: Kenneth MacMillan; *Principal
Dancers:* Deanne Bergsma, Georgina Parkinson, Vergie
Derman, Keith Rosson, Robert Mead

See also *Gezeiten; Symphonie in drei Sätzen;
Symphony in Three Movements*

Overture from *Greeting Prelude* (EWW 93) and *Suite
for Small Orchestra No 2* (EWW 32B) 8 minutes

20 June 1967, London, Sadler's Wells
Company: Western Theatre Ballet
Choreographer: Laverne Mayer; *Costumes:* Elisabeth
Dalton; *Dancers:* Donna Day Washington, Elaine
McDonald, Sarah Page, Simon Mottram, Tony Hulbert,
Brian Burn

See also *Afterthoughts; les Baladins; Capricci; Cous,
Coudes, Corps et Coeurs; Deux Petites Suites;
Eccentrique; Petites Suites*

Par Flux et Marée

See *Gezeiten*

Pas de Poissons from *Scènes de Ballet* (EWW 79)

26 April 1966, Philadelphia, Irvine Auditorium
Company: Pennsylvania Ballet Company
Choreographer: Robert Rodham; *Costumes:* Ruth
Sobotka

Pasdansés from *Suite for Small Orchestra No 1* (EWW
32A), *Scherzo à la Russe* (EWW 78), *Circus Polka*
(EWW 74), *Tango* (EWW 72), *Suite for Small Orchestra
No 2* (EWW 32B), *Fireworks* (EWW 13)

April 1972, Venice, La Fenice
Company: Ballet Théâtre Contemporain
Choreographers: Dirk Saunders and René Goliard;
Scenery: Roman Cieslewicz; *Principal Dancers:* Thérèse
Thoreux, Muriel Belmondo, Itchko Lazarov, Tasuo
Sakai, Odile Carrard, Jean-Claude Giorgini

Peregrine from *The Firebird* (EWW 16)

19 March 1981, Lübeck, Bühnen der Hansestadt
(Studio)
Choreographer: Lajos Horvath; *Costumes:* Vivien
Deuber; *Principal Dancer:* Anna Lavrova

Peter Pan from an unidentified work

21 December 1974, California, Civic Center, Walnut
Creek
Company: Pacific Ballet and ACT
Choreographer: John Pasqualetti; *Libretto:* based on
play by J.M.Barrie

Petites Suites from *Two Suites for Small Orchestra*
(EWW 32A and 32B) 12 minutes

1936, New York, Stadium Concerts
Choreographer & Scenery: José Limon

See also *Afterthoughts; les Baladins; Capricci; Cous,
Coudes, Corps et Coeurs; Deux Petites Suites;
Eccentrique; Overture*

Piano-Rag-Music (EWW 44)) 3 minutes

23 June 1972, New York, NY State Theatre
Company: New York City Ballet
Pianist: Madeleine Malraux; *Choreographer:* Todd
Bolender; *Costumes:* Stanley Simmons; *Lighting:*
Ronald Bates; *Dancers:* Gloria Govrin; John Clifford

See also *The Least Flycatcher*

Pierrot and the Moon from an unidentified work

14 October 1950, New York, YM-YWHA
Company: Ross-Ward Ballet d'Action
Choreographer: Herbert Ross; *Scenery & Costumes:*
John Ward; *Principal Dancers:* Iona McKenzie, Alice
Temkin

Psalmensymphonie from *Symphony of Psalms* (EWW
60) 23 minutes

1979, The Hague
Company: Nederlands Dans Theater
Choreographer: Jiri Kylian; *Scenery:* William Katz

See also *Symphonie de Psaumes*

Pulcinella Variations (EWW 46) 35 minutes

11 July 1968, New York, Metropolitan Opera House
Company: American Ballet Theatre
Choreographer: Michael Smuin; *Scenery:* Jack Brown;
Costumes: Stanley Simmons; *Dancers:* Susan Casey,
Ellen Everett, Diana Weber, Georgina Vidal, Reese
Haworth, John Sowinski, Terry Orr, Michael Smuin

See also *Pulcinella* in Works Composed for the Stage,
and *Games*

Ragtime (EWW 42) 4½ minutes

3 April 1922, London, Royal Opera House
Choreographer: Leonide Massine; *Dancers:* Leonide
Massine, Lydia Lopokhova

Presented as an item in a programme of divertissements.

29 April 1980, Dresden, Staatstheater
Choreographer: Harald Wandtke; *Costumes:* Traute
Mahler & Barbara Schiffner; *Dancers:* Carole Schwab,
Gerald Binke, Dictmar Jacob

See also *Jazz Concert*

Rapid Transit from *Concerto for Two Pianos* (EWW 66)

25 November 1975, New York, Dance Umbrella at
Roundabout Stage One
Company: Lar Lubovitch Company of Dance
Choreographer: Lar Lubovitch; *Lighting:* Beverly
Emmons

See also *Concerto for Two Solo Pianos, Concerto für
zwei Klaviere*

Requiem Canticles (EWW 108) 15 minutes

2 May 1968, New York, NY State Theatre
Company: New York City Ballet
Choreographer: George Balanchine; *Costumes:* Rouben
Ter-Arutunian

Single performance in memory of Martin Luther King.

25 June 1972, New York, NY State Theatre
Company: New York City Ballet
Conductor: Robert Craft; *Choreographer:* Jerome
Robbins; *Lighting:* Ronald Bates; *Principal Dancers:*
Merrill Ashley, Susan Hendl, Bruce Wells, Robert
Maiorano

Rhyme nor Reason retitled from *Dumbarton Oaks* from
Concerto in E flat 'Dumbarton Oaks' (EWW 70)
12 minutes

7 October 1978, London, Sadler's Wells
Company: Sadler's Wells Royal Ballet
Choreographer: Michael Corder; *Dancers:* Jennifer
Jackson, Judith Howe, Deidre Eyden, Michael
Batchelor, Stephen Sheriff

See also *Dumbarton Oaks*

Sans Titre from *Concertino for String Quartet* (EWW
47) 6 minutes

April 1972, Venice, La Fenice
Company: Ballet-Théâtre Contemporain
Choreographer: Lar Lubovitch; *Dancers:* Martine
Parmain, James Urbain

See also *The Time Before the Time After, The
Antagonists*

Scherzo à la Russe (EWW 78) 4 minutes

21 June 1972, New York, NY State Theatre
Company: New York City Ballet
Conductor: Hugo Fiorato; *Choreographer:* George
Balanchine; *Costumes:* Barbara Karinska; *Lighting:*
Ronald Bates; *Principal Dancers:* Karin von Aroldingen,
Kay Mazzo

Scherzo Fantastique (EWW 12) 16 minutes

18 June 1972, New York, NY State Theatre
Company: New York City Ballet
Conductor: Robert Irving; *Choreographer:* Jerome
Robbins; *Lighting:* Ronald Bates; *Dancers:* Gelsey
Kirkland, Bart Cook, Bryan Pitts, Stephen Caras, Victor
Castelli

13 March 1974, Paris, Théâtre national de l'Opéra
Conductor: Manuel Rosenthal; *Choreographer:* Jerome
Robbins; *Principal Dancers:* Noella Pontois, Marc du
Bouays, Jacques Namont, Serge Daubrac

See also *Les Abeilles*

Serenade in A (EWW 54) 12 minutes

21 June 1972, New York, NY State Theatre
Company: New York City Ballet
Pianist: Madeleine Malraux; *Choreographer:* Todd
Bolender; *Costumes:* Stanley Simmons; *Lighting:*
Ronald Bates; *Principal Dancers:* Susan Hendl, Robert
Maiorano, Robert Weiss

Seven and Seven from an unidentified work

1972, Brussels, Théâtre royal de la Monnaie
Company: Ballet du XXe siècle
Choreographer: Paul Mejia; *Scenery & Costumes:*
Joëlle Roustan

Sleeping Beauty by Piotr Tchaikovsky Bluebird *Pas de
Deux* specially orchestrated for Ballet Theatre (EWW
VIII (iii)) 5 minutes

24 June 1940, Philadelphia, Robin Hood Dell
Company: Ballet Theatre
Choreographer: Anton Dolin, after Marius Petipa

Some Dance and Some Duet from *Sonata* (EWW 53)
20 minutes

18 February 1980, Brighton, Gardner Centre Theatre,
University of Sussex
Company: London Contemporary Dance Theatre
Choreographer: Micha Bergese; *Scenery & Costumes:*
Liz da Costa; *Lighting:* Adrian Dightam; *Dancers:* Anca
Frankenhaeuser, Anita Griffin, Patrick Harding-Irmer,
Celia Hulton, Brendon Hughes, Tom Jobe, Michael
Small

Stravinsky Capriccio for Piano and Orchestra (EWW 59)
20 minutes

9 May 1978, San Francisco, Opera House
Company: San Francisco Ballet
Choreographer: Robert Gladstein; *Costumes:* Willa
Kim

See also *Capriccio; Jewels*

Stravinsky Pas de Deux from *Four Norwegian Moods*
(EWW 75) 8 minutes

1 April 1976, San Francisco, War Memorial Opera
House
Company: San Francisco Ballet
Choreographer: Lew Christensen; *Dancers:* Susan
Magno, Keith Martin

Stravinsky: Symphony in C (EWW 71) 28 minutes

9 May 1968, New York, NY State Theatre
Company: New York City Ballet
Choreographer: John Clifford; *Costumes:* John Braden;
Principal Dancers: Anthony Blum, John Prinz, Marnee
Morris, Kay Mazzo, Renée Estopinal

Symphonie de Psaumes (EWW 60) 23 minutes

1977, Brussels, Théâtre royal de la Monnaie
Company: Ballet du XXe siècle
Choreographer: Micha van Hoecke; *Scenery &
Costumes:* Joëlle Roustan & Roger Bernard

See also *Psalmensymphonie*

Symphonie in Drei Sätzen (EWW 82) 24 minutes

21 March 1981, Zurich, Opernhaus
Conductor: André Presser; *Choreographer:* Sara
Leland; *Principal Dancers:* Deborah Dobson, Jonas
Kage, Debra Austin, Reda Sheta, Stephanie Herman,
Peter O'Brien

See also *Olympiad; Gezeiten; Symphony in Three
Movements*

Symphonies d'Instruments à Vent (EWW 48) Subtitled
'L'âme Vivante –II' 12 minutes

12 December 1972, Grenoble, Maison de la Culture
Company: Ballets Félix Blaska
Choreographer: Félix Blaska; *Costumes:* Jacques
Schmidt; *Dancers:* Marie-Laurence Bonnet, Marc
Digout, Aliocha Gorki, Françoise Joullie, Doris Mengus,
Graeme Lloyd Murphy

See also *Myth*

Symphony in E Flat (EWW 9) 30 minutes

20 June 1972, New York, NY State Theatre
Company: New York City Ballet
Conductor: Robert Irving; *Choreographer:* John
Clifford; *Costumes:* Stanley Simmons; *Lighting:* Ronald
Bates; *Principal Dancers:* Gelsey Kirkland, Peter
Martins

Symphony in Three Movements (EWW 82) 24 minutes

7 November 1963, Sunderland, Empire
Company: Nederlands Dans Theater
Choreographer: Hans van Manen; *Scenery:* Nicolas
Wijnberg

18 June 1972, New York, NY State Theatre
Company: New York City Ballet
Conductor: Robert Craft; *Choreographer:* George
Balanchine; *Lighting:* Ronald Bates; *Principal Dancers:*
Sara Leland, Marnee Morris, Lynda Yourth, Helgi
Tomasson, Edward Villella, Robert Weiss

See also *Olympiad; Gezeiten; Symphonie in drei Sätzen*

Tango Tango an ice ballet from *Tango* (EWW 72) and
music by Niels Gade 4½ minutes

21 November 1978, New York, Felt Forum
Choreographer: Peter Martins; *Costumes:* D.D.Ryan;
Dancers: John Curry, JoJo Starbuck

Tilt from *Concerto in D for String Orchestra* (EWW 84) (played twice) 24 minutes

21 January 1972, Scheveningen, Holland, Circustheater
Company: Nederlands Dans Theater
Choreographer: Hans van Manen; *Scenery & Costumes:* Jean-Paul Vroom

See also *Attis und die Nymphe*; *The Cage*; *Concerto in D*; *Kill What I Love*

The Time Before the Time After (After the Time Before) from *Concertino for String Quartet* (EWW 47) 6 minutes

31 October 1972, New York, Brooklyn Academy of Music
Company: Lar Lubovitch Dance Company
Choreographer, Costumes and Lighting: Lar Lubovitch; *Dancers:* Lar Lubovitch, Jeanne Solan

See also *The Antagonists*; *Sans Titre*

Trois Pieces pour Clarinette (EWW 45) 4 minutes

12 December 1972, Grenoble, Maison de la Culture
Company: Ballets Félix Blaska
Choreographer: Félix Blaska; *Costumes:* Jacques Schmidt; *Dancers:* Marie-Laurence Bonnet, Peter Heubi

Two Portraits In two parts: *After Toulouse Lautrec* from an unidentified work by Igor Stravinsky and *Odalisque* by Béla Bartók

1 March 1952, New York YM-YWHA
Choreographer: Marie Marchowsky

Variations from *Variations (Aldous Huxley in Memoriam)* (EWW 106) (played three times) 15 minutes

31 March 1966, New York, NY State Theatre
Company: New York City Ballet
Choreographer: George Balanchine; *Lighting:* Ronald Bates; *Dancers:* Karin von Aroldingen, Karen Batizi, Diane Bradshaw, Marjorie Breler, Elaine Comusdi, Rosemary Dunleavy, Susan Hendl, Ruth Ann King, Jennifer Nairn-Smith, Delia Peters, Donna Sackett, Lynne Stetson, Robert Maiorano, Paul Mejia, Frank Ohman, John Prinz, David Richardson, Michael Steele, Suzanne Farrell

Violin Concerto (EWW 61) 22 minutes

18 June 1972, New York, NY State Theatre
Company: New York City Ballet
Conductor: Robert Irving; *Solo Violin:* Joseph Silverstein; *Choreographer:* George Balanchine; *Lighting:* Ronald Bates; *Principal Dancers:* Karin von Aroldingen, Kay Mazzo, Jean-Pierre Bonnefous, Peter Martins

See also *Balustrade*

Vision

See *Concerto in D*

Wind von West from *Cantata* (EWW 89) 30 minutes

3 December 1975, Wuppertal, Opernhaus
Company: Tanztheater Wuppertal
Choreographer: Pina Bausch; *Scenery & Costumes:* Rolf Borzik

The first part of a sequence of three ballets *Wind von West*, *Der Zweite Frühling* and *Le Sacre du Printemps* under the collective title *Frühlingsopfer*.

See also *Der Zweite Frühling* and *Le Sacre du Printemps* in Works Composed for the Stage

Witch Spell from an unidentified work

3 February 1935, New York, Guild Theatre
Company: Agnes De Mille Company
Choreographer and Costumes: Agnes De Mille

Zig Zag from *Sonata for Two Pianos* (EWW 80) and *The Five Fingers* (EWW 49) 19 minutes

August 1979, Cuyahoga Falls, Ohio, Blossom Music Centre
Company: Pennsylvania Ballet Company
Choreographer: Lar Lubovitch

Der Zweite Frühling from *Waltz (to Erik Satie) from Three Easy Pieces for Piano Duet* (EWW 28), *No 1 of Three Pieces for Clarinet Solo* (EWW 45), *No 2 (Eccentric) and No 3 (Canticle) from Three Pieces for String Quartet (later included in Four Studies for Orchestra)* (EWW 25), *Tango* (EWW 72), *Allegretto from Eight Instrumental Miniatures* (EWW 49A), *No 1 from Five Easy Pieces for Piano Duet* (EWW 32), *Larghetto from Eight Instrumental Miniatures* (EWW 49A)

3 December 1975, Wuppertal, Opernhaus
Company: Tanztheater Wuppertal
Choreographer: Pina Bausch

The second part of a sequence of three ballets: *Wind von West*, *Der Zweite Frühling* and *Le Sacre du Printemps* under the collective title *Frühlingsopfer*.

See also *Wind von West* and *Le Sacre du Printemps* in Works Composed for the Stage

13 Stühle from *Concerto for Piano and Wind Instruments* (EWW 52) 20 minutes

29 November 1960, Cologne, Opernhaus
Company: Ballett der Bühnen der Stadt Köln
Choreographer: Aurel Milloss; *Scenery & Costumes:* Liselotte Erler; *Dancers:* Helga Held, Hugo Delavalle

See also *Arcade*; *Concerto for Piano and Winds*

Bibliography

The most comprehensive bibliographies relating to Stravinsky and his music are to be found in:

Lederman, Minna (ed.) *Stravinsky in the Theatre*, New York, 1975. (ISBN 0-306-80022-5)
This is the first paperback printing in an unabridged republication of the first edition published in New York in 1949. The bibliography of over 600 references was compiled by Paul Magriel.

Stravinsky, Vera and Craft, Robert. *Stravinsky in Pictures and Documents*, New York, 1978.
(ISBN 0-671-24382-9)
This has a selected bibliography, annotated with revealing and corrective remarks, of Russian and English publications since 1971.

White, Eric Walter. *Stravinsky, The Composer and his Works* (2nd edn), London, 1979. (ISBN 0-571-04923-0)
This is the essential work on Stravinsky, containing a biography and a complete register of his compositions. It also contains the fullest bibliography relating to Stravinsky, the man and his music, currently available.

This selected bibliography is divided into four parts:
General reference works;
Catalogues;
Books on particular artists, choreographers, dancers, impresarios, companies.
Periodicals.

General Reference Works

Balanchine, George and Mason, Francis, *Balanchine's Festival of Ballet*, London, 1978.

Beaumont, Cyril W. *Complete Book of Ballets*, London, 1951.

Berezkin, V.I., *Khudozhniki Bolshogo Teatra*, Moscow, 1976.

Caamaño, Roberto, *La historia del Teatro Colon 1908-1968*, Buenos Aires, n.d.

D'Amico, Silvio (ed.), *Enciclopedia dello Spettacolo*, 9 volumes, Rome, 1954-1962.

Dictionary Catalog of the Dance Collection, 10 volumes and annual supplements. The New York Public Library, Boston 1974-80.

Goldner, Nancy, *The Stravinsky Festival of the New York City Ballet*, New York, 1973.

Harewood, The Earl of, *Kobbé's Complete Opera Book*, London, 1966.

Loewenberg, Alfred, *Annals of Opera 1597-1940*, Cambridge, 1943.

Phaidon Book of the Ballet, Oxford, 1981.

Phaidon Book of the Opera, Oxford, 1979.

Riobó, Julio F. and Cucullu, Carlos, *El arte del Ballet en el Teatro Colon*, Buenos Aires, 1945.

Terry, Walter, *Ballet Guide*, Newton Abbot, 1976.

Tintori, Giampiero, *Duecento anni di Teatro alla Scala*, Rome, 1978 (This supesedes *Il Teatro alla Scala*, 2 volumes, Milan, 1964).

Seltsam, William H, *Metropolitan Opera Annals*, ?New York, 1947.

Wenzel, Joachim E, *Gesichte der Hamburger Oper 1678-1978*, Hamburg, 1978.

Catalogues

Collections:

Salmina-Haskell, Clarissa, *Russian Drawings*, Ashmolean Museum, Oxford, 1970.

Salmina Haskell, Clarissa, *Catalogue of Russian Drawings*, Victoria & Albert Museum, HMSO, London 1972.

Exhibitions: (In chronological order)

Ballets Russes de Diaghilew 1909-1929, Musée des Arts Décoratifs, Paris, 1939.

Buckle, Richard, (ed.) *The Diaghilev Exhibition*, Edinburgh, 1954.

Buckle, Richard, (ed.) *The Diaghilev Exhibition*, London, 1954.

Stravinsky and the Dance, The Dance Collection of the New York Public Library, New York, 1962.

Stravinsky and the Theatre, The New York Public Library, New York, 1963.

Russian Stage and Costume Designs for the Ballet, Opera and Theatre, a loan exhibition from the Lobanov-Rostovsky, Oenslager and Riabov Collections. International Exhibitions Foundation, 1967.

Les Ballets Russes de Serge de Diaghilev, 1909-1929, Conseil de l'Europe, Strasbourg, 1969.

Covent Garden, 25 Years of Opera and Ballet, Victoria & Albert Museum, London, 1971.

Buckle, Richard, *Omaggio ai Disegnatori di Diaghilev*, Palazzo Grassi, Venice, 1975.

Visages d'Igor Stravinsky. Musée de Tesse, Le Mans, France, 1976.

1909-1929 Les Ballets Russes de Diaghilev, Centre Culturel du Marais, Paris, 1977.

Russian Painters and the Stage 1884-1965, from the collection of Mr and Mrs Nikita D. Lobanov-Rostovsky, University of Texas, 1978.

Chadd, David and Cage, John, *The Diaghilev Ballet in England*, Sainsbury Centre for Visual Arts, Norwich, 1979.

Lobanov, Nikita D., Lobanov, Nina & Troyen, Aimée, *Russian Theatre and Costume Designs*, Fine Arts Museums, San Francisco, 1980.

Alexandre Benois, 1870-1960, *Drawings for the Ballet*, Hazlitt, Gooden & Fox, London 1980. (With an introduction by Richard Buckle.)

Igor Stravinsky, Musée d'Art Moderne de la Ville de Paris, Festival d'Automne, Paris, 1980.

Spotlight, Victoria & Albert Museum, London, 1981.

Auctions: (In chronological order)

Costumes and Curtains from Diaghilev and de Basil Ballets, Sotheby & Co., London, 1968.

Serge Diaghilev/Max Reinhardt, Sotheby & Co., London 1969.

Serge Diaghilev, Boris Kniaseff, Max Reinhardt, Sotheby & Co., London 1969.

Costumes and Curtains from Diaghilev and de Basil Ballets, Sotheby & Co, 1969.

Designs for Costumes and Decors, Ballet, Opera, Theatre, Parke-Bernet Galleries Inc., New York, 1970.

Ballet, Theatre and Opera Decor and Costume Designs, Portraits and Posters, Sotheby & Co., London, 1971.

Costumes and Curtains from Diaghilev and de Basil Ballets, Sotheby & Co., London, 1973.

Decor and Costume Designs, Portraits, Manuscripts and Posters principally for Ballet, Sotheby & Co., London, 1973.

Ballet and Theatre Material, Sotheby & Co., London, 1975.

Dance, Theatre, Opera, Sotheby Parke Bernet Inc., New York, 1977.

Ballet and Theatre Material, Sotheby & Co., London, 1979.

Dance, Theatre, Opera, Cabaret, Sotheby Parke Bernet, New York, 1979.

Ballet and Theatre Material, Sotheby & Co., London, 1980.

Dance, Theater, Opera, Music Hall, Sotheby Parke Bernet Inc., New York, 1980.

Ballet Designs from the collection of Mr and Mrs John Carr Doughty, Sotheby & Co., London, 1981.

Dance, Theater, Opera, Music Hall, Sotheby Parke Bernet, New York, 1981.

Ballet, Theatre & Music-Hall Material, Sotheby Parke Bernet & Co., London, 1981.

Books

Bablet, Denis, *Les Révolutions scéniques du XXe siècle*, Paris, 1975.

Barr, Alfred H. Jr, *Matisse: His Art and his Public*, London, 1975.

Benois, Alexandre, *Reminiscences of the Russian Ballet*, London, 1941.

Bland, Alexander, *The Royal Ballet – The First 50 Years*, London, 1981. (Contains comprehensive statistics compiled by Sarah C. Woodcock.)

Buckle, Richard, *Diaghilev*, London, 1979. This is the most authoritative and comprehensive biograpby of Serge Diaghilev. Also has an important Bibliography.

Chamot, Mary, *Gontcharova*, Paris, 1972.

Chamot, Mary, *Goncharova Stage Designs and Paintings*, London, 1979.

Clarke, Mary and Crisp, Clement, *Design for Ballet*, London, 1978.

Cooper, Douglas, *Picasso Theatre*, London, 1968.

Hammarstrom, David Lewis, *Behind the Big Top*, Cranbury, New Jersey, 1980.

Horgan, Paul, *Encounters with Stravinsky*, New York, 1972.

Jacquot, J. (ed.), *Les voies de la Création Théâtrale VI*, Paris, 1978.

Kirstein, Lincoln, *Thirty Years – The New York City Ballet*, London, 1979.

Kochno, Boris, *Diaghilev et les Ballets Russes*, Paris, 1973.

Kögler, Horst and others, *John Cranko und das Stuttgarter Ballett*, ?Stuttgart, 1978.

Krassovskaya, Vera, *Russkii Baletnii Teatr nachalo XX veka*, 2 volumes (1 Choreografi, 2 Tantzovchiki), Leningrad, 1971.

Lassaigne, Jacques, *Marc Chagall Dessins et aquarelles pour le Ballet*, Paris, 1969.

Livingstone, Marco, *David Hockney*, London, 1981.

Meyer, Herbert, *Das Nationaltheater Mannheim 1929-79*, Mannheim, 1979.

Payne, Charles, *American Ballet Theatre*, London, 1978.

Pruzhan, Irina Nikolaevna, *Lev Samoilovitch Bakst*, Leningrad, 1975.

Riobó, Julio F. & Cucullu, Carlos, *El Arte del Ballet en el Teatro Colon*, Buenos Aires, 1945.

Souriz E.Y., *Khoreograficheskoe Isskustvo Dvagtzatikh Godov*, Moscow, 1979.

Periodicals

The American Dancer, monthly, 1927-1942, New York. This then became the current *Dance Magazine*.

Ballet, monthly, July/August 1939-October 1952 (not published between November 1939 and December 1945), London.

Dance Chronicle, 1977-   , New York.

Dance and Dancers, monthly, 1950-1980 Vol. XXXI, No 6/7, London.

Dance Index, monthly (sometimes multiple issues), 1942-1948, New York.

Dance Magazine, monthly, January 1924-December 1931, New York.

Dance News, monthly except July and August, 1942-   , New York.

Dance Perspectives, 1959-1976 Vol. 17, No 66, New York.

The Dancing Times, 1894-   , London.

Opera, monthly (Vol. I bi-monthly; Festival issue from 1960), 1950-   , London

Index

The transliteration and spelling of proper names, Russian names in particular, often changes from one printed programme to another. For the sake of clarity and consistency these names have been standardised throughout the text to the version generally used today.

All places of performance are listed separately by country under the heading 'Theatres', following the general index. Page references in bold type denote the main sections on each of the twenty-one works composed for the stage. Those in italic type denote plates or captions to plates.

216

219

221

222

Theatres